Critical Thinking

Also available from Bloomsbury

Introduction to Indian Philosophy, Christopher Bartley
Phenomenology, Michael Lewis and Tanja Staehler
Philosophical Logic, George Englebretsen and Charles Sayward
The Philosophy of History, Mark Day
The Philosophy of Mind, Dale Jacquette
The Philosophy of the Social Sciences, Robert C. Bishop

Forthcoming:

Classical Chinese Philosophy, Im Manyul
Ethics, Robin Attfield
Metaphysics, Jonathan Tallant
Philosophy of Language, Chris Daly
Philosophy of Law, Jeffrey Brand-Ballard
Philosophy of Science, Emma Tobin
Pragmatism, John Capps

Critical Thinking

An Introduction to Reasoning Well

Jamie Carlin Watson
and Robert Arp

B L O O M S B U R Y
LONDON • NEW DELHI • NEW YORK • SYDNEY

Bloomsbury Academic

An imprint of Bloomsbury Publishing Plc

50 Bedford Square
London
WC1B 3DP
UK

1385 Broadway
New York
NY 10018
USA

www.bloomsbury.com

Bloomsbury is a registered trade mark of Bloomsbury Publishing Plc

First published in 2009 by the Continuum International Publishing Group Ltd
Reprinted 2012 (twice)
Reprinted by Bloomsbury Academic 2013 (twice)

© Jamie Carlin Watson and Robert Arp, 2011

British Library Cataloguing-in-Publication Data
A catalogue record for this book is available from the British Library.

ISBN: HB: 978-0-8264-2492-1
PB: 978-0-8264-3951-2

Library of Congress Cataloging-in-Publication Data
A catalog record for this book is available from the Library of Congress.

Arp, Robert.
Critical thinking: an introduction to reasoning well/Robert Arp and
Jamie Carlin Watson.
p. cm.
Includes index.
ISBN 978-0-8264-2492-1 – ISBN 978-0-8264-3951-2
1. Reasoning. 2. Critical thinking. 3. Logic.
I. Watson, Jamie Carlin. II. Title.
BC177.A775 2011
160–dc22
2010028055

Typeset by Newgen Imaging Systems Pvt Ltd, Chennai, India
Printed and bound in Great Britain

Contents

List of Figures

Preface

You shouldn't drink too much.
The Earth is round like an egg.
Dinosaurs once roamed the Earth.
Milk is good for your bones.
It is wrong to get an abortion.
God exists.
Vanilla ice cream is the best.
Zoloft cures depression.

Are any of these claims true? How could you tell? Could you ever be *certain* you were *right*? Is there some method, some set of tools, to help you decide whether to believe any or all of these claims? Thankfully, the answer to the last question is *yes*, and this book is like a beginner's tool set—a starter guide to determining whether these claims, and others, deserve your stamp of approval and assent. As with any basic tool set, this one doesn't have every tool you'll ever need. But just as every starter kit includes a hammer, at least two screwdrivers, and a measuring tape, this one includes the most fundamental and widely used rules of good reasoning.

This book is designed to be *read* and not simply taught from. We attempt to explain each concept simply and thoroughly, and we include many examples and exercises. Our goal has been to write a textbook that could be used individually or in the classroom. It is designed with three types of readers in mind: students in basic reasoning courses, students preparing for graduate school, and people who simply need an edge in their communication skills. But we hope you find it useful no matter where life takes you. In this book, we aim to accomplish three goals:

(1) To help you recognize good and bad reasoning as it happens around you;
(2) To help you excel on examinations which assess your reasoning capacities (e.g., the GRE, GMAT, and LSAT);

and most importantly,

(3) To help you reason better about important decisions in your life.

The book is divided into five main parts. **Part One** is foundational. It explains the basic concepts you will need throughout the other parts, namely, claims, evidence, and arguments. The three remaining parts can be studied in any order, but we have organized them so that they proceed from more abstract, technical principles to more concrete, practical principles.

In **Part Two**, we cover deductive rules of reasoning, including the basic rules of symbolic logic, categorical logic, truth tables, and propositional logic. A grasp of these will increase clarity, precision, and organization in your thought and writing. In **Part Three**, we cover inductive logic and the uncertainty in our evidence. We discuss five basic reasoning strategies used in reasoning about the natural world: enumeration, generalization, analogy, causation, and inference to the best explanation. In addition, we explain over a dozen errors in reasoning, so we can both avoid them in our own arguments and expose them in the arguments of others. And finally, in **Part Four**, we discuss how all these reasoning skills can assist you in the event you decide to take a graduate school entrance exam.

Consult the companion website to this text for answers to some of the exercises, additional exercises, a glossary, help with the Real Life Examples at the end of each chapter, more Real Life Examples, and additional informal fallacies.

Here's to reasoning well!

Jamie Carlin Watson
Robert Arp

Part One
THE BASICS OF GOOD REASONING

The Basic Tools of Reasoning

1

1.1. Claims

All of us have beliefs or opinions about ourselves, the world, and reality as we perceive it: some of us believe abortion is wrong; some are of the opinion that the universe is only thousands of years old; more than half of the people on the planet believe in a god of some kind; most people believe in the verified statistical evidence found in books and journals that "more than half of the people on the planet believe in a god of some kind." We communicate a belief to others by making a **claim.**

A claim expresses a **state of affairs**. A state of affairs is the way the world *is* or *was* or *could be* or *could have been* or *is not*. For instance, I could have been taller than I am. That is one way the world *could have been*. Julius Caesar was emperor of Rome. That is one way the world *was*. And snow is white. That is one way the world *is*. So, states of affairs are the features of reality. Claims express states of affairs. We'll sometimes use brackets "< >" to distinguish a claim from a state of affairs. So the state of affairs, snow is white, is expressed by the claim, <Snow is white.> It is important to note that claims are not restricted to a particular human language. Since we cannot communicate without a human language (English, French, German, etc., also called *natural languages*), claims are expressed in a language. When we are referring to a claim expressed by a sentence in natural language, we'll use quotes, ". . . ," to distinguish it from a claim or a state of affairs.

Now, sentences express claims in a natural language. So a single claim can be expressed by many different sentences. <Snow is white.> can be expressed in English, "Snow is white," German, "Schnee ist weiss," French, "La neige est blanche," Italian, "La neve é bianca," and any other natural language. To see the relationship between claims, states of affairs, and sentences, consider Figure 1.1.

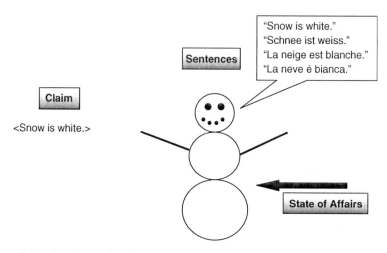

Figure 1.1 Claims, States of Affairs, and Sentences

Given what we've said so far, we can describe a claim as a:

> (1) declarative statement, part of a declarative statement, assertion, proposition, or judgment,
> (2) that expresses something about the world (states of affairs) and is either true or false.

Let's look more closely at these two criteria for a claim.

(1) A claim is a proposition, judgment, declarative statement, or part of a declarative statement.

— It is not a *question*, as in: "What time is it?" or "How do I tie a bowtie?"
— It is not a *suggestion* or *command*, as in: "Hey, let's go to the beach today," or "Shut the door!"
— It is not an *emotive iteration*, as in: "OW, that hurts!" or "Yay, Tigers!"

Claims can be **descriptive**, in which case we have a statement where someone is describing what *is* or *was* or *could be* or *could have been* the case about a person, place, or thing, as in a report or explanation. For example, the following are all descriptive claims, expressed by English sentences:

a. "We are all participating in a critical thinking class right now."
b. "We all could be at the beach."
c. "At least one of us is the professor."
d. "There are more than ten people sitting in this classroom."
e. "Frank is absent today."
f. "He has stomach flu."
g. "Frank is absent today because he has stomach flu." (Notice, there are two claims here, each *part of* a declarative sentence.)
h. "The clock in this room is broken."
i. "We cannot tell what time it is."
j. "The clock in this room is broken, therefore we cannot tell what time it is." (Again, two claims comprising a single declarative sentence.)
k. Hence, "most of us in the classroom are ticked off."

Claims can also be **prescriptive**, that is, they express that some state of affairs *ought to be* or *should be* the case. For example, the following are all prescriptive claims expressed by English sentences:

a. "You should be paying attention in class right now."
b. "It's important to hold the violin under your chin—and not between your legs—for the best sound."
c. "No one should ever abort a fetus."
d. "In the United States, you must drive on the right-hand side of the road."
e. "You have got to stop drinking."
f. "Some really should fix the clock in this room."

Exercises 1.a.

For each of the following English sentences, identify whether it expresses a *descriptive claim, prescriptive claim, question, command, emotive iteration,* or some combination:

1. "Is that Sally?"
2. "That is a Doberman Pincer."
3. "Please close the window . . . "
4. ". . . There are flies accumulating on grandpa's head."
5. In the 1960s *Batman* television show, The Joker screams, "Yikes!"
6. "Is that car a Porsche?"
7. Also from the 1960s *Batman* show, Robin says, "Holy semantics, Batman!"
8. "There's a tear in my beer 'cause I'm cryin' for you dear," song lyric, Hank Williams
9. "How about we try Burger King for once?"
10. "Smoking is bad for your health."
11. "You shouldn't smoke."
12. "That's totally, like, bogus, man!"
13. "It is not the case that she does not like chocolate."
14. "If you build it, they will come."
15. "How much more of this do I have to endure?"
16. "Stop!"
17. "I wish the clock worked."
18. "Is that a real Rolex?"
19. "Stop asking me whether I should wait for you."

Claims can be simple or complex. A **simple claim** communicates one idea, having at least one subject and one predicate, as in:

a. Metallica rocks.
b. Jenny is in the garden.
c. The new edition of Encyclopedia Britannica is out.
d. Two plus two equals five. (Remember, claims can be true or false, so, even though this sentence is not true, it is still a claim.)
e. She lied.
f. Eating candy all day rots your teeth.

A **complex claim** is one or more claims plus an **operator**. An operator is a tool that allows us to express more complicated states of affairs. You are probably familiar with *mathematical* operators like +, —, x, /, and =. Logic has a slightly different set of operators. We'll discuss five (see Figure 1.2).

Operator	Symbol	Example
and	&	It is a cat **and** it is a mammal.
or (sometimes requires "either")	v	It is **either** a cat **or** a skunk.
not	~	It is **not** raining.
if . . . , then . . .	⊃	**If** it is a cat, **then** it is a mammal.
if and only if	≡	He is a bachelor **if and only if** he is single.

Figure 1.2 Logical Operators

Claims that are operated on by "and" are called **conjunctions** because two or more claims are being conjoined. Each claim in a conjunction is called a **conjunct**. Here are a few more examples; the operator appears in bold and the conjuncts are underlined:

    a. <u>John is in grade school</u> **and** <u>he is ten years old.</u>
    b. <u>June went to the movies</u> **and** <u>Frank took the car in for maintenance.</u>
    c. Jack is a hunter, fisherman, and marksman. [This complex claim is comprised of three simple claims conjoined: <u>Jack is a hunter</u> **and** <u>Jack is a fisherman</u> **and** <u>Jack is a marksman.</u> English allows us to simplify by dropping "ands." The operator is *implied* in English, but later, when we translate this sentence into logic we will make it explicit.]
    d. <u>Leo is a lion,</u> **(and)** <u>(Leo is) a constellation,</u> **and** <u>he is an astrological symbol.</u> (Notice that the first "and" and the second "Leo is" are implied in this English expression of a complex claim.)

Claims that are operated on by "or" are called **disjunctions** because two or more claims are being disjoined. Each claim in a disjunction is called a **disjunct**. Here are a few more examples; the operator appears in bold and each disjunct is underlined:

    a. **Either** <u>Jane will do the job</u> **or** <u>Henry will be called in as backup to do the job.</u>
    b. **Either** <u>the budget will be settled</u> **or** <u>the meeting will last past 7:00 pm.</u>
    c. <u>That thing over there is</u> **either** <u>a wolf</u> **or** <u>(that thing over there is) a really large dog.</u>
    d. <u>The sales figures indicate a recession</u> **or** <u>(the sales figures indicate) a problem with our accounting</u> **or** <u>(the sales figures indicate) serious embezzlement.</u>

The "not" operator operates only on single claims, though they may be simple or complex. Claims that are operated on by "not" are called **negations**, because a claim is being negated. Here are few more examples:

a. <u>Jenny is</u> **not** <u>lying</u>. (Notice that the single claim <Jenny is lying> is split by the operator. This happens often.)
b. <u>It is</u> **not** <u>raining</u>.
c. **It is not the case that** <u>George W. Bush rigged the 2000 election</u>.
d. <u>Hercules was</u> **not** <u>a real person</u>.

Claims operated on by "if . . . , then . . . " are called **conditional claims**. This is because the claim following the "then" is conditional on the claim following the "if." They are also called *hypothetical claims* because they do not express the way the world is, but how it could be. For instance, the conditional, <If it is raining, then the sidewalk is wet,> does not express either that it is raining or that the sidewalk is wet, but that (conditionally) if it is raining, then the sidewalk is wet. A conditional claim has two parts: an **antecedent**, which is the claim following the "if" (recall that "ante" means "comes before") and a **consequent**, which is the claim following the "then" (think: what comes after—consequent—the ante). Here are a few examples:

a. **If** <u>you want to get downtown</u>, **then** <u>the best route is the highway.</u>
b. **If** Smith is elected, **then** our taxes will be raised.
c. The tide will rise **if** the moon comes closer to the Earth. (Notice that the "then" is implied and the consequent comes before the antecedent in this English expression of the claim, <If the moon comes closer to the Earth, then the tide will rise.>)
d. All the pins will fall **if** you roll the ball just right. (Again, the consequent comes before the antecedent and the "then" is implied. The claim is, <If you roll the ball just right, then all the pins will fall.>)

Claims operated on by "if and only if" are called **bi-conditionals** because two (hence, the "bi") conditionals (the "if . . . , then . . ." operator) are being conjoined (the "and" operator). Imagine a conditional that is true even if you swap the antecedent for the consequent. For instance:

If <u>Pat is a woman</u>, **then** <u>she has two X chromosomes</u>.

This conditional is also true if we swap the antecedent with the conditional:

If <u>she has two X chromosomes</u>, **then** <u>Pat is a woman</u>.

We will soon see that if two claims are true, we can conjoin them (the "and" operator). Since both of these are true, we can form the conjunction:

> If Pat is a woman, then she has two X chromosomes **and** if she has two X chromosomes, then Pat is a woman.

The result of conjoining two claims (simple or complex) is a conjunction. The bi-conditional operator simplifies this operation. If two conditionals are conjoined, we have a bi-conditional (the "if and only if" operator). Drop the "ifs," "thens," and "and," and replace with "if and only if":

> Pat is a woman **if and only if** she has two X chromosomes.

Here are a few more examples:

a. A person is a bachelor **if and only if** a person is an unmarried male.
b. Utensils go in this drawer **if and only if** they are sharp.
c. A person is alive **if and only if** we can detect brain activity.
d. A person is legally permitted to drink alcohol in the U.S. **if and only if** he or she is 21 years old.

Exercises 1.b.

Identify the following English sentences as expressing *simple* or *complex* claims. If a claim is complex, say whether it is a *conjunction, disjunction, negation, conditional,* or *bi-conditional*:

1. "If the clock is broken in this room tomorrow, I'll scream."
2. "That movie is not the same movie you were just talking about."
3. "Eating the right kinds of foods builds muscles and doing so helps your immune system."
4. "You have to do it or else you'll get in trouble."
5. "You should join the club."
6. "You'll make the team, if you pass the tests."
7. "You don't have to take the final exam if and only if your grade is an "A" going into the final exam."
8. "It would be necessary to invent one, if there were no god."
9. "Either the universe is only thousands of years old or the scientists are right."

Exercises 1.c.

These last three complex claims are trickier because they involve more than one operator. See if you can figure out whether each is a *conjunction, disjunction, negation, conditional,* or *bi-conditional*:

1. "If the case goes to trial, then the lawyer gets his day in court and we get to tell the whole story."
2. "If it rains tomorrow, then we can either go to the mall or hang out here."
3. "He will arrive and she will arrive shortly thereafter if and only if the dog stays and the cat goes."

We will say more about simple and complex claims and show how they are used in reasoning in the following chapters.

(2) A claim expresses something about the world (states of affairs) and is either true or false.[1]

Claims are assertions, declarations, or judgments about whether something is or is not the case. Sally might say: "It is raining right now." Notice that this is the same thing as saying: "It is the case that it is raining right now." John might say: "This shirt is not mine." Notice that this is the same thing as saying: "It is not the case that this shirt is mine" or "It is the case that this shirt is not mine." Consider these assertions, declarations, or judgments where something is communicated that is or is not the case:

    a. Leo Tolstoy wrote *War and Peace*.
    b. It is the case that Edgar Allen Poe wrote *The Murders in the Rue Morgue*.
    c. The United States is not the country with the largest population in the world.
    d. It is not the case that Chicago is the most populous city in the Unites States.
    e. It is the case that she will not be attending the performance tonight.
    f. It is not the case that Jesus Christ lived during the eighteenth century.

Since claims are either true or false, what is communicated in a claim either:

> (A) accurately expresses some state of affairs, that is, the way the world is (a true claim), or
> (B) inaccurately expresses some state of affairs (a false claim).

Most of us agree that a claim is true if and only if it accurately expresses some state of affairs, that is, it corresponds to some feature of reality. If a claim does not correspond to some feature of reality, it is false. This definition of "truth" is called the **correspondence theory of truth**, and this common sense definition is what we utilize in this text. There are other approaches to truth including the *coherence theory of truth* (in a nutshell: a claim is true if it coheres with, or is consistent with, other claims that are true) and the *pragmatic theory of truth* (in a nutshell: a claim is true if it is useful, works, or is prudent).

A claim's status as true or false is known as its **truth value**. The following claims are considered true claims, what they communicate accurately corresponds to some state of affairs in the world, and they have a truth value, "true":

    a. The population in the United States presently is over 200 million.
    b. Charles Darwin wrote *The Origin of Species*.
    c. All whales are mammals.
    d. Most children are born with two feet.
    e. Some snakes are black.

The following claims are considered false claims, what they communicate does not accurately correspond to some state of affairs out there in the world, and they have a truth value, "false":

    f. Greece has the largest population in the world.
    g. William Shakespeare lived in New York City, New York.
    h. All whole numbers are fractions.
    i. Most states in the United States have a city called "Springfield" that is the state's capitol.
    j. Most snakes are venomous.

Notice, when someone writes or says that something is the case, he is saying that the claim expressing some state of affairs is true (the claim corresponds to some state of affairs). Similarly, when someone writes or says something is not the case, he is saying that the claim expressing some state of affairs is false (the claim does not correspond to some state of affairs). Here are some examples of ways to express that a claim is true or false:

a_1. In fact, it is raining outside right now.
a_2. It is the case that it is raining outside right now. **claim: <It is raining outside right now.>**
a_3. It is true that it is raining outside right now.

b_1. This shirt is not mine.
b_2. It is true that <this shirt is not mine>.   **claim: <This shirt is mine.>**
b_3. It is not the case that this shirt is mine.
b_4. It is false that <this shirt is mine>.

c_1. I say that all whales are mammals.
c_2. It is the case that <all whales are mammals>. **claim: <All whales are mammals.>**
c_3. It is true that <all whales are mammals>.

d$_1$. The claim, "Most snakes are venomous," is false.

d$_2$. It is not the case that most snakes are venomous.   **claim: <Most snakes are venomous.>**

d$_3$. It is false that most snakes are venomous.

Exercises 1.d.

For each of the following claims:

(a) Restate the claim with "It is the case that . . ." or "It is not the case that . . ."
(b) State whether the claim is true or false (to the best of your knowledge):

1. "Ricki Lake is still on the air as a talk show host."
2. "It is not raining outside right now."
3. "Dinosaurs did not live 10 thousand years ago."
4. "*Homo sapiens* began roaming Europe about 10 million years ago."
5. "Uncle Fester is Bart's dad on *The Simpsons*."
6. "There are twenty students in this classroom right now."
7. "George Washington was president of the United States twice."

1.2. Evidence

To determine whether a claim is true or false, or likely to be true or false, you need some **evidence**. Evidence provides reasons to believe that a claim is true or false. Evidence can take the form of a claim or set of claims, for instance, the claims: <All men are mortal> and <Socrates was a man>, are evidence for the claim, <Socrates was mortal.> Evidence can also take the form of a psychological state, for instance, the psychological state of seeing a ball as red is evidence for the claim, <The ball is red.> Evidence plays a key role as premises or sets of premises in arguments.

An intuitive way to understand evidence is to divide types of evidence into two categories: **direct** and **indirect**. Direct evidence is evidence that you as a critical thinker have immediate access to, for instance, seeing that something is the case or recognizing that a particular claim follows from a set of claims. This doesn't mean you have direct access to reality; your eyes and ears and taste buds are instruments that can be calibrated differently. So, your picture of reality may be distorted, but whatever picture you're getting is immediately available to you. Indirect evidence, on the other hand, is evidence that you are distanced from by some sort of mediator, for instance, if someone testifies that they saw someone hit your car, you don't have immediate access to that information, but must rely on the witness's testimony. The witness had direct access to the accident; you have mediated access—the testimony is only an indicator of what the witness saw. These categories can be helpful when evaluating the strength of different pieces of evidence. This is one reason that legal courts prefer eyewitness testimony rather than hearsay testimony.

Some examples of **direct evidence** include:

a. **Sensory evidence** (vision, hearing, touch, taste, smell)
b. **Logical entailment** (for example, the rules of inference we will discuss in Chapter 6)
c. **Mathematical entailment** (claims that follow from the rules of arithmetic, geometry, etc.)
d. **Intuitions** (moral or rational)
e. **Introspection** (personal access to your beliefs and feelings)
f. **Definitions** (A definition can provide evidence that some claim is true in virtue of the meaning of the words in the claim. For example, if you understand what the word "bachelor" means, then if someone says that Jack is a bachelor, this is evidence that Jack is unmarried.)

Some examples of **indirect evidence** include:

a. The results of **scientific experiments** (mediated by instruments)
b. **Testimony** (mediated by someone else's sensory evidence or experiments)
c. **Memory** (mediated by time)
d. **Scientific theories** (mediated by lots of experiments and widespread acceptance by scientists)
e. **Specific types of inductive inferences** (mediated by incomplete information; see Chapters 7 and 8)

Evidence is important for (i) forming beliefs about claims, (ii) evaluating beliefs about claims, and (iii) persuading others to adopt claims you believe. It is difficult to form beliefs without evidence. For instance, could you really make yourself believe that there is a large pink elephant in your room right now? Without evidence, it seems extremely difficult. Similarly, it is often difficult to believe contrary to your evidence. For instance, could you force yourself to believe that the dollar in your pocket is really worth $100? Examples like these led philosopher W.K. Clifford (1845–1879) to make the strong claim that, "It is wrong always and everywhere for anyone to believe anything on insufficient evidence" (1877).

Evidence is also important for evaluating claims. Let's say we (Rob and Jamie, the authors of this book) assert that "this chapter was typed on a computer." This claim is supported *for us* by *direct* evidence; we see that we are typing it on a computer. It is also supported by indirect evidence; we *remember* typing it on a computer. This claim can be supported *for you* by indirect evidence; *testimony from us* (whom you may know to be reliable witnesses), *testimony from our wives* (who may have no reason to lie), or your *background beliefs* that, for the most part, books are now written on a computer (with a few exceptions, like novelist Danielle Steele, who still uses a typewriter). The point is that the strength of your belief that we wrote this chapter on a computer depends on the strength of your evidence for this claim.

Finally, evidence is important for convincing others that what you believe is true. If Rob tells you, "Rob Arp is President of the United States," a critical thinker has reasons to believe this is false. For instance, you may be able to gather direct evidence that it is false (you could follow him around noting that he does nothing presidential, plus there don't seem to be any Secret Service people around). Or you may be able to gather indirect evidence that it is false (the inference from your beliefs that you have not seen him on TV, plus the testimony of appropriate authorities on the subject). So, if Rob wants to convince you he is President, he needs to offer new evidence sufficient for removing your confidence in your current evidence.

Exercises 1.e.

To the best of your ability, provide two pieces of evidence for and two against each of the following claims. If you are not aware of any particular evidence, feel free to make it up. The point is to present claims that, if true, obviously support the truth or falsity of the claims below.

1. The Sun's distance from the Earth is about 92,960,00. miles.
2. Rust on metal is caused by a substance that is trapped in the metal and released with moisture.
3. Humans and monkeys evolved from a common ancestor.
4. There is E. coli in your intestines.
5. Men have never walked on the moon.
6. Jack the Ripper likely was a surgeon.

Exercises 1.f.

A bit harder:

7. An all-knowing, all-powerful, all-good god exists.
8. O.J. Simpson killed two people.
9. Bread will nourish you the next time you eat it.

1.3. Arguments

Arguments employ claims as evidence for the truth of other claims. As we have seen, claims can be either true or false and what we should believe about a claim's truth value depends on the evidence we have for or against that claim. Arguments help us organize claims so we can see clearly how well some evidence supports a claim.

Not everyone thinks critically about the claims they make or about the claims others express. As rational beings, it is not enough to make claims; we must be able to explain, justify, or give reasons for the claims we make, as well as the claims of others. When we make a claim and then attempt to support that claim with another claim or claims, we are exercising our reasoning capacities as critically thinking, rational beings, and not mere sheep.

Critical thinking separates us from sheep and other animals, and involves the principles of correct reasoning concerning the formation and evaluation of arguments. Critically thinking individuals offer evidence in the form of **arguments** to articulate their beliefs and persuade others to adopt them.

An argument is:

    (1) one or more claims, called a *premise* (or premises),
    (2) intended to support the truth
    (3) of another claim, called the *conclusion*.

The **conclusion** is the claim in need of support by evidence. The **premises** along with the overall structure of the argument are the claims that support the conclusion. There is at least one premise and only one conclusion in a complete argument, and they typically have two or more premises.

Pay special note to part (2) of this definition. A set of claims is an argument if someone *intends* it to be an argument. Sometimes people express themselves in ways that are not arguments, for instance:

We all went to the store today. We bought candy. We went home right afterward. We went to sleep. Billy slept the longest. Janey got sick.

This is not an argument, but a narrative (a story) comprised of claims. Sometimes people attempt to support a conclusion, but do it poorly. For instance:

> The sky is blue. And the grass is green. Therefore, the fool is on the hill at midnight.

Since the person making these claims *expects* you to believe something (specifically, the fool is on the hill at midnight) on the basis of (he uses "therefore") other claims (the sky is blue and the grass is green), this is an argument, albeit a bad one. The point is: *bad arguments are still arguments*. We can identify them and point out their flaws using the tools you are learning in this book.

One of the best reasons to treat bad arguments as arguments is called **the principle of charity**, which states that one should always investigate the reasons why someone has put forward an argument, even if the argument is poorly-formed, incomplete, or we think it is just downright bad from our perspective. The principle also states that one should try to give "the most charitable reading to" someone's argument (thus the *charity* part of the principle) by filling in implicit elements of the argument and giving the speaker the benefit of the doubt. Since we are finite creatures and do not know everything, it is not always obvious when an argument is bad. In addition, just because a person disagrees with you, does not mean her argument must be bad. In fact—hold on, now—you might be wrong (*gasp!*). It might turn out that an opponent's argument for a claim that you don't accept is *much better than* your argument for an opposing claim. The idea here is that you are only justified in believing a claim if you have been responsible enough to consider the evidence against that claim. This may be a bit extreme; we rarely consider the evidence *against* going to the grocery store when deciding whether we should (unless it's rush hour) or the evidence against taking a flight to a conference when deciding how to get there (unless it's a holiday). Nevertheless, the possibility that you are wrong is a strong reason for adopting the principle of charity.

Another reason to adopt the principle of charity is that it will help you refute your opponents' claims. If you are not aware of your opponents' reasons or have not considered them carefully, how can you respond clearly and forcefully? For this reason, we call the principle of charity *The Godfather Principle*. In the film *The Godfather: Part II* (1974) the protagonist, Michael Corleone tells one of his caporegimes (captains), Frank Pentangeli:

> My father taught me many things. . . . He taught me —
> keep your friends close, and your enemies closer.

The idea is that, if you do not know what your opponents are thinking, you will not be able to respond appropriately or adequately.

Part (2) of our definition of an argument also says that premises support the "truth" of a conclusion. Not all reasons to believe a claim have to do with truth, so some definitions of "argument" may leave this out. For instance, it might be *better for you,* or *more useful to you,* or *more helpful to believe* something that is false. It is reasonable to call these practical premises and conclusions "arguments." But philosophers, like scientists, are interested primarily in what the world is really like—we want to know what is true. Even moral claims—claims about what should be done, or what I ought to do, how things should be—are true or false of the world. Even arguments for negative claims, e.g., "It is not the case that X," are arguments for the *truth* of the claim that it is not the case that X. So, for our purposes, an argument involves premises that are intended to support the *truth* of a conclusion.

Consider an example. You walk into your dorm room and find that the light bulb in your lamp will not come on when you turn the switch. In this scenario, let's say that there are *only two possible explanations* for why the light bulb will not come on:

Either the light bulb is blown or it is not getting electricity. (premise 1)

With this in mind, you investigate to see whether the bulb is blown. For instance, you try it in several different lamps. This is much easier than trying to find a meter and testing the socket for electricity (unless you're an electrician with a meter handy). Suppose you try it in another lamp and it works perfectly. Now, by the evidence of your senses and what it means for a light bulb to work properly, you are justified in believing:

The bulb is not blown. (premise 2)

Given premises 1 and 2, you can now infer the conclusion:

Therefore, it is not getting electricity. (conclusion)

This argument is illustrated in Figure 1.3.

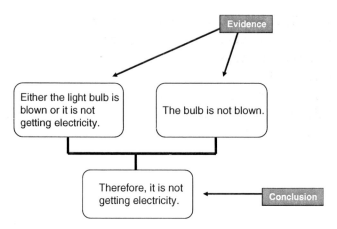

Figure 1.3 The Light Bulb Problem

Here are two more examples of arguments. Note how the premises are supposed to provide support for the conclusion:

EXAMPLE 1:

Premise 1: Ticks wait to trounce on an unsuspecting back or leg.
Premise 2: And anything that does that is just plain insidious.
Conclusion: Ticks certainly are insidious.

EXAMPLE 2:

Premise 1: It's simple: if you want a PlayStation, then you need money;
Premise 2: and if you need money, then you should do your chores.
Conclusion: Hey, if you want a PlayStation, then you should do your chores.

1.4. Identifying arguments

Before we evaluate an argument, we must clearly identify it. Perhaps you recall writing persuasive papers or giving argumentative speeches in high school or college. In those papers and speeches, you had a thesis statement or topic sentence you had to defend or explain. The thesis statement/topic sentence was essentially your argument's conclusion, while your defense/explanation was your argument's premise or premises. Also, your teacher likely had you state your conclusion first, then go on to support your conclusion. This is how you will often find arguments structured in books, magazines, or newspapers. Since arguments are often packaged this way, we need some tools for picking out conclusions and premises.

The first step in identifying an argument is picking out the conclusion. The basic goal of an argument is to *convince or persuade* others of the truth of some claim. So, if someone made the above argument about the problem of the light bulb, presumably he would want others to be convinced or persuaded that the bulb is not getting electricity (for instance, the maintenance department in his building). The same goes for "Ticks certainly are insidious" and "If you want a PlayStation, then you'll have to do your chores": the speaker making those claims wants others to be convinced of their truth.

So, step 1, ask yourself: "Is the author/speaker trying to convince me that some claim is true?" If the answer is yes, then ask, step 2, "What claim, *exactly*, is this person trying to persuade me to accept?" The claim you're being asked to accept is the conclusion. Conclusions can often be identified by **indicating words or phrases**. Consider this argument:

> Daily cocaine use causes brain damage. Brain damage is bad for you. **Therefore,** daily cocaine use is bad for you.

In this example, the word "therefore" indicates that the claim following it is the conclusion of an argument. The claim <daily cocaine use is bad for you> is the conclusion. Not all arguments will have indicating words. For example, if we remove the "therefore" from the cocaine argument and change the order of the claims, as long as the speaker/writer intends it to be an argument, it remains an argument and <daily cocaine use is bad for you> remains the conclusion:

> Daily cocaine use is bad for you. Daily cocaine use causes brain damage. Brain damage is bad for you.

But many times there will be a conclusion indicating word or phrase. Some common conclusion indicating words and phrases are:

Common Conclusion Indicating Words and Phrases:
Hence; Thus; Therefore; So; So that; This shows us that;
We may conclude/deduce/infer that; Entails; Implies;
Consequently; It follows that; It must be the case that

Once you have identified that a set of claims is an argument and you have clearly identified the conclusion, ask, step 3, "What claims are being offered in support of the conclusion?" The claim or claims supporting the truth of the conclusion are the premises. As with conclusions, premises are often accompanied by indicating words or phrases. For instance:

> Because the water trail leads to the sink, the sink is leaking.

In this argument the word "because" indicates that the claim immediately following it is the premise. English grammar gives us a clue about the conclusion. The sentence would be incomplete (a fragment) without more information; it is a dependent (or "subordinate") clause in need of an independent clause:

> Because the water leads to the sink.

Though <the water trail leads to the sink> is a simple claim, the "because" lets you know it is evidence for something, which, in this case, is that <the sink is leaking>. This is the conclusion. What claim are we supposed to accept? That the sink is leaking. What supports this claim? The water trail leads to the sink.

> **Common Premise Indicating Words and Phrases:**
> Because; Since; For; For the reason that; As;
> Due to the fact that; Given that; In that;
> It may be concluded from

A conclusion and premises can be anywhere in a set of claims presented to a person; the conclusion could come first, it could be couched in the middle of a set of premises, or it could be the last thing someone says. Consider these examples:

> (A) Bill says, "That nuclear power plant is not good for our city." He wants you to be convinced of the truth of this claim, and so do you. So, you ask him to support this claim with other claims: you ask for his argument. He goes on:
>
> > "That nuclear power plant is not good for the city . . ." (conclusion) because "it emits all kinds of radiation" (premise) and "that's not good for the city" (premise).
>
> Now, at least, you have a piece of reasoning that the both of you can work with.
>
> ⇨

(B) Sally says, "Johnny is not the killer." She wants you to be convinced of the truth of this claim, and so do you. So, you ask her to support this claim with other claims: you ask for her argument. She goes on:

> "If Johnny were the killer, then there would have been powder residue on his hands right after" (premise). "The police checked his hands, and there was no residue" (premise). So, "Johnny is not the killer" (conclusion).

Again, at least, you have a piece of reasoning that the both of you can work with.

1.5. More exercises

Exercises 1.g.

Identify whether the following claims are simple or complex. If it is complex, identify which operator is being used (hint: there may be more than one operator):

1. That is not a toaster.
2. That woman is good and just.
3. She's either with us or against us.
4. The state of national security in this country is deplorable.
5. Oil prices dropped today by seven dollars and foreign markets rose.
6. If Jack wants to go to the movies and he's broke, then he will have to borrow money from me or Janet.
7. Either we keep health care private or the government will become socialist.
8. It will never work.
9. He's a keeper.
10. The person in black is dancing with me.

Exercises 1.h.

In each of the following arguments, identify whether the evidence offered is direct or indirect and explain your answer:

1. Of course she knows how to cook. Remember, she took all those cooking classes.
2. The test results indicate you have a bacterial infection.
3. Look there (pointing). The hot-air balloon looks like a big eye.
4. Any number greater than two is also greater than one. That's part of what it means to be greater than two.
5. This candle is lemon-scented. Just smell it.
6. The weather man said it is going to rain today. Therefore, I'm taking my rain jacket.
7. Did you see that report on CNN last night? The commentator said that violence is escalating in the Middle East. Man, it must be tough over there.

8. If Bill is taller than Sue and Sue is taller than Dave, then of course Bill is taller than Dave.
9. Every other time you have taken Tylenol it has reduced your pain. So, if you're in pain, you should take Tylenol.
10. I remember that when I was a kid, gasoline was much less expensive.

Exercises 1.i.

Locate the conclusion and premises in the following arguments by asking the questions:

> What claim, exactly, am I being encouraged to believe? (conclusion)
> What claims are supposed to be doing the encouraging? (premises)

Some will have indicating words or phrases and some will not.

1. There's no stamp on that envelope. The Post Office won't deliver it. The Post Office delivers only if there's a stamp.
2. He obviously did not do it, because, if he had, then the door would be open; and it's not.
3. It's illegal, and, in my book, you should not do what's illegal. You shouldn't do it.
4. Since he has to go, and since, if he has to go, then you have to go, I guess, therefore, that you have to go.
5. That my daughter scuffed up the gym floor with black-soled shoes is false for the following reasons: she has never been to that gym and she does not own black-soled shoes.
6. Sally's name is on the inside of the bag, and the bag smells of the same perfume Sally wears. This shows us that Sally was there.
7. John likely trains. Most professional athletes have to train. John is definitely a pro athlete.
8. Green tea has been shown to be good for your health in studies. Green tea likely will be good for my health. I drink green tea.
9. Christians are monotheists. Catholics are monotheists. Catholics are Christians.
10. You're in this room and either a sheep or a critical thinker, and you're no sheep; so, you're a critical thinker.
11. God exists provided there is no evil. God does not exist. There is evil everywhere.
12. Because it's such a difficult project, and because difficult projects require more pay, I'll make sure to pay you more.
13. We can conclude that the butler did it, since either the butler or the driver did it. And, we know the driver didn't do it.
14. Your shoes are muddy. Your hair is wet. Hence, you were out in the garden during the rainstorm.
15. "Because, dude, if I drink, then I am, and because I do drink, dude . . . therefore, dude . . . I am"—One of Rob's drunken Cartesian college friends

Real-Life Example: Reasoning Through a Crime Scene

Chief Gresham arrived on the scene of the grisly murder. Thankfully, officers had roped off the area before any evidence could be disturbed. Gresham began wandering through the carnage in attempt to determine what had happened. On one side of the room lay three bodies near one another, two males and one female, all fully clothed. Laid neatly across the two men was a flagpole with an obelisk on top. The hands of all three people were bound and each had a single gunshot to the head. The gunshot wounds of two victims, the two males, were in the back of the head, but the female's was in her temple. Across the room was another body, male, with a large stab wound in his stomach and a gun in his left hand. The only other items in the room were a couch, a desk chair, a gallon of bleach, a can of white paint, and an empty bookshelf. Though no knife was ever found, Chief Gresham quickly concludes that the crimes were committed by one or more persons in this room. Furthermore, he concludes that the female killed the three men and that the one with the gun killed the female. Gresham has been called to court to testify and he needs your help writing his report. Using only the evidence available to you, construct an argument for Gresham that has the following complex claim as its conclusion:

The female killed the three men, and the man with the gun killed the female.

2   Evaluating Arguments

2.1. Reconstructing arguments

Once you've located an argument (see the previous chapter), it is time to reconstruct it. Arguments are typically found embedded in written paragraphs, in complex orations made by politicians on TV, or in disjointed conversations around the table at a bar. In order to clearly evaluate an argument, it must be extracted from this rhetorical clutter and verbiage. **Reconstructing an argument** involves stripping away everything that is not absolutely necessary to the argument and then arranging the claims so that the premises are clearly distinguishable from conclusion.

2.1.1. Extraneous material

Extraneous material is anything in a paragraph that does not do rational work, that is, words or phrases that do not play a significant role in a premise or a conclusion. Extraneous material makes natural languages rhythmic and rich and explains why Moby Dick is a classic and most dime store romances aren't. Consider this beautiful passage from the book of Proverbs in the Bible:

> My son, if you receive my words and treasure up my commandments with you, making your ear attentive to wisdom and inclining your heart to understanding; yes, if you call out for insight and raise your voice for understanding, if you seek it like silver and search for it as for hidden treasures, then you will understand the fear of the LORD and find the knowledge of God. (Proverbs 2:1–5, ESV)

In this case, extraneous material makes a very simple idea poetic. But the claim, stripped of this material, is a basic conditional:

> If you act wisely and diligently seek knowledge, then you will know God.

Other times, however, extraneous material just gets in the way and government language can be some of the worse. William Zinsser tells the story of a U.S. government document from 1942 explaining preparations to be made for blackouts.[1] In 1942, since the United States had just entered the war, there was a worry about air raids. For protection, people might be ordered to "black out" all windows in a building at night so that light would not shine through turning that building into a target. One blackout order for government offices read as follows:

> Such preparations shall be made as will completely obscure all Federal buildings and non-Federal buildings occupied by the Federal government during an air raid for any period of time from visibility by reason of internal or external illumination.

This sentence is ungainly and it is difficult to interpret its meaning. President Franklin Roosevelt, in a commendable effort to simplify government language, responded, "Tell them that in buildings where they have to keep the work going to put something across the windows." We might put it even more simply as a conditional:

> If you must work through the night, then block the light from shining through the windows.

There is a pretty straightforward list of extraneous material you will want to remove when you begin reconstructing an argument:

---

(1) Set up or background phrases:
Once again . . .; It pains me to have to relate to you . . .; To begin . . .; Let me just say a few words about . . .; X was born on February . . .; Let me give it to you straight . . .; It has recently come to my attention . . .; Stop me if you've heard this . . .; As you are well aware . . .; etc.

(2) Expressions of personal feeling or commentary:
It happens over and over . . .; Some of the worst X . . .; . . . X rears its ugly head . . .; It's pretty obvious . . .; It should be clear that . . .; No one could doubt . . .; I can't believe . . .; You know, it's really frustrating when . . .; It's really sad that . . .; Descartes was a great philosopher who . . .; I would like to propose that . . .; etc.

(3) Transition phrases:
In addition . . .; . . . which leads me to my next point . . .; On one hand . . . , on the other hand . . .; . . . insofar as . . .; . . . naturally . . .; . . . of course . . .; Didn't you know, . . .; You know, . . .; That raises the question . . . (not "begs the question," the latter is a fallacy, see Chapter 18); . . . which leads us to ask . . .; . . . which raises another point . . .; etc.

Leaders of organizations have a nasty talent for using lots of words without saying much of anything at all. You can construct whole presentations out of extraneous material. Imagine being welcomed into an organization with the following speech:

> I would like to begin our time together by welcoming our newcomers. We are sincerely looking forward to getting to know you all and to sharing with one another our knowledge and abilities so we can move ahead and be the best we can be. In addition, I look forward to hearing all your great new ideas and learning about the experiences you are bringing to the table. Of course, we have a long history of quality and achievement, and we're looking once again to the future; we're dreaming big so that our tradition of excellence will further extend our reputation into this community and into our world.

Some would call this "politispeak" or "politalk." Good reasoners call it *nonsense*.

2.1.2. Implicit claims

Often, when people are reasoning, they **explicitly** omit a premise or conclusion in their argument, but the premise or conclusion is there, nonetheless; it is **implicit**. Consider this simple argument:

---

(1) "If you are innocent, then we would not have caught you with your hand in the cookie jar. But, alas, we did catch you."

We immediately see that the arguer intends you to believe, "You are not innocent" or "It's not the case that you are innocent." But, of course, that claim is not explicit in the argument; it is an **implicit conclusion**. Here are a few more simple arguments with implicit conclusions:

---

(2) "His mom told him to do it or else he'd get a good beating, and he hasn't been beaten."

P1: Do it or else he'd get a good beating.
P2: He hasn't been beaten.
C: Thus, he did it.

(3) "If you want to go downtown, you'll need to take the bus; and if you want to take the bus, you'd better put a rush on it to get to that station!"

P1: If you want to go downtown, you'll need to take the bus.
P2: If you want to take the bus, you'd better put a rush on it to get to that station.
C: We can conclude that if you want to go downtown, then you'd better put a rush on it to get to that station.

(4) "FIXO has been shown to fix all of these tough problems, and you have a similar problem."

P1: FIXO has been shown to fix all of these tough problems.
P2: You have a similar problem.
C: FIXO will fix your problem.

Here are a few simple arguments with **implicit premises**:

---

(5) "If you do it that way, you'll get wet. Oops! You got wet."

P1: If you do it that way, you'll get wet.
P2: You did it that way.
C: You got wet.

(6) "A person makes it into the academy only if he or she passes the course. She didn't make it in.

P1: A person makes it into the academy only if he or she passes the course.
P2: She did not pass the course.
C: She didn't make it in.

(7) "Holding the substance like that is dangerous. You should not do that."

P1: Holding the substance like that is dangerous.
P2: You should not do whatever is dangerous.
C: You should not do that (hold the substance that way).

Keep an eye out for implicit claims that are part of an argument. As a critical thinker, your goal is to lay out, explicitly, all of the premises and conclusions in an argument. So, anytime you come across an implicit premise or conclusion, make it explicit!

In the first chapter, we noted that a claim is distinct from a question. Actually, however, there are times when *questions can be disguised claims*, and, hence, may be a premise or a conclusion in an argument. In other words, sometimes questions are implicit premises or conclusions. Consider these two arguments:

---

(1) "Why should we have to pay for the plumbing bill? We rent this place, we don't own. Plus, the toilet has been causing us problems since we moved in."

(2) "You're a good boy, right Johnny? And good boys shouldn't hit, should they?"

In argument (1), the question is actually a masked claim that is also the conclusion, and goes something like this: "We should not have to pay for the plumbing bill." In argument (2), the first question is a masked claim that goes something like "Johnny is a good boy," while the second question is a masked claim that goes like "Good boys shouldn't hit." Also, in (2) there is an implicit conclusion: "Johnny shouldn't hit." We can lay these arguments out, explicitly, in argument form:

---

(1) "Why should we have to pay for the plumbing bill? We rent this place, we don't own. Plus, the toilet has been causing us problems since we moved in."

P1: We rent this place, we don't own.
P2: The toilet has been causing us problems since we moved in.
C: We should not have to pay for the plumbing bill.

(2) "You're a good boy, right Johnny? And good boys shouldn't hit, should they?"

P1: Johnny is a good boy.
P2: Good boys shouldn't hit.
C: Johnny shouldn't hit.

2.1.3. Ambiguity and vagueness

Once you've eliminated extraneous material from an argument and identified any implicit premises or conclusions, you can focus on the words and phrases that are doing rational work. But not all words and phrases that are doing that work are clear. They can be ambiguous or vague.

A word or phrase is *ambiguous* if it has more than one clear interpretation. For instance, the word "law" has several clear meanings: criminal law, civil law, moral law, natural law, etc. The trick is figuring out what the arguer means. There are two types of ambiguity: *lexical* and *syntactic*.

Lexical Ambiguity: A word is lexically ambiguous if it has *more than one clear meaning*, as we have seen with "law." "Bank" is also lexically ambiguous because it could mean "a river bank" or "a savings bank" or a mass of something, such as "a computer bank" or "a bank of clouds." The word "human" might mean "a being with a certain sort of DNA" or it might mean "a being with a certain set of mental states": e.g., self-aware and rational.

If a crime happened in a lab, we can imagine someone telling the police, "He was assaulted by the lab mice." This claim is lexically ambiguous because the word "by" can have more than one meaning. Our witness might have meant that the victim was assaulted *near* the area where the lab mice are kept, or, however strange, the lab mice assaulted the victim.

Some common lexically ambiguous words include:

match	(make the same; a fire starter; a game)
hard	(difficult; resistant; tough)
pen	(a writing tool; to enclose)
draw	(to pull out; to represent with a pencil or pen)
chip	(golf technique; poker money; contribute)
head	(leader; body part)
suit	(clothing; legal proceeding)
mouse	(rodent; computer hardware)
virus	(illness; malicious computer program)

To resolve lexical ambiguity, make sure your terms are properly qualified. If you mean "moral law," say "moral law," and not just "law." If you mean "river bank," use "river bank," and not just "bank." Context will often make clear what an arguer means (legislators rarely discuss natural laws), but it is never a bad form to be precise when constructing an argument.

Syntactic Ambiguity: A phrase is syntactically (or "structurally") ambiguous if *the arrangement of words allows for more than one clear interpretation.* For instance, "I cancelled my travel plans to play golf," might mean, "my travel plans included playing golf but I cancelled those plans," or it might mean, "I cancelled my travel plans *in order to* play golf." Notice that specifying the type of travel in this example will not help. For instance, I might have said, "I cancelled my vacation to play golf." Since golf is typically a leisure activity, we might associate it with a vacation. But I might still have meant, "I cancelled my (family) vacation to play golf (with my friends)." And if you knew I was a competitive golfer, playing golf would not necessarily indicate an activity associated with leisure or a vacation.

Consider also, "The community has been helping assault victims." Notice that, in a case of syntactic ambiguity, the ambiguity does not result from just one word, but from the way the words are arranged. We hope the speaker means the community has been helping victims of assault and not helping *to assault* victims. Also, imagine reading a novel with the line, "The child was lost in the hall." Out of context it is not clear what happened. It might be that a child went missing in the hall, or that a child died in the hall, or that a child in the hall could not find her way.

Since sentences can be arranged in a number of ways, there is not a set of common syntactic ambiguities, but here are a few more examples:

Murderer gets fifteen years in Luggage case.

– The murderer involved in the "Luggage Case" is sentences to fifteen years in prison.
– The murderer is sentenced to spend fifteen years in a luggage case.

Supreme Court tries stabbing suspect.

– The Supreme Court places stabbing suspect on trial.
– The Supreme Court tries to stab a suspect.

Committee's head discovers hidden arms.

– The committee's head finds weapons that were hidden.
– The committee's head finds appendages of which he wasn't aware.

Sister sues after wrongful death.

– After her wrongful death, the nun sues.
– After a woman's wrongful death, her sister sues.

To eliminate syntactic ambiguity, you must rely heavily on context. If either or all meanings could be legitimate interpretations, you may have to assume one meaning just for the sake of argument. If one is more plausible, explain why. If both or all interpretations are plausible, you may have to construct different arguments for each.

Vagueness: A word or phrase that's *vague* has a clear meaning, but not precisely defined truth conditions. A word's **truth conditions** are those conditions on which we could say for sure that the claim in which the word is used is true or false. For instance, we all know what it means for someone to be "bald"—in fact, at 40, Rob is definitely going bald! But *at what point* does someone become bald? How many hairs can be left and someone still be considered bald? The same goes for "dry." Sitting at my desk, I would consider myself dry, but that doesn't mean there are no water molecules on my skin. So what does it mean? How many water molecules must I have on my skin before I am no longer dry?

Consider the word, "obscene." Supreme Court Justice Potter Stewart, speaking in his official capacity as Justice, said of "obscenity" that he could not define it, "But I know it when I see it." That a group of highly educated, legally trained men could not accurately define "obscenity" is quite a testimony to the word's vagueness (perhaps if they'd had some women justices . . .). But it has a clear meaning; we all know what a speaker means when he says something is "obscene." But what actually counts? That's more difficult.

Some words are both vague and ambiguous, so don't be surprised that some words that are commonly lexically ambiguous are also commonly vague. Some common vague terms include:

tall/short	(Napoleon would be short today, but not when he was alive.)
close/far	(If you live in Montana, 80 miles is nearby; if you live in NYC, not so much.)
weak/strong	(Schwarzenegger won Mr. Universe, but he's got nothing on a grizzly bear.)
soft/hard	(I thought my dog's fur was soft until I got a cat.)
fat/thin	(Let's face it, the painter Reubens would think today's fashion models are emaciated.)
pile or heap	(Just how many grains of sand does it take to make a "pile"? The world may never know.)

Eliminating vagueness is not easy. You will almost always have to find a different, more precise word. If you cannot find an alternative, you can sometimes stipulate what you mean by a word. For instance, you might begin, "By 'pile' I mean five or more grains of sand" or "I will use 'fat' to mean someone who is more than twenty pounds over their ideal body weight. And by 'ideal body weight,' I mean the calculation. . . ." Sometimes an alternative is not available and stipulation will not help. If this is the case, your argument will be inescapably vague. If you find yourself with an inescapably vague argument, be sure to note the vagueness and allow that an unforeseen resolution may alter the conclusion.

2.1.4. Argument form

After you have removed extraneous material, identified implicit claims, and resolved any issues with ambiguity or vagueness, it is helpful to organize the claims in the argument so that the premises are clearly distinct from the conclusion. The standard way of organizing the claims of an argument is called **argument form**. To put an argument in argument form, number the premises and list them one on top of the other. Draw a line, and then list the conclusion below the line. Here are a few examples:

(A) "The government is out to get us, since we're taxed everywhere we turn and our privacy rights are constantly being violated."

In Argument Form:
Premise 1: (Since) "we are taxed everywhere we turn"
Premise 2: (Since) "our privacy rights are constantly being violated"

Conclusion: (So) "the government is out to get us"

(B) "Sam lost the golf clubs, and he lost the score card. He'll never make it as a caddy. Oh, and he showed up late to the club house, too."

In Argument Form:
P1: (Because) "Sam lost the golf clubs"
P2: (Since) "Sam lost the score card"
P3: (For the reason that . . .) "Sam showed up late to the club house"

Conclusion: (Thus, Hence, This shows us that . . .) "Sam will never make it as a caddy"

(C) "Every comic book reader I've ever met has been a geek. They're all geeks!"

In Argument Form:
P1: (Since) "Every comic book reading person I've ever met has been a geek"

Conclusion: (Therefore, Ergo, we can conclude that . . .) "All comic book reading persons are geeks"

2.2. Two types of arguments

There are two basic types of arguments: **deductive** and **inductive**. In a deductive argument, an arguer's conclusion follows from his premise(s) with *certainty* so that, if all of the premises are true, then the conclusion must be true, without any doubt whatsoever. **NOTE WELL: This is *not* to say that the conclusion *is* true or that the premise(s) *are* true.** We are only saying: the argument is structured such that, *if* all premises are true, *then* the conclusion is true.

In a deductive argument, the conclusion follows with certainty from the premises. If an arguer constructs such an argument, her argument is **valid**.

If an argument is valid, the premises entail the conclusion; it is not possible for the premises to be true and the conclusion to be false.

A conclusion *follows* from a premise if, independent of any other considerations, someone is justified in accepting the conclusion given in the premises. A conclusion can follow from premises with more or less likelihood, that is, with a greater or lesser degree of **relative probability**. Relative probability is the likelihood that the conclusion is true *given* (assuming) that the premises are true. If a conclusion follows from premises with certainty, that is, if the conclusion has a relative probability of 1, or 100%, the argument is valid. If the conclusion follows from the premises with a likelihood less than certainty, that is, it has a relative probability less than 1, or between 0 and 99.999999999%, it is **invalid**.

Recently, while Rob was in a comic book shop, he overheard two ten-year-old boys talking about their desire for the copy of *Batman* #1 (Spring, 1940) that was in a locked display case—a very difficult comic book to find. One of the boys put forward a deductive argument that went something like this:

Premise 1: If we both do our chores, then we'll get $200.00 (total) from our parents;
Premise 2: And if we get $200.00, then we'll be able to buy this copy of *Batman* #1;
Conclusion: So, if we both do our chores, then we'll be able to buy a copy of *Batman* #1.

Provided that the two premises are true, we can see that the conclusion absolutely must be true. Here are a few more deductive arguments in standard argument form:

P1: If it's a cat, then it's a mammal.
P2: If it's a mammal, then it's warm-blooded.
C: Therefore, if it's a cat, then it's warm-blooded.

P1: It's either the soup or salad for you,
P2: And you did not opt for the soup.
C: So, it's salad for you.

P1: If the project is complete, then we would see the final step.
P2: Since we do not see the final step.
C: We can conclude that the project is not complete.

In each of these examples, just as with the *Batman #1* argument above, if all the premises are true, then the conclusion has to be true:

Exercises 2.a.

For each of the following incomplete arguments, fill in the missing premises or conclusions to construct valid deductive arguments:

P1: All Christians are monotheists.
P2: . . .
C: Therefore, all Christians believe in one god.

P1: If people are wicked, then they should be wicked.
P2: Because people are wicked,
C: . . .

P1: You're serious or you're lying.
P2: . . .
C: Hence, you're lying.

P1: If it rains we stay, and if it snows we go.
P2: It either rains or snows.
C: . . .

In an inductive argument, a conclusion follows from a set of premises with some degree of likelihood or probability so that, if the degree is high enough and if all of the premises are true, then the conclusion likely or probably is true. If the arguer achieves her goal and the conclusion follows from the premises with a *high degree of likelihood*, the argument is **strong**. On the other hand, the conclusion does not follow with a high degree of probability, the argument is **weak**.

It is important to see that the strength of an inductive argument has nothing to do with the truth of the premises. As we said with deductive arguments, we do not mean that the premises *are* true, only that, *if* they are, the conclusion is also likely true. However, in an inductive argument, it is still possible that the conclusion is false *even if the premises are true*. This means that *all inductive arguments are invalid*.

It is important to note that, just because an argument is invalid, doesn't mean it is a bad argument. We just cannot evaluate it as if it were deductive. We need to see whether it has inductive strength. It may turn out to be a good inductive argument (although still invalid, as we have defined the term above).

Jamie's friend ordered a book from a certain book shop, assuming it would arrive in good shape, without the cover ripped. Jamie's friend reasoned like this:

> P1: In the past, when I received a book from this book shop, it was in good shape, without the cover ripped.
> P2: And because this book order is similar to the last,
> C: (It is therefore likely that) I'll receive this book that I just ordered in good shape, without the cover ripped.

The conclusion is <I'll receive this book that I just ordered in good shape without the cover ripped>. Provided the premises are true, the conclusion is probably or likely true, but not certainly true. It makes sense to conclude that his book would arrive in good shape, without the cover ripped, given his past experience with the book shop. But the truth concerning his success in getting a book in good shape in the past does not guarantee with certainty or without a doubt that he *will* get this book in good shape. It's still possible that someone at the shop, say, accidentally rips the cover without knowing it prior to shipping or purposefully wants to deceive Jamie's friend with a book copy that has a two-inch rip in the cover, so the conclusion is merely probable or likely. In order to let others know this conclusion follows only with some degree of probability, and not with certainty, we include phrases like, "it is likely that," "probably," "there's a good chance that." In fact, Jamie's friend did get the book in good shape, but he needn't *necessarily* have received it that way.

Consider the kind of reasoning someone may have utilized just before Joel Schumacher's *Batman and Robin* came out in 1997. Because of the wild financial success of *Batman Forever* in 1995, someone might have concluded that *Batman and Robin* would be just as successful. No one would bet their life on this conclusion, but the filmmakers risked millions on it. Surprisingly—and to the dismay of the investors and many Batman fans—*Batman and Robin* was a financial failure and heavily criticized by many people. This is an example of inductive reasoning where it seemed as if the conclusion was going to be true, but turned out to be false in the end.

How can you tell whether an argument is strong or weak? An argument is generally strong if the probability that the conclusion is true given the premises is greater than 50%. This doesn't mean you should always believe a conclusion that is more than 50% likely given the premises. For instance, if one conclusion is 52% likely given a set of premises, and another is 65% given the same premises, though both are strong, the latter is clearly stronger.

Sometimes determining strength will be a matter of calculating the percentages. This is possible when you have real numbers, for instance, from scientific or statistical data (though these numbers can be tricky, see chapter 9). But even when you don't have real numbers, there are some indicator words that will help you decide whether an inductive argument is strong. Consider the following two arguments:

A.

P1: Most members of Congress voted to invade Iraq.
P2: John Kerry is a member of Congress.
C: Therefore, (it is likely that) Kerry voted to invade Iraq.

B.

P1: Many members of Congress voted to invade Iraq.
P2: John Kerry is a member of Congress.
C: Therefore, (it is likely that) Kerry voted to invade Iraq.

Since "most" means "more than 50%," the left argument is strong. Since "many" does not indicate anything with respect to percentage or likelihood, the right argument is not strong. If 100,000 people vote for a governor, that's a good many, even if it's only 40% of the voters.

Here are two more examples:

C.

P1: Almost all Republicans are conservative.

P2: John McCain is a Republican.
C: Therefore, (it is likely that) McCain is conservative.

D.

P1: A significant percentage of Republicans are conservative.
P2: John McCain is a Republican.
C: Therefore, (it is likely that) McCain is conservative.

Since "almost all" means "more than 50%," the left argument is strong. Since "a significant percentage" does not indicate what percentage counts as "significant," the right argument is not strong. 30% is not typically considered an insignificant amount, but it is not sufficient for making an argument strong.

There are instances where the 50% marker is not the best indicator of strength. Given what we know about biology and physics, it may be less than 50% likely that Darwinian evolution is true or that the Big Bang was anything like what physicists say it was. There may not even be enough evidence to make an informed judgment about their likelihoods. But since these inferences are based on the best evidence available and since there are no alternative explanations with higher likelihoods, the arguments for these views are strong. Something similar happens when you are arguing from a difference in percentages. If one hypothesis yields results that are 30% different from another hypothesis, then, even if the likelihood of both hypotheses is lower than 50%, the fact that there is a difference can be used to construct a strong argument about the hypotheses. So evaluating the strength of an argument sometimes requires an understanding of the context in which the argument is made.

Strong Quantifiers:	Weak Quantifiers:
Most	Some
Almost all	A few
It is likely that	It is possible that
Most likely	Somewhat likely
The majority	A percentage
Almost definitely	Could be
Highly probable	Many
More often than not	A significant percentage

Exercises 2.b.

For each of the following inductive arguments, explain whether the conclusion is (a) highly likely, (b) somewhat likely, (c) somewhat unlikely, or (d) highly unlikely:

1.
P1: Rover the dog bit me last year when I tried to pet him.
P2: Rover has been castrated and has been much calmer in the past three months.
C: Rover will bite me when I try to pet him today.

2.
P1: Jones had sex with Brown's wife.
P2: Brown told Jones he was going to kill Jones.
P3: Jones was murdered.
C: Brown is the murderer.

3.
P1: Watches are complex and have watch-makers.
P2: The universe is complex like a watch.
C: The universe has a universe-maker.

4.
P1: The sign on Interstate 95 says the town is 1 mile away.
C: The town is, in fact, 1 mile away.

5.
P1: Frank loves Jane
P2: Jane loves Tom.
C: Frank loves Tom.

2.3. Good and bad arguments

As critical thinkers, it is not enough to put forward arguments—we have to make sure that the arguments are good, and by "good" we mean, they conform to the principles of correct reasoning. Remember that critical thinkers are concerned with the principles of correct reasoning concerning the formation and evaluation of arguments. Recall this argument:

> P1: Every comic book reading person I've ever met has been a geek.
> C: So, every comic reading person is a geek.

Not only is this a mean-spirited form of reasoning (poor comic book geeks!), anyone can see that the conclusion does not follow from the premise. First, we do not know how many comic-book-reading people you've met, and second, we do not know how many comic book readers there are. This is an example of a **bad argument**—believe it or not, there are plenty of comic readers who are *not* geeks; and it is unlikely that anyone could know the vast majority of comic readers. Yet millions of racists, ageists, sexists, anti-comic bookists, and every other kind of extreme "ists" reason this way.

Both deductive and inductive arguments can be good or bad. Try to explain what is wrong with these arguments:

P1: My friend knows a person of X ethnic background who is rude.
P2: My sister knows a person of X ethnic background who is rude.
C: So, people of X ethnic background are all rude.

P1: The problem could be the wheel, the crank shaft, or both.
P2: We just found out that the wheel is the problem.
C: So, it's not the crank shaft.

P1: Almost all of the beans in this bag are red.
C: Hence, the next one I pull out definitely will not be red.

Whether someone intends to offer a deductive or an inductive argument, for that argument to be **good**, it must meet two conditions:

> (1) the conclusion must follow from the premise(s)—*absolutely* follow from the premise(s) with a deductive argument, or *likely* follow from the premise(s) with an inductive argument, and
> (2) all of the premises must be true.

If either one of these conditions (or both) is missing, then the argument is bad and should be rejected. We can draw an analogy with the battery on your car. The battery has two terminals. As long as both cables are connected, the car will start. If one or both of the cables is disconnected, the car won't start. The same goes for an argument: there are two conditions, and both must be met in order to successfully support a conclusion. Consider the following diagram:

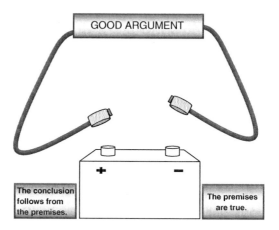

2.3.1. Good deductive arguments

The term **valid argument** is reserved for deductive arguments where a conclusion does, indeed, follow from premises with certainty (it is called **invalid** if the conclusion does not follow with certainty). You will find that "valid" has two uses in contemporary English: one means "legitimate," for instance, when someone says, "You've got a valid point" or "That claim is valid"; the other refers to the structure of an argument and means, "the conclusion follows necessarily from the premises." When evaluating arguments, only the second use is legitimate. **NOTE WELL:** This means that *claims are never valid or invalid*. Only a deductive argument where the conclusion necessarily follows from the premise(s) is valid. Claims are true or false; arguments are valid or invalid. All inductive arguments are invalid.

Example of a valid argument:

P1: All chemists are scientists.
P2: All scientists utilize the scientific method.
C: This shows us that all chemists utilize the scientific method.

Example of an invalid argument:

P1: All cats are mammals.
P2: All warm-blooded animals are mammals.
C: So, all cats are warm-blooded.

When an argument is valid and all the premises are true, the argument is a good, **sound argument**. The conclusion, then, is without a doubt, absolutely, positively true.

Examples of sound arguments:

P1: Our Sun is a star.
P2: All stars are composed of helium.
C: Our Sun is composed of helium.

P1: The famous attack on Pearl Harbor by the Japanese occurred on either 12/07/412 or 12/07/51.
P2: All warm-blooded animals are mammals.
C: So, all cats are warm-blooded.

Examples of valid, *unsound* arguments:

P1: All green things float.
P2: All ducks are green.
C: So, all ducks float.

P1: If it is round, then it is red.
P2: If it is a car, then it is round.
C: Therefore, all cars are red.

2.3.2. Good inductive arguments

The phrase **strong argument** is reserved for an argument where a conclusion likely will follow from premises (and **weak argument** if the conclusion likely does not follow). For our purposes, claims are never strong. Only philosophers correctly use "strong" of claims when they say things like, "You made a strong point" or "That claim is too strong." When philosophers talk about a "strong claim," they mean one that is very difficult to support, for instance, "God does not exist." By "weak claim," they mean one that is much easier to support, for instance, "The evidence for God's existence is inconclusive." We will not discuss strong or weak claims, only strong or weak arguments—that is, the likelihood of a conclusion's being true given the premises. And only an inductive argument where the conclusion likely follows from the premise(s) is strong or weak. Claims are true or false; inductive arguments are strong or weak. Consider the following examples:

A strong argument:

P1: The Tigers beat all of the other teams during the season.
P2: The Tigers have the best stats overall.
P3: The championship game is about to begin, and all of the Tiger teammates are in good health.
C: (It is very likely that) the Tigers will win the championship game.

A weak argument:

P1: The Tigers beat all of the other teams during the season.
P2: The Tigers have the best stats overall.
P3: The championship game is about to begin, and all of the Tiger teammates are in good health.
C: (We can infer that) the last-place Lions will win the championship game.

A weak argument:

P1: Frank is a Democrat.
P2: In the past, many Democrats have voted for bill X. [remember "many" is a weak quantifier]
C: (So,) Frank will vote for bill X.

When an argument is strong and all the premises are true, the argument is **cogent** (kō-jent). In a cogent argument, the conclusion most likely or probably is true. Conversely, in the inductive realm of reasoning if an argument is weak, all the premises are not true, or both, then the argument in **uncogent**.

Examples of cogent arguments:

P1: The scans show it to be a benign tumor.
P2: The specialist thinks it's a benign tumor.
P3: The patient has symptoms indicating that indicate it's a benign tumor.
C: Thus, the tumor is probably benign.

P1: The Sun rose today.
P2: The Sun rose all the days before.
C: Hence, the Sun will probably rise tomorrow.

Examples of strong, *uncogent* arguments:

P1: Most Americans are communists.
P2: Osama Bin Laden is an American.
C: Therefore, Bin Laden is probably a communist.

P1: Almost all private corporations are run by greedy profiteers.
P2: The U.S. Department of Education is a private corporation.
C: The U.S. Department of Education is run by greedy profiteers.

Absolute truth and probable truth are good things, so sound arguments and cogent arguments are, by definition, good arguments in the deductive and inductive realms, respectively.

Thus, as critically thinking creatures we must always go through the two-step procedure of checking our own arguments—and the arguments of others—to see if:

(1) the conclusion follows from the premises (Is the argument deductively valid or, if it is invalid, is it inductively strong?)
(2) all of the premises are true (Does your audience have reasons to believe the premises are true?)

If an argument fails to meet either (1) or (2) or both, then we should reject it; we do not have reasons to believe the conclusion. (This doesn't mean the conclusion is false; only that we do not yet have reasons to believe it.)

Good Deductive Argument = Sound Argument =
(1) Valid and (2) All Premises are True
Good Inductive Argument = Cogent Argument =
(1) Strong and (2) All Premises are True

Recall our ten-year-old's argument for doing chores in order to buy *Batman #1*:

> P1: If we both do our chores, then we'll get $200.00 (total) from our parents;
> P2: And if we get $200.00, then we'll be able to buy a copy of *Batman #1*;
> C: So, if we both do our chores, then we'll be able to buy a copy of *Batman #1*.

This argument might be bad because Premise 2 is not obviously true, given the information. It's not clear whether with $200.00 they'll be able to buy this particular copy *Batman #1*. Now, it's true the boy probably would not formulate this particular argument had the store not advertised it as $200, but we should question the truth of these premises (especially once you find out that a copy of *Batman #1* went for over $65,000 on Ebay).

In this case, if we find out that the store has a $10,000 price tag on the issue and the boy is just hoping to bargain with the owner, the conclusion, "If we both do our chores, then we'll be able to buy a *Batman #1*" is not supported by one of the reasons given (premise 2 is false). The argument is valid, but unsound. On the other hand, if premise 2 is true and if the boys really are able to come up with $200, then the conclusion must be true. The argument is sound.

Now, recall this argument from Jamie's friend:

> P1: In the past, when I received a book from this book shop, it was in good shape, without the cover ripped.
> P2: And because this book order is similar to the last one where I received a book in good shape,
> C: Therefore, it is likely that I'll receive this book that I just ordered in good shape, without the cover ripped.

Unfortunately, one good experience with a book-seller does not tell us much about whether the next experience will be favorable. What we call the "sample size" is just too small. Just as every bad chef can whip up one good meal every now and then and every good car manufacturer can accidentally produce one lemon, one instance of something is not representative of the majority of instances. In this argument, though the premises are true, the conclusion does not follow with much strength; and it certainly does not follow with a likelihood greater than 50%.

What this argument needs is more information. What is Jamie's friend who found a whole host of reviews about this bookseller and these reviews were mostly positive?

P1: In the past, when I received a book from this book shop, it was in good shape, without the cover ripped.

P2: This book order is similar to the last one where I received a book in good shape.

P3: Out of 6,738 reviews of this bookseller, 97% were positive.

C: Therefore, it is likely that I'll receive this book that I just ordered in good shape, without the cover ripped.

This new information increases the likelihood that Jamie's friend will receive the book in good condition. Now, it does not tell us much about whether the cover will be ripped. Perhaps his friend is buying a used book and the seller tells him that the cover is ripped. Perhaps a book can be in "good" condition with a ripped cover, whereas if the seller had said "excellent" condition, this would indicate a non-ripped cover as well. With this information, we now have a strong argument for the conclusion that the book will arrive in good condition, but it is still weak with respect to whether the cover is ripped.

The following argument is another example of a bad deductive argument:

P1: Our Sun is a star.

P2: All stars are cube-shaped.

C: Thus, our Sun is cube-shaped.

Even though it is valid (if the premises are true, the conclusion must be true), one of the premises is false.

Similarly, the following argument is a bad inductive argument because, even though it is strong, one of the premises is false (P2):

> P1: Most Republicans are conservative.
> P2: Barack Obama is a Republican.
> C: Thus, Obama likely is conservative.

And finally, consider one more bad argument:

> P1: Grass is green.
> P2: The sky is blue.
> C: The fool is on the hill at midnight.

What do we make of an argument like this? Clearly it's nonsense. But, since it is being offered as an argument, we must (for the sake of charity) treat it like one. Use our two-step process. Is the argument valid? No, the premises do not guarantee the conclusion. Is it at least strong? No, the premises do not grant strength to the conclusion greater than 50%. In fact, this is an inductive argument because the conclusion follows with some degree of probability less than 1, but that degree is zero. Given the premises, the conclusion is 0% likely. (Its *relative* probability is 0%; this doesn't mean that its objective probability is 0%—we may have independent evidence that increases its probability, but *given these premises*, it is 0% likely to be true.) Therefore, though the premises are true, since the argument is weak, it is a bad inductive argument.

2.4. Simple and complex arguments

In Chapter 1, we looked at the basics of reasoning, which included a description of claims and arguments. All of the arguments in the previous chapter, when laid out in argument form, were **simple arguments**. Simple arguments are arguments with only one conclusion, for instance:

Simple Arguments:

P1: If the floor is flooded, then we need to trudge through water.
P2: The floor is flooded.
C: Thus, we need to trudge through water.

P1: Either your eyes are in the blue spectrum or in the brown spectrum.
P2: Since your eyes are not in the brown spectrum . . .
C: we can conclude that your eyes are in the blue spectrum.

P1: Brown birds forage.
P2: Blue birds are a lot like brown birds.
C: It is likely that blue birds forage, too.

However, many arguments have two or more conclusions, and one conclusion will serve as the premise for a further conclusion. We will call arguments with more than one conclusion, **complex arguments**.

Consider the following simple argument:

P1: Daily pot-smoking causes brain damage.
P2: Daily pot-smoking impairs thinking.
P3: Anything that causes brain damage and impairs thinking is bad for you.
C: Daily pot-smoking is bad for you.

As critical thinkers, you are not always only going to want evidence for the truth of a conclusion, sometimes you will also need: (a) to provide evidence for the truth of the premises, or (b) to use that conclusion in another argument. In fact, most discussions and debates involve both (a) and (b). Consider this complex argument that builds on the simple argument above:

P1: Daily pot-smoking causes brain damage.
P2: Daily pot-smoking impairs thinking.
P3: Anything that causes brain damage and impairs thinking is bad for you.
C1: Daily pot-smoking is bad for you.

C1: Daily pot-smoking is bad for you.
P4: You should not do what is bad for you.
C2: You should not smoke pot daily.

Note how the conclusion of the first argument is used as the premise in the second argument. This is an example of (b) and is typical of reasoning that involves many different claims. In addition, if someone is asked to justify the premises of the first argument above, she might offer the following complex argument:

An Example of a Complex Argument:

P5: In study A, reported in a reputable journal, daily pot-smoking caused brain damage in 78% of subjects.
P6: In study B, reported in a reputable journal, daily pot-smoking caused brain damage in 82% of subjects.
P7: In study C, reported in a reputable journal, daily pot-smoking caused brain damage in 70% of subjects.
P8: In study D, reported in a reputable book, daily pot-smoking caused brain damage in 87% of subjects.
P9: In study E, reported in a reputable book, daily pot-smoking caused brain damage in 77% of subjects.
P1(C3): Daily pot-smoking causes brain damage.

P1: Daily pot-smoking causes brain damage.
P2: Daily pot-smoking impairs thinking.
P3: Anything that causes brain damage and impairs thinking is bad for you.
C1: Daily pot-smoking is bad for you.

C1: Daily pot-smoking is bad for you.
P4: You should not do what is bad for you.
C2: Daily pot-smoking is something you should not do.

In this case, someone is asking for justification for the claim that, "Daily pot-smoking causes brain damage." Our new argument in support of (P1) does this. Don't worry that the numbers are out of order; just make sure you label the premises so that they are easy to identify. When arguments get this complicated, most philosophers drop the Ps and Cs and just use numbers. Since you can clearly identify conclusions as the claim below the line, this helps keep things simple:

An Example of a Complex Argument:

7: In study A, reported in a reputable journal, daily pot-smoking caused brain damage in 78% of subjects.

8: In study B, reported in a reputable journal, daily pot-smoking caused brain damage in 82% of subjects.

9: In study C, reported in a reputable journal, daily pot-smoking caused brain damage in 70% of subjects.

10: In study D, reported in a reputable book, daily pot-smoking caused brain damage in 87% of subjects.

11: In study E, reported in a reputable book, daily pot-smoking caused brain damage in 77% of subjects.

1: Daily pot-smoking causes brain damage.

1: Daily pot-smoking causes brain damage.

2: Daily pot-smoking impairs thinking.

3: Anything that causes brain damage and impairs thinking is bad for you.

4: Daily pot-smoking is bad for you.

4: Daily pot-smoking is bad for you.

5: You should not do what is bad for you.

6: Daily pot-smoking is something you should not do.

You may also need an argument for, "Daily pot-smoking impairs thinking," and "Anything that causes brain damage and impairs thinking is bad for you," and "You should not do what is bad for you." Just remember, *if you are making the claim, the burden is on you to support it.*

Consider this complex argument presented in conversational language:

> "Hey John, it looks as if we can't go sledding. If it's above freezing, it is too wet to sled and if it is raining, it's above freezing. And, of course, it's raining!"

To see the structure of this complex argument clearly, we can break it up into two simple arguments and place each in argument form, like this, noting how the conclusion of the first simple argument acts as the premise in the second simple argument:

1: It is raining.
2: If it is raining, then it is above freezing.
3: It is above freezing.

3: It is above freezing.
4: If it is above freezing, it is too wet to sled.
5: It is too wet to sled.

One important thing to notice about this complex argument is that there is an *ultimate conclusion*, or final conclusion that the speaker wants to make: "It is too wet to sled," or, in other words, "We can't go sledding." In all complex arguments, there will be an ultimate conclusion that can be identified, usually when the complex argument is reconstructed.

Now consider this complex argument presented in conversational language:

"Well officer, in answer to your question: if he took the highway, then he would have run into the road block. He didn't run into the road block, so he didn't take the highway. Now, if he didn't go the highway route, he must have gone back roads. I guess he took the back roads, then. But taking back roads will slow him down. So, he must be moving slowly."

To see the structure of this complex argument clearly, we can organize it into three simple arguments and place each in argument form, like this:

1: If he took the highway, then he would have run into the road block.
2: He didn't run into the road block.
3: So, he didn't take the highway.

3: He didn't take the highway.
4: If he didn't take the highway, then he must have gone back roads.
5: He must have gone back roads.

5: He must have gone back roads.
6: If he goes back roads, he will be moving slowly.
7: So, he must be moving slowly.

Look at the following complex arguments and determine how the conclusion of one argument is acting as the premise of another argument. Place the simple arguments that comprise this complex argument in argument form the way we have done for the examples above:

Complex Argument 1:
"The law will be passed. Everyone I have spoken to about it who is involved in the voting process is in favor of the law's tenets. Now, if the law is passed, there will be backlash. And, if there's backlash then feathers will be ruffled, no doubt. So, we know that if the law is passed, feathers will be ruffled."

Complex Argument 2:
"John's artwork is the best. And the best is likely to win. It shows symmetry, it shows hard work, and, above all, it shows passion. The passion is displayed in his use of light and shade, as well as in his choice of colors."

2.5. More exercises

Exercises 2.c.

Each of the following claims involves an ambiguity. Write out each possible meaning so that the ambiguity is resolved. Identify which type of ambiguity is being committed.

1. He could not draw his sword.
2. He couldn't find the match.
3. He lost his suit.
4. She caught a virus.
5. She mastered the art of writing and speaking at the university.
6. He asked her about the universe in his kitchen.
7. The bystanders were struck by the angry words.
8. She got sick eating potato chips.

Exercises 2.d.

Each of the following claims includes a vague term. Rewrite the claim to eliminate the vagueness.

1. The old man was bald.
2. She was the tallest woman.
3. Reubens mostly painted fat women.
4. Her skin was completely dry.
5. The painting was still wet.
6. Cook it until it is done.
7. Just watch until the good part, then you can turn it off.

Exercises 2.e.

In these arguments, identify whether the underlined claim is a premise or a conclusion. Remember to not only look for premise and conclusion indicating words, but also ask yourself the questions:

> What claim, exactly, am I trying to be convinced of? (conclusion)
> What claims are intended to convince me? (premises)

1. The post office delivers only if there is a stamp and given that the letter lacks a stamp, the post office will not deliver.
2. Most people make it via the road in 11 minutes. He took the road, so he will make it in about that time.
3. Philosophy entails critical thinking. Philosophy entails arguing. Critical thinking entails arguing.
4. Only band members are allowed on the stage. You're not allowed onstage since you are not a band member.
5. I will get either liberty or death. They will not give me liberty. They will give me death.
6. The universe must be billions of years old because there is plenty of evidence in textbooks.
7. Moral responsibility requires free acts. Free acts imply the falsity of determinism. Thus, if we are morally responsible, determinism must be_____.
8. He believes only in the visible; the soul is not visible, so you see, he won't believe in it.
9. The polls put Bush ahead right now. He is sure to win later. [The argument is missing a premise. What could it be?]
10. God either is not powerful enough or good enough to prevent evil. God is good. Hence, either evil exists and God is not powerful enough to prevent it or God is powerful enough to prevent it and evil does not exist.
11. Most of the beans in this bag are red. The next one I pull out will be red.
12. You will have good health since you're drinking tea and tea is linked to good health in studies.
13. The dog did not attack. It must be that the man wasn't a stranger. [This argument is missing a premise. What could it be?]
14. Even though it is possible to lose, they are sure to win the game. They are up so many points.
15. The kitty is asleep, as her eyes are closed. [This argument is missing a premise. What could it be?]

Exercises 2.f.

Now, go back through the arguments above and:

(a) place them into argument form, and
(b) identify whether the argument is deductive or inductive.

Exercises 2.g.

For the following arguments:

  (a) locate the conclusions and premises of the argument
  (b) place the argument in argument form
  (c) identify the argument as simple or complex and deductive or inductive
  (d) assess the argument as either a good deductive argument (sound = valid and all premises true) or a good inductive argument (cogent = strong and all premises are true)

1. "Bill Clinton was actually a bad president, maybe one of the worst we have ever had. He had sex with an intern, for Christ's sake, and any president that does that, in my book, is bad news . . . "
   [Note: "bad" is vague; clarify when you reconstruct]
2. "Siberian tigers are an endangered species. We should set up more programs to protect Siberian tigers, since any animal that is endangered should be protected."
3. "Van Halen's version of "You Really Got Me" will probably go down in history as more significant than The Kinks' version of the same song. Eddie Van Halen's guitar work is amazing. David Lee Roth has more charisma in his voice than the lead singer from The Kinks. And, Alex's drumming can't be beat (pun intended!)."
4. "In China, just prior to an earthquake, not only did a bunch of snakes suddenly wake up from hibernation, but dozens of fish were seen leaping from lakes and rivers, so I heard. Maybe animals can predict earthquakes. Also, it is reported that cows and horses have refused to enter barns just before an earthquake. And, pet-owners give accounts of their pets acting strangely just before the onset of an earthquake."
5. "Spiders keep pesky insects away. You should stop killing every spider you see. And they mostly pose no threat to us, too."
6. Critical thinking is the key to a successful future. Your college allows you to take a critical thinking course to fulfill a core course requirement. Since you want a successful future, you should take the critical thinking course. Why do I think it is key to a successful future? Lawyers, doctors, and engineers are successful people. And people who master critical thinking skills have a much higher chance of becoming a lawyer, doctor, or engineer.
7. The provost said that complying with the new regulations will allow us to keep enrollment high. If we keep enrollment high, we will be able to meet our budget. If we are able to meet our budget, you get to keep your job. Since you want to keep your job, you should help us comply with the new regulations. The new regulations help keep enrollment high because those regulations mean we are accredited and many students only choose colleges who are accredited.

Real-Life Example: A Logic Problem

The following problem can be worked out individually or as a group activity. Try it to test your deductive reasoning abilities.

6 friends—Andy, Ben, Carol, Dawn, Edith and Frank—are snacking around a round table, and each had either a fruit or a vegetable and each had only one of the following snacks: apples, bananas, cranberries, dates, eggplant (a vegetable) or figs. From the information provided below, try to figure out where each person sat and what snack they had. Try to construct clues using complex claims and deductive arguments:

1. The man to the right of the date-eater will only eat vegetables.
2. Dawn is directly across from the eggplant-eater.
3. Andy loves monkey food and is to the left of Dawn.
4. The apple-eater, who is two seats over from Andy, is across from the cranberry-eater.
5. Frank is across from the fig-eater and to the right of Edith.
6. Carol is allergic to apples.

Part Two
DEDUCTIVE REASONING

Thinking and Reasoning with Categories

3

3.1. Categories of things

Humans are natural classifiers, sorting all kinds of things into categories so as to better understand, predict, and control reality. A **category** is a class, group, or set containing things (or members or elements) that share some feature or characteristic in common. We can construct a category of things that are dogs, a category of things that are human, a category of things that are red and left shoes, a category of things that are in one's memory plus the number 2, a category of things that taste sweet and fly, and on and on. In fact, it's possible to classify anything that exists or you can think of into one category or another. Consider this claim:

"I think I saw a black cat sitting on the window sill of that vacant house."

It is possible to categorize the various things in this claim like this:

a. There is the category of **things I think I saw**
   e.g., I think I saw water on the road, I think I saw a mouse scurry, etc.

b. There is the category of **things that are black**
   e.g., black cats, black bats, black rats, black rocks, black socks, black blocks, etc.

c. There is the category of **things that are cats**
   e.g., Garfield, Morris, Fluffy, Xantippe (Jamie's cat), etc.

d. There is the category of **things that are black cats**
   e.g., Grover (my friend's black cat), Janey (my other friend's black cat), etc.

e. There is the category of **things that are sitting**
   e.g., Rob, right now as he is typing this chapter, My Uncle Jed on the back porch, etc.

f. There is the category of **things that are sitting on the window sill of that vacant house**
   e.g., a black cat, maybe a plant, too, etc.

g. There is the category of **things that are window sills**
   e.g., the ones in the vacant house, the ones in the White House, etc.

h. There is the category of **things that are vacant**
   e.g., this house, that room, etc.

i. There is the category of **things that are houses**
   e.g., the White House, the house on Elm and Main in Central City, Iowa, etc.

j. There is the category of **things that are vacant houses**
   e.g., this vacant house, that vacant house, etc.

* There is also the category of: **things that are *that* vacant house,** which contains only one thing, namely, that particular vacant house.

* There is the category of: **things that are me** doing the thinking, which contains only one thing, the "me" noted in the category.

An easy way to visualize categories of things is with a circle and little rectangles in the circle, where the circle represents the category, type, class, group, or set of things, and the little rectangles in the circle represent the individuals, things, or **members** in that category. Also, we can use a capital letter to represent the category itself as in, say, *C* for the category of cats, *B* for the category of black things, *H* for the category of houses, etc. Usually, people will choose the first letter of the word that designates the category. You just have to make sure that you know what category the letter is symbolizing.

Sometimes, this can be confusing to keep straight, so be aware of this. The following represent a few of the categories from our cat example:

the category of things that are cats

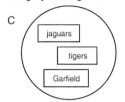

the category of things that are black

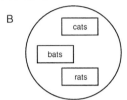

the category of things that are houses

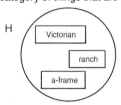

the category of things that are me

Exercises 3.a.

In each of the following claims, identify as many categories of things as you can, by using the "things that are BLANK" format, as we have done above:

1. Aristotle was an Ancient Greek philosopher who wrote many treatises.
2. Rob has seen a few mailboxes painted like R2–D2, but most are blue.
3. Dinosaurs, like the Stegosaurus, roamed the Earth during the Jurassic Period.
4. People who are not handicapped but who take handicapped persons' parking spots belong in jail.

3.2. Relating categories to one another

Not only do we categorize things, we make assertions about the relationships between and among categories. For example, consider the category of things that are snakes and the category of things that are venomous. Now, think of all the things that are snakes, like pythons, boa constrictors, vipers, etc. and all of the things that are venomous, like jellyfishes, stingrays, spiders, etc. In trying to accurately represent reality, we might assert that some members of the category of snakes belong in, or are in, the category of things that are venomous, which turns out to be true. Think of rattlesnakes or asps, which are venomous snakes. Using circles again to represent categories of things, and little rectangles to represent the things or members in the categories, and capital letters to represent categories, we can visualize the claim, "Some snakes are venomous" like this:

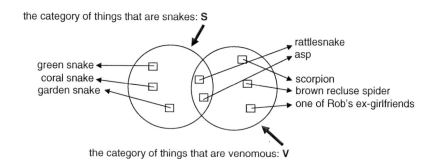

Notice that there are other snakes that are non-venomous, like green snakes and garden snakes, and there are other venomous things, like scorpions and one of Rob's ex-girlfriends (a little critical thinking humor, here). Further, not only can we say that "Some venomous things are snakes"—and, essentially, we are saying the same thing as "Some snakes are venomous"—but it is also the case that both claims are true when we look at reality.

To diagram this claim, we don't really need to identify all non-venomous snakes or all venomous things; we can focus only on venomous snakes. The Venn Diagram for "Some venomous things are snakes," looks like this:

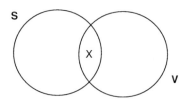

(The "X" indicates, "at least one"; see "I-Claim" below.) Therefore, the diagram expresses a claim, and, in this case, the claim is true. The diagram we use is modeled after what are known as **Venn diagrams**, named after the famous logician, John Venn (1834–1923). We will continue to talk more about Venn diagrams as this chapter progresses.

We can also assert that two categories of things have nothing to do with one another, that is, they have no members in common. For instance, consider the claim, "No dogs are cats." Using circles again to represent categories of things, little rectangles to represent the members in the categories, and capital letters to represent categories, we can add a shaded black area to represent a void or nothing, we can visualize the claim "no dogs are cats" like this:

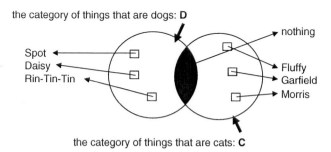

Notice *D* and *C* intersect one another in football-shaped area (an American football, that is, not a soccer ball). Notice also that the shaded black area in that intersection of *D* and *C* pictorially represents the fact that nothing in the category of dogs is in the category of cats, and vice versa. Further, not only can we say that "No dogs are cats"—and, essentially, we are saying the same thing as "No cats are dogs"—but it is also the case that both claims are true in reality. In this case, as before, the diagram expresses a true claim.

3.3. Standard-form categorical claims

In Western history, the famous Greek philosopher, Aristotle (384–322 BCE), is usually credited with reformulated typical categorical claims into what is known as *standard-form categorical claims*. The idea is that any claim a person makes can be translated into one of four basic types of claim: **A-claim, E-claim, I-claim**, and **O-claim**. We'll explain each type, give several examples of claims translated into each type, and then show how each example can be pictorially represented with a Venn diagram.

The *A*-claim

A standard-form categorical *A*-claim has this form:

All *A*s are *B*s.

and its diagram is drawn like this:

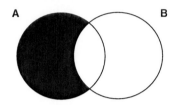

Notice that the football-looking intersection between *A* and *B* is left un-shaded, while the rest of the *A* circle is shaded in. This expresses that there is no member of *A* (shaded area = nothing) that is not a member of *B*, or again, all *A*s are *B*s.

Consider the *A*-claim: All lawyers are jerks. Its diagram would look like this:

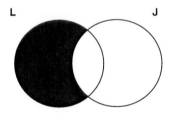

The shaded area indicates that everything in the category of lawyers is also in the category of jerks.

Exercises 3.b.

Venn diagram the following A-claims using the capital letters given:

1. All cats (*C*) are mammals (*M*).
2. All Catholics (*C*) are Christians (*X*).
3. All voters in the United States (*U*) are at least 1. years old (*E*).
4. All things that are living (*L*) are things that require water (*W*).
5. All AC/DC songs (*A*) are songs that rock (*R*).

Rewrite each of the following claims as A-claims, then Venn diagram:

1. Every human is an air-breather.
2. Items in this bin are on sale.
3. Dinosaurs are extinct.
4. Clocks tell time.
5. Calculators perform calculations.

The E-claim

A standard-form categorical E-claim has this form:

No As are Bs.

and its diagram is drawn like this:

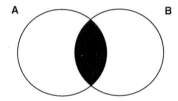

Notice that the football-looking intersection between categories A and B is shaded. This diagram expresses that there is no member of A (shaded area = nothing) that is a member of B or, again, No As are Bs.

Consider the E-claim: No men are one-thousand feet tall. The Venn diagram for this claim looks like this:

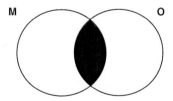

The shaded area indicates that there are no men in the category of things that are one-thousand feet tall.

Exercises 3.c.

Venn diagram the following E-claims using the capital letters given:

1. No cats (*C*) are fish (*F*).
2. No Christians (*C*) are polytheists (*P*).
3. No voters in the United States (*U*) are under 1. years old (*E*).
4. No things that are made by humans (*H*) are things that can be in two places at once (*T*).
5. Nothing in that can (*C*) is edible (*E*).

Rewrite each of the following claims as E-claims, then Venn diagram:

1. Every human male cannot give birth.
2. Nothing in this drawer is sharp-edged.
3. There are no U.S. Civil War veterans who are living.
4. No illegal immigrants deserve access to our health care system.
5. All felons are prohibited from voting.

The *I*-claim

A standard-form categorical *I*-claim has this form:

Some *A*s are *B*s.

and its diagram is drawn like this:

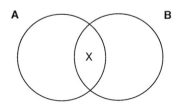

Notice that the football-looking intersection between *A* and *B* has an "X" in it, indicating that there is at least *one* member of *A* that is also a member of *B*. When we say "Some" here, we mean "at least one"; however, there could also be more than one. There is no shading because we do not know whether there are any *B*s that are not *A*s or whether there are any *A*s that are not *B*s. *I*-claims tell us only that some *A*s are *B*s. In addition, this diagram would be the same for the *I*-claim: Some *B*s are *A*s.

Exercises 3.d.

Venn diagram the following *I*-claims using the capital letters given:

1. Some cats (*A*) are de-clawed (*B*).
2. Some Christians (*A*) are Presbyterian (*B*).
3. Some voters in the United Kingdom (*A*) are over 9. years old (*B*).
4. Some things that are made by humans (*A*) are things that will last 1,00. years (*B*).
5. Some Democrats (*A*) are conservative (*B*).

Rewrite each of the following claims as *I*-claims, then Venn diagram:

1. There are lots of human males that are brown-haired.
2. There are fire hydrants that are painted yellow.
3. Some like it hot!
4. I know at least one 30-year-old man who likes Lady Gaga, and that's me.
5. C'mon, at least some Mormons are rational.

The *O*-claim

A standard-form categorical *O*-claim has this form:

Some *A*s are not *B*s

and its diagram is drawn like this:

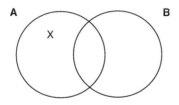

Notice that the category *A* has an X in it, but there is no X in the area where *A* and *B* intersect (the football-shaped area), indicating that there is at least one *A* that is not a *B*.

Exercises 3.e.

Venn diagram each of the following O-claims using the capital letters provided:

1. Some students at this college (*A*) are not sophomores (*B*).
2. Some tables (*A*) are not four-legged (*B*).

3. Some members of the Labour Party (*A*) are not very liberal (*B*).
4. Some pottery that have been made by the ancient Greeks (*A*) are not things that will ever be discovered intact (*B*).
5. Some Muslims (*A*) are not violent (*B*).

Rewrite each of the following claims as *O*-claims, then Venn diagram:

1. A few of the students are not going to the show.
2. There are U.S. mailboxes that aren't painted the standard blue.
3. Yech! Some of those grapes did not taste sweet.
4. Hey, there are a few non-religious conservatives.
5. At least some of our students are not rational.

Exercises 3.f.

Rewrite each of the following claims as an *A*-, *E*-, *I*-, or *O*-claim. Then draw diagrams for the following claims using circles, capital letters, and, where needed, a shaded area or an "X". We've done the second for you:

1. Jane, Mona, and Sue are women.
2. Some women are firefighters.
3. Jill and Sheri (both women) are firefighters.
4. Jack, Frank, and Jim (all men) are firefighters.
5. Jerry is a Catholic.
6. Shelly and Zoe (both women) are not Hindu.
7. No Catholics are Hindu.
8. Some CEOs are not greedy.
9. Everyone in Virginia is in the Eastern Time Zone.
10. We've heard that no one in England works past 3PM.

2. Some women are firefighters.

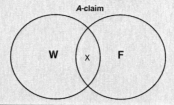

A-claim

Notice that we don't need a shaded area in this diagram. Some women are not firefighters, some firefighters are not women. But some women are both. This is indicated with an "X" in the football-shaped section.

3.4. Translation tips

You've already had a little practice translating English variations on categorical claims into standard-form categorical claims, but you may still be unclear how those translations work. In this section, we will explain some examples of various translation difficulties and offer some tips that may help you translate common expressions into standard categorical form.

Sometimes someone will actually say, "All *As* are *Bs*" or "Some *As* are *Bs*," etc., but people don't usually speak sentences in standard categorical form. Consider these common claims:

> 1. Junk food is unhealthy for people.
> 2. Abortions are immoral actions.
> 3. Metal music rocks!
> 4. Country music sucks!
> 5. Believe it or not, peanuts are not nuts.
> 6. Several checks bounced.
> 7. Lots of people are not afraid to speak in public.

There aren't any strict rules for translating, but there are some useful guidelines. For instance, if someone else is making the claim, make sure you interpret the claim charitably. In number 1, "Junk food is unhealthy for people," does the speaker mean *all* junk food or just *some*? If you cannot ask the speaker to be more specific, this is a judgment call. The more charitable interpretation is probably "some," since it is (i) not clear what is intended by "junk food," and (ii) "all" is a very strong quantifier that is difficult to justify unless the claim is definitional (e.g., *All* bachelors are unmarried . . . by definition).

3.4.1. Most?

What happens when a speaker means "most" instead of just "some"? "Most" is a strong quantifier, and we saw in Chapter 2 that the difference in meaning between "most" and "some" can determine the difference between a strong and a weak inductive argument. However, for the purpose of categorical logic, "most" and "some" will look the same on a Venn diagram. Since we don't know exactly how many there are, the best we can do is indicate that some are, recognizing that some is consistent with most. For instance, if we know that *most* Labour Party members are liberal, then we know that *some* are. The same does not hold true going the other direction. If we know that some Labour Party members are conservative, we do not know whether most are; though it is still *possible* that most are. So, for the purposes of categorical logic, "Some *A*s are *B*s" is equivalent to "Most *A*s are *B*s."

3.4.2. Four parts of categorical claims

There are four parts to every categorical claim: (i) a **quantifier**, (ii) a subject, (iii) a copula, and (iv) a predicate or object. When translating, the first thing you do is to identify which elements of the claim correspond to which part of a categorical claim:

Quantifier	Subject	Copula	Predicate/Object
All; No; Some	things	are (not)	other things.

Begin by identifying the categories involved and distinguishing the subject from the predicate. For instance, in number 1 above, the categories are most likely: subject: "things that are junk food" and predicate: "things that are unhealthy for people." The subject is the "category of things that are BLANK" and the object, too, is another "category of things that are BLANK." Recall, also, the circle as representing a certain category (or set) with little rectangles representing the things (elements) inside of it, which is helpful in imaging what is logically taking place when we classify things into categories, as well as relate categories to one another. Further, remember to make sure that you know what category the letter you are using is symbolizing.

Keep in mind, too, that the object of the claim is a category of things that are predicated of the subject, in that it could be a person, place, or thing (noun), as well as an action (verb) or quality (adjective or adverb) *that is being categorized*. So, consider that "Cats are mammals" gets translated as "All cats are mammals." Simple enough. However, "Cats have brains" does not get translated as "All cats are brains;" rather, it gets translated as "All cats (things that are cats) are things that *have brains*." Also, "Cats arch their backs" gets translated as "All cats are things that arch their backs" and not "All cats are backs." So, again, in number 1 above, the categories are most likely: subject: "things that are junk food" and predicate: "things that are unhealthy for people":

Quantifier	Subject	Copula	Predicate/Object
All; No; Some	things that are junk food	are (not)	things that are unhealthy for people.

Next, identify the copula. As we have interpreted it, this claim is positive; there is no "not" involved. So, the resulting translation is: "things that are junk food **are** things that are unhealthy for people."

It is important to see that this need not have been the case. We could have interpreted the second category as: "things that are healthy for people." If we had, our copula would be negative; our translation would read, instead, "things that are junk food **are not** things that are healthy for people." Both are legitimate interpretations and we will see that these claims are actually **logically equivalent**, which means that one is true if and only if the other is true. We will continue with both so this is clearer:

Quantifier	Subject	Copula	Predicate/Object
All; No; Some	things that are junk food	are	things that are unhealthy for people.
All; No; Some	things that are junk food	are not	things that are healthy for people.

Finally, identify the copula. "No" is not an option, so we are left to choose between "all" and "some." "All" would probably be too strong, depending on what the speaker means by "junk food" and "unhealthy." Therefore, charity should lead us to interpret it as "some":

Quantifier	Subject	Copula	Predicate/Object
Some	things that are junk food	are	things that are unhealthy for people.
Some	things that are junk food	are not	things that are healthy for people.

Now, let's diagram both. The first is an *I*-claim and is, therefore, diagrammed like this:

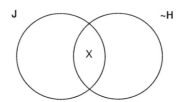

The tilde (~) before the *H* represents the word "not," so "~*H*" is the category of things that are not healthy for people." The second is an *O*-claim, and its diagram looks like this:

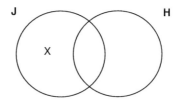

These claims are logically equivalent because the category of "things that are healthy" is **mutually exclusive** with the "category of things that are unhealthy"; there is nothing that can be in both categories at the same time under the same conditions or we would have a contradiction. So, if something is in the category of things that are unhealthy, it is not in the category of things that are healthy under this particular set of circumstances. Therefore, our diagrams are logically equivalent and both interpretations are legitimate.

Here are some further examples of standard-form categorical claims parsed into the four elements of a categorical claim:

Quantifier	Subject	Copula	Predicate/Object
A: All	cats	are	mammals.
E: No	dogs	are	insects.
I: Some	heaters	are	oil-fueled.
O: Some	people	are not	good listeners.

Exercises 3.g.

For the following seven claims, organize each into the four elements of a standard-form categorical claim, then Venn diagram.

1. Junk food is unhealthy for people.
2. Abortions are immoral actions.
3. Metal music rocks!
4. Country music does not rock!
5. Believe it or not, peanuts are not nuts.
6. Several checks bounced.
7. Lots of people are not afraid to speak in public.

3.4.3. Singular expressions and proper nouns

Singular expressions are expressions that refer to a single thing, like "this cat," "that dog," or "the house right there on 1st Ave. and Main Street," while proper nouns refer to even more specific things beginning with a capital letter like the state of Georgia, Michael Jackson, Kleenex, and Young Harris College. When translating a singular expression and/or a proper noun, consider the singular or specific thing to be *something in a category all by itself*. Thus, the following are translated:

1. "This cat lives in the neighborhood":
   All things that are *this cat* are things that live in the neighborhood

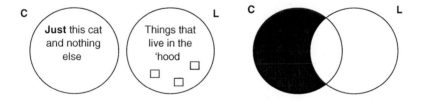

2. "Michael Jackson is no longer alive":
   No things that are *Michael Jackson* are things that are alive

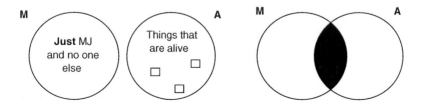

3. "Jane Doe is on the street":
All things that are *Jane Doe* are things that are on the street

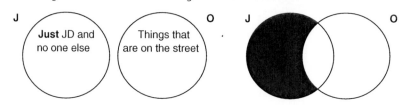

A few more examples:

a. Jenny hugged Jim.
All things that are Jenny (just her in the category) are things that hugged Jim.
All *J*s are *H*s.

b. Metallica put on an awesome show.
All things that are Metallica (just them in the category) are things that put on an awesome show.
All *M*s are *P*s.

c. Hey, these brownies are awesome!
All things that are these brownies (just them) are things that are awesome.
All *B*s are *A*s.

d. There are people in that house.
Some people are things in that house.
Some *P*s are *I*s.

3.4.4. Time and place

Categorizing claims made about time and place can be difficult, but always remember the simple rules that:

(a) When talking about a time (sometimes, always, never, every time, when), think in terms of the category of All, No, or Some **"*times that* are BLANK"** as in:

"There are times when I am sad." becomes:
Some times are times when I am sad.

Some *T*s are *S*s.

(b) When talking about a place (some place, everywhere, nowhere, wherever, where), think in terms of the category of All, No, or Some *"places where* BLANK" as in:

> "Ghosts exist nowhere" becomes:
> No places are places where ghosts exist.
>
> **No *Ps* are *Gs*.**

Here are more examples of how to categorize time and place:

> **Time:**
>
> a. "At no time should he be allowed in," becomes:
>   No times are times when he should be allowed in.
>   No *Ts* are *Ss*.
>
> b. "Whenever I eat, I usually burp," becomes:
>   All times when I eat are times when I usually burp.
>   All *Ts* are *Us*.
>
> c. "Every time I call her, she hangs up," becomes:
>   All times I call her are times when she hangs up.
>   All *Ts* are *Hs*.

> **Place:**
>
> a. "Gravity is everywhere," becomes:
>   All places are places where there is gravity.
>   All *Ps* are *Gs*.
>
> b. "The keys are someplace," becomes:
>   Some place is/are place(s) where the keys are.
>   Some *Ps* are *Ks*.
>
> c. "Here is where we are on the map," becomes:
>   All places that are here are places where we are on the map.
>   All *Hs* are *Ms*.

3.4.5. Conditional claims

Conditional claims have the "If . . . (antecedent), then . . . (consequent)" format, as in "If it is a cat, then it is a mammal." The way to translate these claims is straightforward: They are always translated as *A*-claims with the antecedent taking the "All *A*s" spot, and the consequent taking the " . . . are *B*s" spot. So, the claim, "If it is a Bluegill, then it is a fish," becomes: All things that are Bluegills are things that are fish.

This also works with events, though it is a bit more awkward. For instance, the claim, "If it is raining, then the sidewalk is wet," becomes: All events that are raining are events in which the sidewalk is wet. This is not as clear as we would like, since the "are" here indicates a *causal* relationship (the rain causes the sidewalk to be wet) instead of a *property* relationship (Bluegill have the property of being fish). This is one of the limitations of categorical logic that we will discuss at the end of this chapter. Here are a few more examples:

a. "If it is a cat, then it is a mammal," becomes:
   All cats are mammals.
   All *C*s are *M*s.

b. "If it's 10pm, then it's time for bed," becomes:
   All times that are 10pm are times when it's time for bed.
   All *T*s are *B*s.

c. "If he is elected, then our taxes will be raised," becomes:
   All times he is elected are times when our taxes will be raised.
   All *E*s are *T*s.

3.5. Syllogisms and testing for validity with Venn diagrams

Now that you have a clear sense of how to Venn diagram categorical claims, we can finally see why this is useful. Their primary function is to allow us to evaluate arguments that include categorical claims as premises. For instance, consider the following argument:

A.
P1: All squirrels are rodents.
P2: All rodents are mammals.
C: Therefore, all squirrels are mammals.

Both premises are *A*-claims and it is fairly easy to see that, if the premises are true, the conclusion must be true, so the argument is deductively valid. But what happens when the quantifiers aren't so clear?

Consider this next argument:

B.
P1: No dogs are meowers.
P2: All normal cats are meowers.
C: No dogs are cats.

To evaluate arguments like this, we'll use a method called the **Venn diagram method** of testing for validity, named, of course, after John Venn. We can use the Venn diagram method to evaluate arguments that meet exactly two conditions[1]:

1. **There are three standard categorical claims arranged as a syllogism.**
2. **There are three or fewer categories.**

Condition 1: There are three standard categorical claims arranged as a syllogism.

All the arguments we can evaluate with Venn diagrams are *syllogisms*. A **syllogism** is an argument made up of exactly *one* conclusion and *two* premises. If all the claims in the syllogism meet the conditions for a standard-form categorical claim, the argument is called a **categorical syllogism**. Recall that all arguments are either valid or invalid, since a conclusion will either follow necessarily from the premises (a valid argument) or it will follow with some degree of probability (an invalid argument). There a whopping 256 possible types of syllogisms that can be constructed out of standard-form categorical claims; most of them are invalid.

Condition 2: There are three and only three categories.

It is also important to notice that the Venn diagram method *only* works for arguments that include up to three categories of things. In our first two examples above, the first has the three categories: squirrels, rodents, and mammals. The second has dogs, cats, meowers. If there are *four or more* categories, the Venn method will not deliver accurate results. The following examples illustrate these difficulties:

P1: All dogs are mammals.
P2: No turtles are amphibians.
C: Therefore, . . . ?

(We can derive valid conclusions from these premises, for instance, we could say that both are true: "All dogs are mammals *and* no turtles are amphibians," as well as a number of trivial claims. But we could not use the Venn diagram method to determine the validity of those arguments.)

P1: All humans are thinkers.
P2: All thinking machines are calculators.
C: Hence, . . . ?

(Notice: there are actually four categories of things in this syllogism: 1. humans, 2. thinkers, 3. thinking machines, and 4. calculators.)

And don't let anyone convince you that this conclusion follows:

P1: All great artists are well-trained persons.
P2: All persons are human-born.
C: So, all great artists are human-born.

(There are actually four categories of things here: (1) great artists, (2) well-trained persons, (3) persons, and (4) human-born things.)

Once you discover that your argument meets the conditions of a categorical syllogism, you can evaluate it using the Venn diagram method. The method has two steps:

1. Diagram both premises (but not the conclusion).
2. Check to see if the conclusion is depicted in the resulting diagram.

Consider, again, example B:

B.
P1: No dogs are meowers.
P2: All normal cats are meowers.
C: No dogs are cats.

In order to evaluate this argument with the Venn diagram method, begin by diagramming both premises:

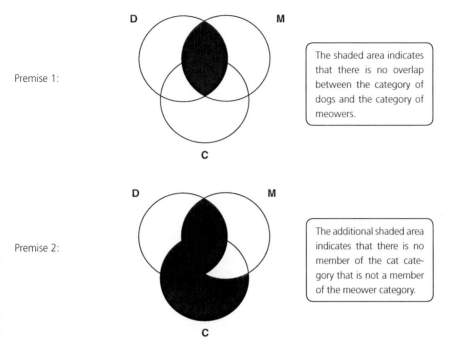

Premise 1:

The shaded area indicates that there is no overlap between the category of dogs and the category of meowers.

Premise 2:

The additional shaded area indicates that there is no member of the cat category that is not a member of the meower category.

Now that both premises are diagrammed, check to see whether the conclusion ("No dogs are cats.") is diagrammed. If we were to diagram this claim independently of the argument, it would look like this:

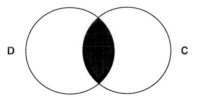

Is this diagrammed above? Yes. The overlapping area between "D" and "C" is completely blocked out, indicating that there is no member of the dog category that is a member of the cat category; thus, no dogs are cats. Since diagramming the premises results in the diagram of the conclusion, the argument is valid.

If diagramming the premises of a syllogism does not result in the diagram of the conclusion, the argument is invalid. Consider the following argument:

C.
P1: All mothers are female.
P2: Some females are bankers.
P3: Some mothers are bankers.

Begin, as before, by diagramming the first two premises:

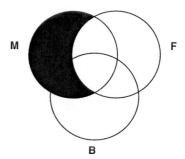

Now we ask whether the conclusion is diagrammed. In this case, the answer is no:

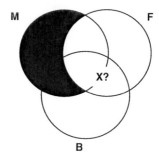

Even though some females are bankers—indicated by the "X?"—we have no idea whether the X applies just to females or also females who are mothers—indicated by placing the "X?" on the "M" line. Since the conclusion is not clearly diagrammed, this argument is invalid.

Let's look at another example:

D.
P1: Some rodents are mammals.
P2: Some mammals have fins.
C: Some rodents have fins.

Begin by diagramming both premises:

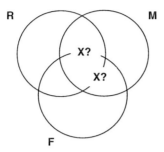

In this argument, we cannot tell whether the rodents in the mammal category are also included in the fin category. Similarly, we cannot tell whether the mammals in the fin category are also included in the rodent category. Since these questions are not answered by the diagram, the conclusion is not clearly diagrammed; therefore, the argument is invalid.

Let's look at two more examples; then you can try it yourself. Consider the argument:

E.
P1: All Catholics are Christian.
P2: Most Christians are monotheists.
C: Hence, all Catholics are monotheists.

Diagram both premises:

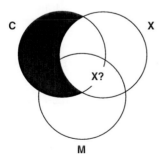

We're using "X" for "Christian" because the Greek word for "Christ" begins with the Greek letter *chi*, "X": *Xpistos*.

"Most" implies "at least some," so we read premise 2 as an *I*-claim. But it is not clear on which side of the Catholic line we should place our "X." Therefore, if these premises are true, it is possible that there are some Catholics who are not monotheists, which would make our conclusion false. Our conclusion is not diagrammed, so this argument is invalid.

Consider one more:

F.
P1: All voters are registered persons.
P2: Some teens are voters.
C: So, some teens are registered persons.

Diagram both premises:

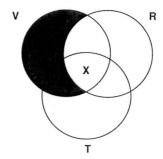

In this case, it is clear where the "some teens" from our *I*-claim goes: in the pool of voters. Since it happens that all voters belong to the category of registered persons, then some teens fall into this category as well. As it turns out, this is our conclusion: some teens are registered persons. This is clearly represented in the diagram; therefore, the argument is valid.

3.6. The limitations of categorical logic

There are two major limitations of categorical logic that worry philosophers. First, as we have noted, categorical logic cannot be used to evaluate arguments including more than three categories.

The second major limitation is that the quantifier "some" is ambiguous between "some are" and "some are not." For instance, does the claim, "Some politicians are liars," imply that some are not? If it doesn't, the following argument is invalid:

G.
P1: All politicians are public figures.
P2: All public figures are liars.
C: Thus, some politicians are liars.

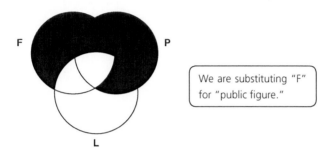

We are substituting "F" for "public figure."

Since the conclusion is not diagrammed, the argument is invalid. We cannot infer that there really are any politicians who are liars (that is, from these premises—we may know for other reasons). The premises tell us something about the members of the categories "politicians," "public figures," and "liars." But what if there aren't any members? For instance, "All unicorns have one horn," can be diagrammed, but this doesn't tell us whether there *are* any unicorns. The same goes for, "All centarians are over 100 years old," "All Martians are aliens," etc.

Nevertheless, the father of categorical logic, Aristotle, argued that we should assume there are some members of the categories we pick out. This is called an **existential assumption** (the assumption that something exists). So, without the existential assumption, the above argument is invalid. But with the existential assumption, we get the following diagram:

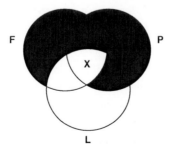

Why can we put an "X" here, even though the premises do not indicate one? Aristotle argued that the premises implicitly indicate an existential assumption. If it is true that "All politicians are public figures," there must be some politicians and some public figures.

The problem is that it is not clear when we should and when we should not make an existential assumption. You might think it is irrelevant. To test for validity, we simply assume the premises are true, so even if our claims are about mythical creatures, we assume they are true in order to test for validity. In this case, we make the existential assumption, then show that one of the premises is false. But this does not always work. Consider this argument:

H.
P1: No professional football players have Ph.D.s.
P2: Some football players are not ballet dancers.
P3: Some football players are ballet dancers.

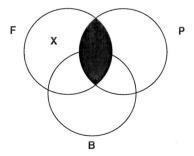

In this argument, both premises may be true. The conclusion is not explicitly diagrammed. But if we make an existential assumption, we must conclude that, "Some football players are not ballet dancers," implies that some are. But, surely this does not follow necessarily from the premises. The claim, "Some diamonds are valuable," is consistent with "All diamonds are valuable." Both can be true because "some" just means "at least one." Therefore, "Some diamonds are valuable," doesn't imply that, "Some diamonds are not valuable." Similarly, just because some professional football players are not ballet dancers, we cannot infer that some are. That some professional football players are not ballet dancers is consistent with both, "Some professional football players are ballet dancers," and "No professional football players are ballet dancers." There is no principled way to decide whether to make an existential assumption. Because of this, philosophers are skeptical of the power of categorical logic.

Despite its limitation to arguments with three categories and its ambiguity about existential assumptions, categorical logic can still be useful. We must simply recognize and compensate for its limitations.

3.7. More exercises

Exercises 3.h.

In the following claims, identify as many categories of things as you can, by using the "the category of things that are [BLANK]" format:

1. The honey bee lives in a community.
2. 80. of the people polled think that Frank is doing a lousy job.
3. She sells seashells at the seashore.
4. Logic is the science of sound reasoning.
5. Jen told me that Al Gore claimed that he invented the Internet.

Exercises 3.i.

Translate each of the following claims into one of the four standard-form categorical claims: A-claim, E-claim, I-claim, or O-claim, then Venn diagram.

1. Some primates have hair.
2. She placed the keys in the drawer.
3. Some fruits are not edible.
4. If you build it, they will come.
5. The only thing we have to fear is fear itself.
6. The timing is off here.
7. Nothing Frank and John have produced has been of top quality.
8. If it barks, then it's not a duck.
9. They concluded the show with a bang.
10. Some polls indicated that John would not win in tomorrow's election.
11. His stats have been unmatched.
12. Some men discovered that pearl.
13. Water splashed him again.
14. Only the strong survive.
15. He does not want help.

Exercises 3.j.

For each of the following arguments:

(i) Translate the claims into standard-form categorical claims: A-claim, E-claim, I-claim, or O-claim;

(ii) organize the claims into a categorical syllogism (one conclusion and two premises);

(iii) use the Venn diagram method to test for validity, indicating whether the argument is valid or invalid. ⇨

1. Idiots make bad choices. There are a few idiots who are living next door. So, I guess some people living next door make bad choices.
2. Dinosaurs are extinct. Some extinct things are not fossilized. Hence, some fossilized things are not dinosaurs.
3. Metallica rocks. If it rocks, it rolls too. Metallica does not roll.
4. There are a few cats that are tabby cats. All cats are sweet. So, there are a few sweet things that are tabby cats.
5. Atheists are unbelievers, and some unbelievers are baptized persons; so some baptized persons are atheists.
6. Teens are not professional drivers. Some teens, however, are people who are good at simulated driving. Therefore, some people who are good at simulated driving are not professional drivers.
7. There are bears that aren't brown. Bears are hibernating animals. Thus, there are hibernating animals that aren't brown.
8. Minds calculate. Computers calculate. Therefore, minds are computers.
9. Exercising is good for you. Some activities are not exercising. So, some exercising is not good for you.
10. Catholics are not Muslims. Some Muslims are Shiite. Some Shiites are not Catholic.
11. Starbucks serves coffee. Some coffee is decaf. So, Starbucks serves decaf coffee.
12. Most airplanes have a transponder. All airplanes are winged vehicles. Therefore, some winged vehicles have a transponder.
13. No news is good news. Good news travels fast. Thus, no news travels fast!
14. No voters are persons under eighteen. All infants are persons under eighteen. Thus, no infants are voters.
15. All cats are mammals. Some mammals are not indigenous to Africa. So, some cats are not indigenous to Africa.

Real-Life Example: Mexican Holy Week

Read the following news report. Then, using information from the article, construct and Venn diagram two valid categorical syllogisms, one with the conclusion:

C: All Catholic officials in Mexico City are at risk from cartel violence.

and another with the conclusion:

C: No Catholic officials in Mexico City are afraid of cartel violence.

Mexican clergy in trafficking areas won't change Holy Week activities.
March 29, 2010 – Catholic News Service

MEXICO CITY (CNS) — Catholic officials in some of the regions hit hardest by the violence attributed to narcotics-trafficking cartels said they have no plans to alter or cancel Holy Week events. They also called on Catholics to work toward spiritual renewal during Holy Week, instead of dedicating the popular Mexican vacation

⇨

period to leisure activities. Archbishop Felipe Aguirre Franco of Acapulco — the destination for hoards of Mexico City residents during Holy Week — called on visitors to the coastal city to "not fall into excesses (and) not participate in pagan festivals and drunkenness that, instead of honoring the passion and death of Christ, desecrate the sacred and truly Holy Week." Palm Sunday activities kicked off Holy Week as violence attributed to the cartels escalated. The death toll has reached nearly 2,400 so far this year, the Mexico City newspaper Reforma reported, and innocent bystanders increasingly have been caught in the conflict. In Acapulco, which has a population of about 725,000, 32 deaths were recorded during the three-day weekend ending March 15. The head of one decapitated victim was left in front of a parish. Still, Father Juan Carlos Flores, spokesman for the Archdiocese of Acapulco, said Holy Week activities would proceed as planned. In the northern city of Monterrey, Catholic officials also said they would not cancel Holy Week events, even though the region has been plagued by events such as presumed cartel members hijacking vehicles to block expressways and the early morning deaths of two graduate students as soldiers chased criminals cutting through the campus of an elite university. In Ciudad Juarez, where the violence has been most intense, the diocese planned a normal schedule of Holy Week events, although some of the hours were adjusted to coincide with daylight hours, said Father Hesiquio Trevizo, diocesan spokesman.

4 Basic Propositional Logic

4.1. A new language

As we have seen, categorical logic is useful only to a certain point. It will not work if we have more or less than three categories of things. In addition, it does not suggest a way to resolve the problem of "some are not." Does "some are not" imply that "some are" or does it leave open the possibility that "all are not"? Aristotle thought the former. But why should *we*? If both are consistent with the structure of categorical logic, then either is legitimate. But then, we get very different results depending on which we choose, and reality will not permit a claim to be both true and false at the same time in the same way. So we need a *stronger* logical system—a system that does not suffer from these deficiencies.

Thankfully, logicians in the twentieth century developed such a system. They call it **propositional logic**—it is the logic of *claims* or *propositions* rather than the logic of *categories*. It allows us all the power of categorical logic plus more—though, propositional logic is more difficult when it comes to categories. In this book, we will just cover some of the basics of propositional logic.

The material in this chapter is more difficult than anything in the rest of the book, so prepare yourself to spend lots of time with the exercises. It might help to think of the classroom as an orientation tool. In the classroom, you'll leans some of the basics of reasoning and watch your instructor work with the concepts. Between classes, you will want to work through the text on your own and come to class to get clarification on any concepts you don't understand and to overcome any difficulties you're having. Like mathematics, the majority of logic is learned by working problems over and over.

Learning propositional logic is learning a new language. You will learn to translate your natural language (English, French, etc.) into a new language, called a *formal language*. Your natural language allows you to use words in new and interesting ways, to introduce unique phrases, to modify grammatical rules as trends come and go, and to make exceptions. Formal languages, on the other hand, are very rigid; even new phrases must follow the "grammar" of the language very strictly, and there are no exceptions. Despite its stodginess, the rigidity of formal languages makes them perfect for expressing very precise, technical claims, such as those found in math, philosophy, science, and even religion.

4.2. Translating English claims into the language of propositional logic

Let's start with the basics: translating claims expressed in English sentences into claims expressed in sentences of propositional logic. In this book, we'll only be concerned with translating *whole simple* claims and their logical relationships. In more advanced logic courses you will translate each part of a claim: properties, relations, quantifiers, variables, and constants.

Whole simple claims are translated using single capital letters. For instance, the simple claim, <It is a cat>, can be translated: C. The simple claim, <It is a mammal>, can be translated: M. You may choose whatever capital letter you like, but it helps to pick a letter that will help you remember what claim is being translated. Here are some examples of whole simple claims translated into propositional logic:

Sentence of English	Sentence of propositional logic
Dan is a lawyer.	D
The company is broke.	C
It will be a sad day when the corporations finally collapse.	S
It is imperative that we find out who took the company's latest sales reports.	I

Notice that a simple claim need not be short. But it must convey only one simple claim, that is, it *must not include any operator*: **and; or; not; if . . ., then . . .; if and only if.**

If a claim does include an operator, you must translate the operator using its corresponding symbol. But, whereas you can choose the letters when translating claims, you cannot for operators. These are fixed and they are the five operators we first encountered in Chapter 1.

4.3. Translating claims with operators

The five operators from Chapter 1 help us express relationships among simple claims by allowing us to construct complex claims. Recall Figure 1.2:

Operator	Symbol	Example
and	&	It is a cat **and** it is a mammal.
or (sometimes requires "either")	V	It is **either** a cat **or** a skunk.
not	~	It is **not** raining.
if . . . , then . . .	⊃	**If** it is a cat, **then** it is a mammal.
if and only if	≡	He is a bachelor **if and only if** he is single.

Figure 1.2 Logical Operators

If we translate <It is a cat> as C, and <It is a mammal.> as M, the first example in Figure 1.2 becomes:

(C & M)

(C & M) is a complex claim. The parentheses are not needed in this example, since we can see clearly what the claim expresses. But as complex claims become more complicated, parentheses will help us read them correctly. The claim <Either it is a cat or it is a skunk.> can be translated:

(C v S)

So now we can add a new column to our chart:

Operator	Symbol	Example	Translation
And	&	It is a cat **and** it is a mammal.	(C & M)
or (sometimes requires "either")	v	It is **either** a cat **or** a skunk.	(C v S)
Not	~	It is **not** raining.	~R
if . . . , then . . .	⊃	**If** it is a cat, **then** it is a mammal.	(C ⊃ M)
if and only if	≡	He is a bachelor **if and only if** he is single.	(B ≡ S)

Translating becomes more complicated when multiple complex claims are joined with operators. For instance, consider two complex claims:

<If it is a cat, then it is a mammal.>

and

<If it is a duck, then it is a bird.>

If we were to conjoin these claims, the result would be a complex claim stated:

<If it is a cat, then it is a mammal and if it is a duck, then it is a bird.>

How would we translate this claim? Without parentheses, our translation would lose any meaning. Consider: we might first translate the simple claims as:

C ⊃ M
D ⊃ B

We might then try to conjoin them as follows:

C ⊃ M & D ⊃ B

But, unfortunately, this result is ambiguous. It does not adequately represent our original claim because it has more than one possible meaning and only one of these accurately represents the original. As written, the claim might mean:

> **A. If it is the case that, if it is a cat, then it is a mammal and it is a duck, then it is a bird.**

or:

> **B. If it is a cat, then if it is a mammal and it's a duck, then it is a bird.**

or:

> **C. If it is a cat, then it is a mammal and if it is a duck, then it is a bird.**

Since only the last expresses what we really mean, we need to add something to our translation in order to make this clear. To keep your complex claims intelligible, mark off the component claims with parentheses. Translated into propositional logic, A, B, and C would look as follows:

> A. ((C ⊃ (M & D)) ⊃ B)
> B. (C ⊃ ((M & D) ⊃ B))
> C. ((C ⊃ M) & (D ⊃ B))

A sentence of propositional logic that is not ambiguous is called a **well-formed formula (WFF)**. There is *only one way* to interpret that claim. This is what gives logic its advantage over natural languages; it removes ambiguity. A WFF can be expressed in one of three ways:

Well-Formed Formulas (WFFs)

1. Any simple claim is a WFF.
   Example: "Pete left"; translation: L.

2. Any negated WFF (a claim operated on by "~") is a WFF.
   Example 1: "She did not go"; translation: ~G.
   Example 2: "It did not rain or sleet"; translation: ~(R v S)

3. Any two WFFs joined with an operator and enclosed in parentheses is also a WFF.
   Example 1: "It is wet and cold"; translation: (W & C)
   Example 2: "Either it is wet and cold or my eyes are playing tricks"; translation: ((W & C) v T)

Notice that our original attempt at translating our claim is not a WFF:

C ⊃ M & D ⊃ B

It contains the WFFs, C, M, D, and B, and these are joined with operators, but since they are not properly enclosed in parentheses, the resulting complex claim is not a WFF. The disambiguated interpretations of this claim (A, B, and C) are all WFFs. Because they are WFFs, it is easy to see which accurately expresses our original claim: If it is a cat, then it is a mammal and if it is a duck, then it is a bird: ((C ⊃ M) & (D ⊃ B)).

When complex claims are joined with operators, the resulting claim will still be a complex claim defined by one (and only one) operator. The operator that defines a complex claim is called the *major operator*. For example, the complex claim, ~F, is defined by its only operator, a negation. So, in this case, its only operator is also its major operator. Alternatively, the claim ((C ⊃ M) & (D ⊃ B)) is defined by its major operator, which is "&", so the complex claim is a conjunction. The two if . . ., then . . . claims are minor operators. In this claim, each conditional claim is a conjunct in a conjunction. Remember that a conjunction is simply two claims joined with the "&" operator:

(P & Q)

This is also true for whatever claims stand in for P and Q. Each of the following complex claims is a conjunction. On the left you will see a conjunction; on the right, we have underlined each conjunct and placed the major operator in bold:

((A v B) & (C & D))	⟶	(<u>(A v B)</u> **&** <u>(C & D)</u>)
(((A & B) v C) & (D ⊃ (E v C)))	⟶	(<u>((A & B) v C)</u> **&** <u>(D ⊃ (E v C))</u>)
(A & (B ⊃ ((C v D) & B)))	⟶	(<u>A</u> **&** <u>(B ⊃ ((C v D) & B))</u>)

Here are four examples of complex claims with conditionals as the major operator:

(~A ⊃ B)	⟶	(<u>~A</u> ⊃ <u>B</u>)
((A & B) ⊃ (B v ~C))	⟶	(<u>(A & B)</u> ⊃ <u>(B v ~C)</u>)
(((A ⊃ B) v C) ⊃ D)	⟶	(<u>((A ⊃ B) v C)</u> ⊃ <u>D</u>)
((A ≡ ~B) ⊃ ((C & D) v A))	⟶	(<u>(A ≡ ~B)</u> ⊃ <u>((C & D) v A)</u>)

Remember, every complex claim has a single (unique) major operator, and it might be any of our five operators. For instance, the claim:

~((A v B) ≡ ((C v ~D) & (A ⊃ D)) ⊃ ((C v D) v ~A))

is a negation, that is, the negation operator at the beginning is the major operator. However complex the claim, if there is a negation on the outside of all the parentheses, the claim is defined as a negation. That is its major operator.

TIP for identifying major operators:
The operator enclosed in the least number of parentheses is the major operator.

4.4. Translation examples

1. If I ride with Tim, he will take the long route and stop for coffee.

Right	*Wrong*	*Wrong*	*Wrong*
(R ⊃ (T & S))	(R ⊃ S)	(R ⊃ T)	((T & S) ⊃ R)

2. The sun will not rise tomorrow.

Right	*Wrong*	*Wrong*	*Wrong*
~S	(S & R)	N	~(S & R)

3. Either he will do a good job and get a raise or he will remain in middle-management forever.

Right	*Wrong*	*Wrong*	*Wrong*
((G & R) v M)	(G & R v M)	(G v M)	(G & (R v M))

4. An object is gold if and only if it has atomic number 79.

Right	*Wrong*	*Wrong*	*Wrong*
(G ≡ A)	(A ⊃ G)	(G ⊃ A)	(G)

5. If it will either rain or snow, then I will either need an umbrella or a parka.

Right	*Wrong*	*Wrong*	*Wrong*
((R v S) ⊃ (U v P))	(R v S ⊃ U v P)	(R ⊃ U)	(R ⊃ (U v P))

6. Oil prices are astronomical.

Right	*Wrong*	*Wrong*	*Wrong*
O	(O ⊃ A)	(O & A)	(O ≡ A)

7. Jim is a male if and only if he has a Y chromosome.

Right	*Wrong*	*Wrong*	*Wrong*
(M ≡ Y)	(M ⊃ Y)	(Y ⊃ M)	(M)

8. Either I go to John's and she goes home, or I go to her house and she stays at John's.

Right	*Wrong*	*Wrong*	*Wrong*
((J & G) v (H & S))	(J v S)	(J & G v H & S)	(J & (G v H) & S)

9. She hasn't called in hours.

Right	*Wrong*	*Wrong*	*Wrong*
~S	S	~(S & H)	(~S ⊃ H)

10. If God exists, then there is no unnecessary evil in the world.

Right	*Right*	*Wrong*	*Wrong*	*Wrong*
(G ⊃ ~U)	(~G v ~U)	(U ⊃ G)	(~U ⊃ G)	(G ⊃ U)

4.5. Basic translation exercises

Exercises 4.a.

Translate the following simple and complex English sentences into claims of propositional logic. If the claim is complex, also identify the major operator.

1. It is either a cat or a skunk.
2. It flies.
3. If it flies, it is either a bird or a plane.
4. It looks very strange for a bird or plane.
5. Either it is a bird and it is deformed or it is a plane and it's very small.
6. If it is a bird and it is deformed, then someone either burned it or painted it.
7. It is not a plane.
8. If someone burned it, it would not be hopping around so happily.
9. It is hopping around happily.
10. If it was not burned, then someone must have painted it.

Exercises 4.b.

Using the interpretations provided, translate the following claims of propositional logic into English:

11. [T = I throw the ball; W = The window will break.]

    (T ⊃ W)

12. [R = You're a Republican; D = You're a Democrat.]

    (((R v D) & ~R) ⊃ D)

13. [R = It is raining; S = The sidewalks are wet.]

    (((R ⊃ S) & R) ⊃ S)   ⇨

14. [S = It snowed; R = The roof collapsed.]

    $(((S \supset R) \;\&\; {\sim}R) \supset {\sim}S)$

15. [R = It is raining; B = I bring my umbrella; W = I get wet.]

    $((R \;\&\; {\sim}B) \supset W)$

16. [B = The dog will bite; F = The dog is friendly; P = I will pet the dog.]

    $((B \lor F) \;\&\; ((F \supset P) \;\&\; (B \supset {\sim}P)))$

17. [P = I pay for the ticket; K = I get kicked out.]

    $({\sim}({\sim}P \supset K) \supset {\sim}P)$

18. [P = I am a professor; D = I have a Ph.D.; T = I have teaching experience.]

    $(P \equiv (D \;\&\; T))$

19. [P = He went to the park; R = He went to the restaurant; S = He is on the swings; J = He is on the jungle gym.]

    $((P \lor R) \;\&\; ((P \supset (S \lor J))))$

20. [D = She is a (medical) doctor; M = She went to medical school; L = She is licensed; I = She is immoral; H = She is a hack.]

    $((D \equiv M) \;\&\; (({\sim}L \supset (I \lor H))))$

4.6. Tips for translating

When English words express operators explicitly (for instance, when "&" is expressed as "and," or when "v" is expressed as "or"), translation is fairly straightforward. But because English offers so many ways to express the same operators, it is helpful to identify some of the more common alternatives.

Alternative ways to say "&":

but

P but Q.	(P & Q)
He is a nice guy but he is a liar.	(N & L)
She went to the station but she didn't take her dog.	(S & ~T)

however

P, however, Q.	(P &Q)
He went there after work. However, he drove the company truck.	(A & D)
She didn't go to the store; however, she did stop to get the mail.	(~S & M)

furthermore

P. Furthermore, Q.	(P & Q)
It's not right. Furthermore, it has bad consequences.	(~R & B)
The policy was fast-tracked through the committee. Furthermore, it was approved.	(F & A)

moreover

P. Moreover, Q.	(P &Q)
The roof is leaking. Moreover, the wall is cracked.	(L & C)
The door does not block sound; moreover, it doesn't keep out cold.	(~B & ~K)

in addition

P. In addition, Q. In addition to P, Q.	(P &Q)
She wants the TV. In addition, she wants both chairs.	(T & C)
In addition to the cooler, bring some ice.	(C & I)

yet

P, yet Q.	(P &Q)
He is bitter, yet tolerable.	(B & T)
It was a long winter. Yet, it was an enjoyable one.	(L & E)

although

P, although Q. Although P, Q.	(P &Q)
Although she was angry, she was nice to me.	(A & N)
The door was locked although I told you not to lock it.	(L & T)

An alternative way to say "v":

unless

P unless Q / if not Q, then P	(P v Q)
She's going to leave unless you say something.	(L v S)
You should stop doing that unless you want a knuckle sandwich.	(S v K)

Alternative ways to say "~":

Not P.	~P
It is not the case that space is two-dimensional.	~S
He isn't buying your argument.	~B
She didn't win.	~W

Alternative ways to say "⊃":

if

P if Q	(Q ⊃ P)
The cab is available if the light is on.	(L ⊃ A)
The sidewalks are wet if it has been raining.	(R ⊃ S)
It is a female if it is a mother.	(M ⊃ F)

only if

P only if Q	(P ⊃ Q)
The cab is available only if the light is on.	(A ⊃ L)
It has been raining only if the sidewalks are wet.	(S ⊃ R)
It's a cat only if it is a mammal.	(C ⊃ M)

necessary condition

P is necessary for Q	(Q ⊃ P)
Being a mammal is necessary for being a cat.	(C ⊃ M)
It is necessary that she complete the course in order to move on.	(M ⊃ C)

sufficient for

P is sufficient for Q	(P ⊃ Q)
Being a cat is sufficient for being a mammal.	(C ⊃ M)
Being a tree is sufficient for being a plant.	(T ⊃ P)

Alternative ways to say "≡":

just in case

P just in case Q.	(P ≡ Q)
He's a bachelor just in case he is an unmarried adult male.	(B ≡ U)
She is a woman just in case she has two X chromosomes.	(W ≡ X)

just if

P just if Q.	(P ≡ Q)
I'm going to the party just if she goes.	(I ≡ S)
He's a lawyer just if he's been to law school and has passed the bar.	(L ≡ (S & B))

necessary and sufficient

P is necessary and sufficient for Q.	(P ≡ Q)
The cab's light's being on is necessary and sufficient for the cab's being available.	(A ≡ L)
Being a single adult male is necessary and sufficient for being a bachelor.	(S ≡ B)

Other difficult English expressions:

neither . . . nor . . . / not . . . and not . . .	**(~P & ~Q)**
It's both not round and not green.	(~R & ~G)
She is neither happy nor rich.	(~H & ~ R)
It's not raining or snowing.	(~R & ~S)
It's not easy or painless.	(~E & ~P)

not both / it is not the case that p and q	**~(P & Q)**
You cannot have both ice cream and a candy bar.	~(I & C)
You either get it or you don't.	~(G & ~G)
It is not both cool and warm at the same time.	~(C & W)

not p and q	**(~P & Q)**
It's not easy and she likes it.	(~E & L)
It's not fun but it's a paycheck.	(~F & P)
You shouldn't look, but you should duck.	(~L & D)

p unless q / if not p, then q	(P v Q) or (~P ⊃ Q)
She won't go unless he does.	(~S v H) or (~~S ⊃ H)
The sign is on unless we're closed.	(S v C) or (~S ⊃ C)
The glass will break unless he grabs it.	(B v G) or (~B ⊃ G)

except when (same as "p unless q")	(P v Q) or (~Q **à P)*
She teaches except when she is sick.	(T v S) or (~T ⊃ S)
The door is open unless I am out.	(D v O) or (~D ⊃ O)
Students don't fail except when they skip class.	(~F v S) or (~~F ⊃ S)

4.7. More difficult translation exercises

Exercises 4.c.

Translate each of the following into claims of propositional logic.

1. The tide is coming in. Moreover, it's getting dark.
2. Unless you want to spend the night in jail, you should come home.
3. Passing 130 semester hours of courses in the right distribution is necessary and sufficient for graduating college.
4. You can have candy or bananas, but not both.
5. He's a lawyer, but he is also a nice guy, and if you ask nicely, he might even work for free.
6. You are a male just if you have a Y chromosome, but you're a man just in case you're over 18.
7. If it is not the case that I'm held accountable for my actions, then there is no real reason to care about morality.
8. You shouldn't lie. However, if an innocent person's life is at stake and lying would prevent her death, then you should lie.
9. Number 8 contains a contradiction. It cannot be the case that both "You should lie" and "Sometimes, you should lie."
10. The president of the company is neither good nor prudent. Furthermore, if he doesn't stop complaining, we will replace him.

4.8. Rules of inference and their value

What does all this translation do for us? Two things. First, it helps us make our claims clear and precise. Second, it helps us evaluate arguments. After our claims are translated into the symbols of propositional logic, we can evaluate the connection between the premises and the conclusion without the meaning of our English words getting in the way.

In Chapter 2, we introduced some intuitive cases where a conclusion follows from a premise or set of premises with certainty. For example:

P1: If it is raining, then the sidewalk is wet.   P1: Either it is the starter or the battery.
P2: It is raining.   P2: It is not the battery.
C: Therefore, the sidewalk is wet.   C: Therefore, it is the starter.

If we translate these arguments, we get:

P1: (R ⊃ S)   P1: (S v B)
P2: R   P2: ~B
C: S   C: S

Of course, in these examples, it is easy to see that the conclusion follows with certainty. But why does it follow with certainty? Consider some alternatives:

1.	**2.**	**3.**	**4.**
P1: (R ⊃ S)	P1: (R ⊃ S)	P1: (S v B)	P1: (S v B)
P2: S	P2: ~R	P2: S	P2: B
C: R	C: ~S	C: ~B	C: ~S

Without replacing these symbols with English words, it might be pretty difficult to determine whether arguments 1–4 are valid (recall from Chapter 2: an argument is **valid** if it is not possible for the premises to be true and the conclusion false). As it turns out, none of these four is valid. In addition, the whole motivation for developing a formal language is that it often isn't clear when an argument in English (or French or German) is valid. Consider the following argument in English:

P1: If the experiment yields diphenhydramine or hydrochloric acid, then either we
     made a mistake in judgment or a mistake in our experimental controls.
P2: The experiment did not yield diphenhydramine or hydrochloric acid.
C: We didn't make a mistake in judgment or a mistake in experimental controls.

Is this argument valid? It may be difficult to say if you are unfamiliar with logical forms. Nevertheless, let us translate this English claim into our simple propositional language:

P1: ((D v H) ⊃ (J v C))
P2: ~(D v H)
C: ~(J v C)

Even if you don't know what "diphenhydramine" is, we can look at the argument's form and determine that it is *not valid*. Notice that both premise 2s have the same form as premise 2 of example 2 above:

P1: ((D v H) ⊃ (J v C))   P1: (R ⊃ S)
P2: ~(D v H)   P2: ~R
C: ~(J v C)   C: ~S

> To see this comparison more clearly, imagine that "R" just means "(D v H)" and that "S" just means "(J v C)".

If that earlier argument is invalid then, since this argument has the same form, it must also be invalid.

So, how can we be sure we are drawing appropriate inferences, that is, how do we know when the form is right? For that, we need to establish some **rules of inference**. Once we understand these rules, we will be able to construct valid arguments and evaluate whether an argument is valid without needing to translate the claims into English. In the next chapter, we'll introduce some basic rules of inference and show you how to use them.

4.9. More exercises

Exercises 4.d.

Translate the following complex claims into propositional logic:

1. If you want to run for president, you must be both at least 35 years old and a naturally born citizen of the United States.
2. The writing is on the wall and the check is in the mail, and if this is true, then you only have two choices: pack it in now or stick around for the long haul.
3. You shouldn't be telling me what to do unless you think you can take responsibility for my running this company into the ground or for turning it into a Fortune 500 company.
4. If it's not the case that you're sick and it is not the case that your kids or spouse is sick, then you should be getting dressed for work or risk not getting that promotion.
5. ". . . [T]he proscribing any citizen as unworthy the public confidence by laying on him an incapacity of being called to offices of trust or emolument, unless he profess or renounce this or that religious opinion, is depriving him injudiciously of those privileges and advantages to which, in common with his fellow-citizens, he has a natural right . . ." (From "A Bill for Establishing Religious Freedom," Thomas Jefferson, 1779).

⇨

6. "All that up to the present time I have accepted as most true and certain I have learned either from the senses or through the senses; but it is sometimes proved to me that these senses are deceptive, and it is wiser not to trust entirely to anything by which we have once been deceived." (From *Meditations on First Philosophy*, by René Descartes, meditation 1.)

7. "[During the Enlightenment] Opposition to belief in God increased because it was used by princes ruling by God's grace, by cardinals, bishops, and priests as a means of preventing the diffusion of the 'light of reason' and of keeping the people in tutelage and servitude." (From *Does God Exist?* by Hans Küng, §A.II.4.)

8. "If my letters are condemned in Rome, then what I condemn in them is condemned in heaven." (From *Pensées*, fr. 919, by Blaise Pascal trans. W. F. Trotter.)

9. "The framework of bones being the same in the hand of a man, wing of a bat, fin of the porpoise, and leg of the horse,—the same number of vertebrae forming the neck of the giraffe and of the elephant,—and innumerable other such facts, at once explain themselves on the theory of descent with slow and slight successive modifications." (From *The Origin of Species*, 1st edition, by Charles Darwin, Chapter XIV.)

10. "Well, sir, it's surprising, but it well may be a fact that neither of them does know exactly what that bird is, and that nobody in all this whole wide sweet world knows what it is, saving and excepting only your humble servant, Caspar Gutman, Esquire." (From *The Maltese Falcon*, by Dasheill Hammett, Chapter 11.)

Exercises 4.e.

Using the translation guide, translate the following sentences of propositional logic into English:

1. [D = It is the dog; B = It is the bird; F = It is the fish.]

   (~D ⊃ (B v F))

2. [H = It is hot; S = I am sick; T = The thermostat is working.]

   ((~H & S) v ~T)

3. [A = It is always raining; D = It is at least depressing; F = It is fun.]

   ((~A ⊃ D) & (D ⊃ ~F))

4. [C = I am cleaning the bathroom; W = You are washing dishes; S = You are scrubbing the floors.]

   (C ⊃ (W v S))

5. [B = We're going to Bonnaroo; A = Annie can go; D = You agree to drive half the time.]

   (B ⊃ (A ≡ D))

Exercises 4.f.

For the following three claims, construct your own translation guide for each, then translate into English:

1. ((P ⊃ Q) & R)
2. ((S v L) ⊃ ~H)
3. ((A ⊃ B) v (C ⊃ D))

Exercises 4.g.

Reformulate the following arguments, removing extraneous material and rhetorical devices, then translate them into propositional logic:

1. A government-sponsored health-care program requires heavily taxing all citizens. Excessive taxation is no different than stealing from hard-working people. Stealing from people is immoral. Therefore, government-sponsored health-care is immoral.
2. "If within the same church miracles took place on the side of those in error, this would lead to error. The schism is obvious, the miracle is obvious, but schism is a clearer sign of error than a miracle is of truth: therefore the miracle cannot lead to error. But apart from schism error is not as obvious as a miracle; therefore the miracle would lead to error." (From *Pensées*, fr. 878, by Blaise Pascal, trans. A. J. Krailsheimer.)
3. "When we put together three things—first, the natural attraction between opposite sexes; secondly, the wife's entire dependence on the husband, every privilege or pleasure she has being either his gift, or depending entirely on his will; and lastly, that the principle object of human pursuit, consideration, and all objects of social ambition, can in general be sought or obtained by her only through him, it would be a miracle if the object of being attractive to men had not become the polar star of feminine education and formation of character." (From *The Subjection of Women*, by John Stuart Mill, Chapter 1.)

   [Hint: Mill is arguing that the education system of his day encourages women to be wholly dependent on men. His conclusion has a bit of rhetorical flourish: Given these cultural facts, how could you expect any different?]

4. ". . . [O]ur civil rights have no dependence on our religious opinions, any more than our opinions in physics or geometry; and therefore the proscribing any citizen as unworthy the public confidence by laying on him an incapacity of being called to offices of trust or emolument, unless he profess or renounce this or that religious opinion, is depriving him injudiciously of those privileges and advantages to which, in common with his fellow-citizens, he has a natural right . . ." (From "A Bill for Establishing Religious Freedom," Thomas Jefferson, 1779). ⇨

5. 1. "If it could be demonstrated that any complex organ existed which could not possibly have been formed by numerous, successive, slight modifications, my theory would absolutely break down." (Charles Darwin, *The Origin of Species*, 6th ed., p. 154). 2. "An irreducibly complex system cannot be produced directly . . . by slight, successive modifications of a precursor system . . . " (Michael Behe, *Darwin's Black Box*, p. 39.) 3. " . . . [T]he blood-clotting system fits the definition of irreducible complexity." (Michael Behe, *Darwin's Black Box*, p. 86.) 4. "Faced with such complexity beneath even simple phenomena, Darwinian theory falls silent." (Michael Behe, *Darwin's Black Box*, p. 97).

6. 1. Brigid bought a newspaper called *The Call*, then disappeared. 2. Brigid and Joel Cairo are both after the Maltese Falcon. 3. Joel Cairo had the same copy of *The Call* and had ripped out a section listing the arrival of ships into the local port. 4. The section Cairo had ripped out included a ship called the *La Paloma* and five other ships. 5. The *La Paloma* burned last night. 6. Therefore, a good place to look for clues as to Brigid's disappearance would be the *La Paloma*. (Adapted from *The Maltese Falcon*, by Dasheill Hammett.)

7. " . . . [T]he fact that restricting access to abortion has tragic side effects does not, in itself, show that the restrictions are unjustified, since murder is wrong regardless of the consequences of prohibiting it." (Mary Anne Warren, "On the Moral and Legal Status of Abortion," 1973.)

8. "According to the Humanitarian theory [of punishment], to punish a man because he deserves it . . . is mere revenge and, therefore, barbarous and immoral. . . . My contention is that this doctrine . . . really means that each one of us, from the moment he breaks the law, is deprived of the rights of a human being. The reason is this. The Humanitarian theory removes from Punishment the concept of Desert. But the concept of Desert is the only connecting link between punishment and justice. It is only as deserved or undeserved that a sentence can be just or unjust." (C. S. Lewis, "The Humanitarian Theory of Punishment," *God in the Dock*, pp. 287–88.)

Real-Life Example: Translating a Legal Document

People who write legal documents attempt to capture all the formality of formal language in a natural language. They attempt to remove any and all ambiguities from the language by carefully qualifying every term. The result is often a jumble of rigid verbiage with no rhythm or intuitive meaning. Without some training it can be a maddening translation exercise. Thankfully, with a little practice with propositional logic, you can breeze through many legal documents. And what's more, you can evaluate them for internal consistency.

Case Study A: A Rental Agreement

Using the tools of propositional logic, translate the following section of a standard rental agreement into propositional logic. Add, as a premise, the assumption that you signed the agreement and have been living in the apartment for three months of a twelve month lease. In addition, for whatever reason, you want to be released from the lease and have done everything except find a replacement tenant. From the agreement and these premises, what are your responsibilities to the landlord?

SECURITY DEPOSIT: Unless otherwise stated, the original Security Deposit is equal to the rent rate and, along with the first month's rent, must be paid by certified funds (money order, cashier's check or certified check). The Security deposit will NOT be refunded unless tenant completes the term of the lease AND meets all other conditions of the lease.

RELEASE FROM LEASE: We may, as a courtesy, release the Tenant from the balance of the lease provided the following conditions are met:

- — Tenant forfeits security deposit
- — Tenant prepays $250.00 towards the cost of the releasing fee and other expenses incurred in re-leasing which may include, but is not limited to, advertising, re-keying locks, cleaning, utility, etc. Tenant remains responsible for all re-leasing costs incurred.
- — A satisfactory replacement tenant has been approved by Mountain Properties and has paid the security deposit and first month's rent. Existing Tenant is responsible to pay all rent up to the day the Replacement tenant starts paying rent.

Case Study B: Selection from the Endangered Species Act, 1973, singed into United States law by the 108th U.S. Congress, Section 4 (a) (3).

In the following section of the Endangered Species Act, use parentheses to distinguish complex claims, then replace English operators with operators of propositional logic (or add operators where necessary). After you're finished, rewrite the paragraph in your own words.

(3)(A) The Secretary, by regulation promulgated in accordance with subsection (b) and to the maximum extent prudent and determinable—(i) shall, concurrently with making a determination under paragraph (1) that a species is an endangered species or a threatened species, designate any habitat of such species which is then considered to be critical habitat; and (ii) may, from time-to-time thereafter as appropriate, revise such designation. (B)(i) The Secretary shall not designate as critical habitat any lands or other geographical areas owned or controlled by the Department of Defense, or designated for its use, that are subject to an integrated natural resources management plan prepared under section 101of

⇨

the Sikes Act (16 U.S.C. 670a), if the Secretary determines 5 in writing that such plan provides a benefit to the species for which critical habitat is proposed for designation. (ii) Nothing in this paragraph affects the requirement to consult under section 7(a)(2) with respect to an agency action (as that term is defined in that section). (iii) Nothing in this paragraph affects the obligation of the Department of Defense to comply with section 9, including the prohibition preventing extinction and taking of endangered species and threatened species. (b) BASIS FOR DETERMINATIONS.—(1)(A) The Secretary shall make determinations required by subsection (a)(1) solely on the basis of the best scientific and commercial data available to him after conducting a review of the status of the species and after taking into account those efforts, if any, being made by any State or foreign nation, or any political subdivision of a State or foreign nation, to protect such species, whether by predator control, protection of habitat and food supply, or other conservation practices, within any area under its jurisdiction, or on the high seas. (B) In carrying out this section, the Secretary shall give consideration to species which have been— (i) designated as requiring protection from unrestricted commerce by any foreign nation, or pursuant to any international agreement; or (ii) identified as in danger of extinction, or likely to become so within the foreseeable future, by any State agency or by any agency of a foreign nation that is responsible for the conservation of fish or wildlife or plants. (2) The Secretary shall designate critical habitat, and make revisions thereto, under subsection (a)(3) on the basis of the best scientific data available and after taking into consideration the economic impact, the impact on national security, and any other relevant impact, of specifying any particular area as critical habitat. The Secretary may exclude any area from critical habitat if he determines that the benefits of such exclusion outweigh the benefits of specifying such area as part of the critical habitat, unless he determines, based on the best scientific and commercial data available, that the failure to designate such area as critical habitat will result in the extinction of the species concerned. (3)(A) To the maximum extent practicable, within 90 days after receiving the petition of an interested person under section 553(e) of title 5, United States Code, to add a species to, or to remove a species from, either of the lists published under subsection (c), the Secretary shall make a finding as to whether the petition presents substantial scientific or commercial information indicating that the petitioned action may be warranted. If such a petition is found to present such information, the Secretary shall promptly commence a review of the status of the species concerned. The Secretary shall promptly publish each finding made under this subparagraph in the Federal Register. (B) Within 12 months after receiving a petition that is found under subparagraph (A) to present substantial information indicating that the petitioned action may be warranted, the Secretary shall make one of the following findings: (i) The petitioned action is not warranted, in which case the Secretary shall promptly publish such finding in the Federal Register. (ii) The petitioned action is warranted, in which case the Secretary shall promptly publish in the Federal Register a general notice and the complete text of a proposed regulation to implement such action in accordance with paragraph (5). 6 (iii) The petitioned action is warranted, but that— (I) the immediate proposal and timely promulgation of a final regulation implementing the petitioned action in accordance with paragraphs (5) and (6) is precluded by pending proposals to

⇨

determine whether any species is an endangered species or a threatened species, and (II) expeditious progress is being made to add qualified species to either of the lists published under subsection (c) and to remove from such lists species for which the protections of the Act are no longer necessary, in which case the Secretary shall promptly publish such finding in the Federal Register, together with a description and evaluation of the reasons and data on which the finding is based. (C)(i) A petition with respect to which a finding is made under subparagraph (B)(iii) shall be treated as a petition that is resubmitted to the Secretary under subparagraph (A) on the date of such finding and that presents substantial scientific or commercial information that the petitioned action may be warranted. (ii) Any negative finding described in subparagraph (A) and any finding described in subparagraph (B)(i) or (iii) shall be subject to judicial review. (iii) The Secretary shall implement a system to monitor effectively the status of all species with respect to which a finding is made under subparagraph (B)(iii) and shall make prompt use of the authority under paragraph 7 to prevent a significant risk to the well being of any such species. (D)(i) To the maximum extent practicable, within 90 days after receiving the petition of an interested person under section 553(e) of title 5, United States Code, to revise a critical habitat designation, the Secretary shall make a finding as to whether the petition presents substantial scientific information indicating that the revision may be warranted. The Secretary shall promptly publish such finding in the Federal Register. (ii) Within 12 months after receiving a petition that is found under clause (i) to present substantial information indicating that the requested revision may be warranted, the Secretary shall determine how he intends to proceed with the requested revision, and shall promptly publish notice of such intention in the Federal Register.

Truth Tables

5.1. Constructing truth tables

A **truth table** is a tool for expressing the logical relationships among claims and, therefore, allows us to test the validity of arguments. Truth tables express these relationships in terms of the claims' truth-values. In other words, truth tables express their *truth-functional* relations. A truth table shows *every possible* truth-functional relationship among a set of claims. For instance, a single claim only has two possible truth values: true or false.

Consider the claim, "It is a cat." Let's translate that into symbolic logic using the constant "C." C can be true or false, and we construct a truth table by listing the possible truth-values underneath the claim. Therefore, the truth table for C looks like this:

C
T   (line 1)
F   (line 2)

(column)

In a truth table, there are *columns*, which are vertical, up-and-down rows containing truth values (either T or F). There are also lines, which are the horizontal, left-to-right rows containing truth values.

Now, imagine that C is not alone. Let's conjoin C with the claim, "It is a mammal," symbolized by "M," so that we now have: (C & M). The truth table for (C & M) shows every possible combination of truth values of C and M. The truth-values are listed vertically and the combinations are read horizontally. So we begin by listing all the possible combinations of C and M vertically underneath them:

C	&	M
T	?	T
T	?	F
F	?	T
F	?	F

In order to know all the possible truth values for (C & M), we need to know what makes any conjunction (&) true or false. Since we know that a conjunction is only true if both conjuncts are true, our truth table looks like this:

C	&	M
T	**T**	T
T	**F**	F
F	**F**	T
F	**F**	F

You might have noticed that the truth table for (C & M) has two more lines than the truth table for C. Every time we add a new claim to a truth table you will need to add lines. If we had added another C or another M, we would not need to add lines. But if we added another claim, let's say, "D," we would. Consider the following two truth tables:

1 ((C & M) & C)

T	T	T	T	T
T	F	F	F	T
F	F	T	F	F
F	F	F	F	F

2 ((C & M) & D)

T	T	T	T	T
T	T	T	F	F
T	F	F	F	T
T	F	F	F	F
F	F	T	F	T
F	F	T	F	F
F	F	F	F	T
F	F	F	F	F

Notice that, in 2, since we already know all the possible truth-value combinations of C, we just repeat them under the second C. But in 2, we have a new set of combinations. To know how many lines to add for each new variable, use 2^x, where x stands for the number of simple claims (that is, don't count repeated claims):

$$2^{\text{the number of simple claims}}$$

So for truth table:

C
T
F

we have 2^1, which tells us we need two lines, one for true and one for false. In this table:

C	&	M
T	**T**	T
T	**F**	F
F	**F**	T
F	**F**	F

we have 2^2, which tells us we need four lines. And in this table:

((C	&	M)	&	D)
T	T	T	**T**	T
T	T	T	**F**	F
T	F	F	**F**	T
T	F	F	**F**	F
F	F	T	**F**	T
F	F	T	**F**	F
F	F	F	**F**	T
F	F	F	**F**	F

we have 2^3, which tells us we need eight lines.

There are two more things to know about constructing a truth table. The first is how to list truth-values underneath claims. All of your truth tables will have an even number of lines, so start with the far left column and label the first half of the lines as true and the second half as false. In the next column to the right, cut the pattern in half, labeling the first ¼ as true, the second ¼ as false, the third ¼ as true, and so on. In the next column to the right, cut the pattern in half again. Continue decreasing the pattern by half until you reach a column where the lines alternate T, F, T, F, etc.

The second thing to know is which operators to start with when completing your table. Begin by locating the major operator. Remember the major operator is the operator that determines what the complex claim is called, e.g., a "conjunction," a "disjunction," a "conditional," etc. When completing your table, you will end with the major operator. For instance, here:

```
((C & M) & D)
 T  T  T  T
 T  T  T  F  F
 T  F  F  F  T
 T  F  F  F  F
 F  F  T  F  T
 F  F  T  F  F
 F  F  F  F  T
 F  F  F  F  F
```

you would start by filling in the column under the first "&," that is, the (C & M) column. Then fill in the column under the second "&," that is, the ((C & M) & D) column. Once you've constructed a couple on your own, this becomes obvious. Notice that you couldn't fill in the column under the second "&" without knowing what is in the column under the first "&."

In the next section, we'll see how truth tables express the relationships among claims connected with our remaining four operators. In section 7.3, we'll see how to use truth tables to test short arguments for validity. In section 7.4, we'll see how to test long arguments for validity.

5.2. Using truth tables to express relationships among claims

By showing the truth-functional relationships among claims and operators, truth tables show exactly why our operators do the work they do in a complex claim. Consider the truth table for a simple claim, "A":

A
T
F

If we introduce the negation (~) operator on this simple claim, we can see that all of A's possible truth-values change:

~A
F T
T F

This is obvious when you consider any claim ("It is a cat," "Submarines are boats," "The sky is black") and its negation ("It is not a cat," "Submarines are not boats," "The sky is not black"). So, for any claim, no matter how complex, if a negation is added to that claim, change all of its possible truth values. For instance, consider the claim:

((((A v B) & (C & D)) ⊃ E) ≡ F)

The major operator of this monster is a bi-conditional (≡). Imagine that the truth-values under the bi-conditional begin, T, F, F, F . . . :

((((A v B) & (C & D)) ⊃ E) ≡ F)
                         T
                         F
                         F
                         F
                      . . .

If we then add a negation to the claim (which then becomes the major operator), we change all the truth-values to their opposites (their "contradictories"):

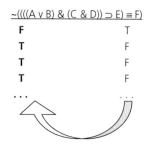

~((((A v B) & (C & D)) ⊃ E) ≡ F)

F	T
T	F
T	F
T	F
. . .	. . .

TIP: For simple claims that are operated on, for example, with a negation, always list the truth-values for a simple claim first, then change it according to the operator. Don't try to guess ahead and list only the truth-values for the negated claim, leaving out the column for the simple claim. You'll almost certainly lost track and get confused as arguments get longer.

We've already seen several examples of the truth table for the conjunction (&):

A	&	B
T	**T**	T
T	**F**	F
F	**F**	T
F	**F**	F

Conjunctions are true if and only if both conjuncts are true. If either, or both, of the conjuncts is/are false, the conjunction is false.

Disjunctions are much more forgiving than conjunctions. With a disjunction, as long as both disjuncts are not false, the disjunction is true:

A	v	B
T	**T**	T
T	**T**	F
F	**T**	T
F	**F**	F

This is most intuitive when one disjunct is true and one is false (lines 2 and 3 of the table). For instance, "Either the sky is blue or the moon is made of green cheese," or "Either pigs fly or you did not win the lottery." Also, "Either Texas is on the west coast or California is on the west coast."

It is also pretty easy to see that a disjunction is false if both disjuncts are false. For example, the disjunction, "Either the moon is made of green cheese or Texas is on the west coast," is false. The same goes for: "Either pigs fly or grass is blue."

Things are less clear when we consider a disjunction where both disjuncts are true. For instance, "Either Texas is on the west coast or California is on the west coast." Some people might say this disjunction is false, because true disjunctions *require* that one disjunct be false. But whether this is true depends on whether you interpret the "or" (v) as *inclusive* or *exclusive*.

An *exclusive* "or" requires that one disjunct be false. An *inclusive* "or" allows that both disjuncts can be true. There are reasons for preferring the exclusive "or," for instance, because there are disjunctions where it is impossible that both disjuncts are true. In the disjunction, "Either it is raining or it isn't," both disjuncts cannot be true. The same goes for any claim and its negation: "Either it is a cat or it isn't," "Either you will win the lottery or you won't," "Either God exists or he doesn't."

But logicians prefer the inclusive "or." In most cases, it is possible for both disjuncts to be true: "He's either a dad or he's a soccer player, and he might be both," "Either she really likes cookies or she's a surfer, and she might be both." In addition, the inclusive "or" can accommodate the cases of exclusive disjuncts. For instance, "Either it is raining or it isn't, and it can't be both," and "He's either a insane or a liar, but he can't be both," can be translated using the inclusive "or" as follows:

$$((R \lor \sim R) \ \& \sim (R \ \& \sim R)) \qquad\qquad ((I \lor L) \ \& \sim (I \ \& \ L))$$

Conditionals are probably the most difficult operator to fully understand. We use them constantly and, most of the time, we use them correctly. Logically, however, they have some characteristics that are not intuitive at first glance. In addition, getting a good grasp on these relations will help you avoid numerous mistakes and fallacies.

As with the disjunction, there is only one combination of truth-values that make the operator false. With the disjunction, it was when both disjuncts were false. With the conditional, it is when the antecedent is true and the consequent is false. Here is the truth table for the conditional:

A	⊃	B
T	**T**	T
T	**F**	F
F	**T**	T
F	**T**	F

It is easy to see why a conditional is true if both the antecedent and the consequent are true: If that animal is a dog, then it is a mammal. If it is true that that animal is a dog and that that animal is a mammal, the conditional is true.

But things get muddy when considering the other possibilities. Consider the claim, "If you are caught stealing, you will go to jail." Both the antecedent and consequent may be true (we hope not). But there are other possibilities as well. You might go to jail without having been caught stealing. For instance, if you started a fight or sold drugs or were wrongly accused of murder. This would be an instance of line 3 on the truth table for the conditional. It remains true that if you are caught stealing, you will go to jail. But it turns out that you went to jail for some other reason.

It's also possible that both the antecedent and the consequent are false (which we hope is the case for anyone reading this). If you were neither caught stealing and your aren't in jail, the conditional is still true. *You do* go to jail, *if you are* caught stealing. But you are neither.

However, if it is possible that you are caught stealing but did not go to jail, then the conditional is false. Some exception keeps it from being true. Perhaps the officer knows you and your family and decides to let you off this time. If this is the case, the conditional is false. It might be true most of the time, but in this case, it is false.

Consider this claim: "If it snows, the roof on the shed will collapse." This conditional is true if, given that it snows, the roof collapses. It is also true if a strong wind collapses the roof but it doesn't snow. It is also true if it neither snows nor the roof collapses. It is a conditional, in a literal sense; the truth of one claim is conditional upon another.

This leads to an important distinction in logic: the difference between a **necessary condition** and a **sufficient condition**. In the theft case, "getting caught" is *sufficient* for "going to jail," but it isn't *necessary* for going to jail, since you could go to jail for any number of reasons. In the snow case, "snowing" is *sufficient* for the "roof collapsing," but not *necessary*, since lots of other events could cause the roof to collapse. However, if the conditionals are true, "going to jail" and the "roof collapsing" are *necessary* for "getting caught" and "snowing," respectively. Here's the trick: the antecedent of any conditional is a sufficient condition; the consequent of any conditional is a necessary condition.

> WARNING: Do not confuse necessary conditions with necessary claims. A necessary claim is true no matter what, unconditionally. A necessary condition is a claim on which the truth of another claim depends. Any claim can be a necessary condition if it is the consequent of a conditional. Only certain claims are necessarily true: 2 + 2 = 4; all bachelors are unmarried; everything is self-identical; no claim is both true and false at the same time.

Once you get the hang of conditionals, the bi-conditional ($\equiv$) will come naturally. A bi-conditional is just a conditional that works in both directions—it is *two conditionals conjoined* together. For instance: $(A \equiv B)$ means the same as $((A \supset B) \mathbin{\&} (B \subset A))$. A bi-conditional is an "if and only if" claim. So the bi-conditional: "A human is a man *if and only if* it has an Y chromosome," means the same as: "If a human is a man, then it has a Y chromosome, and if a human has a Y chromosome, then it is a man." In addition, the bi-conditional, "An object is an electron *if and only if* it has -1.602×10^{-19} Coulombs charge," means the same as, "If an object is an electron, then it has it has -1.602×10^{-19} Coulombs charge, and if an object has -1.602×10^{-19} Coulombs charge, then it is an electron."

The truth table for a bi-conditional looks like this:

A	≡	B
T	**T**	T
T	**F**	F
F	**F**	T
F	**T**	F

If both sides of a bi-conditional are true, the bi-conditional is true. If both sides are false, the bi-conditional is also true. For instance, there are two chairs plus two chairs if and only if there are four chairs. If there are five chairs, then, though both sides of the bi-conditional are false, the bi-conditional remains true.

If either side of the bi-conditional is false, the bi-conditional is false. Since a bi-conditional is just two conditionals conjoined, it follows the rules of conditionals and conjunctions. If one side of a bi-conditional is false, it is equivalent to one of the following truth tables:

((A ⊃ B) & (B ⊃ A))   or   ((A ⊃ B) & (B ⊃ A))
  F T T **F** T F F   T F F **F** F T T

Now that you know the truth tables for all of the operators, use them to figure out the truth-value of the following claims. The first two are completed for you:

Exercises 5.a.

Using truth-tables, construct a truth table for each of the following complex claims. We've constructed the first two for you.

1. ~ (P v Q)

F	T	T	T
F	T	T	F
F	F	T	T
T	F	F	F

2. ~((A v B) & (C v A))

F	T	T	T	T	T	T	T
F	T	T	T	T	F	T	T
F	T	T	F	T	T	T	T
F	T	T	F	T	F	T	T
F	F	T	T	T	T	T	F
T	F	T	T	F	F	F	F
T	F	F	F	F	T	T	F
T	F	F	F	F	F	F	F

Notice that the main operator of this claim is the negation (~), so don't forget to change all the values under the conjunction (&) column.

3. (P ≡ (Q ⊃ R))   4. (W & ~P)   5. (~Q ⊃ R)
6. ~(P & Q)   7. (W v (A v B))   8. (A v (B ⊃ C))
9. ~(A ⊃ ~B)   10. ~(T ≡ (U & ~V))

5.3. Using truth tables to evaluate short arguments

Truth-tables allow us to evaluate an argument's validity. Remember that validity means: necessarily, if the premises are true, the conclusion is true. If it is *even possible* that all the premises are true and the conclusion is false, the argument is invalid.

The validity of any argument can be evaluated using truth-tables. Consider the following argument:

(p1) If Jim is a liberal, then either he will vote for the Democratic candidate or he will not vote.
(p2) Jim is a liberal.
(p3) Jim always votes on principle.
c) Therefore, Jim will vote for the Democratic candidate.

Begin by translating the argument in to propositional logic:

(p1) If (L) Jim is a liberal, then either (D) he will vote for the Democratic candidate or (~V) he will not vote.
(p2) (L) Jim is a liberal.
(p3) (~~V) Jim always votes on principle.
c) Therefore, (D) Jim will vote for the Democratic candidate.

In purely symbolic form, we have:

(p1) (L ⊃ (D v ~V))
(p2) L
(p3) ~~V
c) D

Next, list the premises side-by-side horizontally, separating them with a semi-colon (;). Then list the conclusion horizontally at the far right after the conclusion sign (/∴):

(L ⊃ (D v ~V)) ; L ; ~~V /∴ D

Now, construct the truth-table. There are only three unique claims, L, D, and V. Therefore, you will need 2^3 lines, which is 8 lines. Being by labeling the truth-values of the claims according to our pattern:

(L	⊃	(D v~V)) ;	L ;	~~V /∴	D
T	T	T	T	T	T
T	T	F	T	F	T
T	F	T	T	T	F
T	F	F	T	F	F
F	T	T	F	T	T
F	T	F	F	F	T
F	F	T	F	T	F
F	F	F	F	F	F

Next, fill in the truth values for the complex claims, according to the relationships set out in section 7.2:

(L ⊃ (D	v	~V)) ;	L ;	~~V /∴	D
T T T	T	F T	T	T F T	T
T T T	T	T F	T	F T F	T
T F F	F	F T	T	T F T	F
T T F	T	T F	T	F T F	F
F T T	T	F T	F	T F T	T
F T T	T	T F	F	F T F	T
F T F	F	F T	F	T F T	F
F T F	T	T F	F	F T F	F

With this truth table complete, we can now evaluate the argument for validity. To evaluate the argument, simply check to see if there is any line where all the premises are true and the conclusion is false. If there is even one line like that, the argument is invalid. If there is not, the argument is valid. You can save time by starting with the conclusion column. Find the lines where the conclusion is false, then look left along that line to see whether all the premises are true. This means you won't need to check every line, only those lines where the conclusion is false. In this argument, check lines 3 and 4 and 7 and 8, since those are the lines where the conclusion is false.

(L ⊃ (D v ~V)) ; L ; ~~V /∴ D
T T T   TFT   T   TFT   T
T T T   TTF   T   FTF   T
T **F** F   FFT   **T**   TFT   **F**
T **T** F   TTF   **T**   FTF   **F**
F T T   TFT   F   TFT   T
F T T   TTF   F   FTF   T
F **T** F   FFT   **F**   TFT   **F**
F **T** F   TTF   **F**   FTF   **F**

The only values you need to compare are those of the major operators of the premise(s) with the truth value of the conclusion. As we can see, there are no lines where all the premises are true and the conclusion is false. *This argument is valid.*

Let's look at three more short arguments:

(A v C) ; (C v D) /∴ D
T T T   T T T   T
T T T   T T F   F
T T F   F T T   T
T T F   F F F   F
F T T   T T T   T
F T T   T T F   F
F F F   F T T   T
F F F   F F F   F

(A v C) ; (C v D) /∴ D
T T T   T T T   T
T **T** T   T **T** F   **F** ←
T T F   F T T   T
T **T** F   F **F** F   **F**
F T T   T T T   T
F **T** T   T **T** F   **F** ←
F F F   F T T   T
F **F** F   F **F** F   **F**

This argument is invalid.

(A ⊃ B) ; (B v A) /.: ~A
```
T T T   T T T   F T
T F F   F T T   F T
F T T   T T F   T F
F T F   F F F   T F
```

(A ⊃ B) ; (B v A) /.: ~A
```
T T T   T T T   F T     ←
T F F   F T T   F T
F T T   T T F   T F
F T F   F F F   T F
```

This argument is invalid.

((B v D) ; ~B /.: D
```
 T T T   F T   T
 T T F   F T   F
 F T T   T F   T
 F F F   T F   F
```

((B v D) ; ~B /.: D
```
 T T T   F T   T
 T T F   F T   F
 F T T   T F   T
 F F F   T F   F
```

This argument is valid.

Exercises 5.b.

Using truth tables, test each of the following arguments for validity:

1. ((P ⊃ Q) & P) /.: Q

2. (L ⊃ ~L) /.: ~L

3. (M ≡ ~N) ; ~(N & ~M) /.: (M ⊃ N)

4. (A ≡ ~B) /.: (B v A)

5. (A ⊃ A) /.: A

6. ((B v D) v E) ; ~B ; ~E /.: D

7. ~R ; (S ⊃ R) /.: ~S

8. ~S ; (S ⊃ R) /.: ~R

9. ((A & B) v (C v D)) ; ~ (C v D) /.: A

10. (H ⊃ I) ; (J ≡ H) ; (~I v H) /.: (J ≡ I)

5.4. Using truth tables to evaluate long arguments

Any argument that includes more than four simple claims becomes really long and cumbersome. Thankfully, there is a way to abbreviate the truth table method for long arguments, which we'll call "the short method." By the way, the short method works for short arguments, too, but you have to understand the "long method" before you can really understand why the short method works. So, section 7.3 was a hand-cramping, necessary evil.

To begin, remember with the long method that, once we constructed the full truth table for an argument, we were only concerned with the lines where the conclusion was false. So, instead of constructing a full table, we'll just construct the lines where the conclusions are false and then attempt to make all the premises true. If we cannot do this, the argument is valid.

To begin, simply construct all the ways the conclusion can be false. If the conclusion is a simple claim, just label it false. For example, consider the following argument:

(((A & B) ⊃ (C v D)) & E) /.: D

Since the conclusion is a simple claim, "D," begin constructing your truth table by labeling D with an "F":

<u>(((A & B) ⊃ (C v D)) & E) /.: D</u>
                                  F

Since the truth value for D must be consistent throughout the argument, go ahead and label any other instance of D with an "F":

<u>(((A & B) ⊃ (C v D)) & E) /.: D</u>
                   F   F

Now, simply try to make the rest of the premises true, beginning with the major operator(s). In this case, there is only one premise, with a conjunction (&) as the major operator. In order to be true, a conjunction must have two true conjuncts. Since the second conjunct is a simple claim, "E," just label E as "true":

(((A & B) ⊃ (C v D)) & E) /∴ D
              F   T   F

The first conjunct is a bit trickier. The first conjunct is a conditional (⊃). We know that the only way a conditional can be false is if the antecedent is true and the consequent is false. So, all we have to do is find one combination of truth-values that does not end up in this configuration. As it turns out, any of the following will do:

(((A & B) ⊃ (C v D)) & E) /∴ D
```
T F F T F  F F  T T    F
F F T T F  F F  T T    F
F F F T F  F F  T T    F
T T T T T  T T  T T    F
```

Remember, when testing for validity, all you need to find is ONE line where the premises are truth and the conclusion is false. Therefore, once you find one, you're done; the argument is invalid. We need not have constructed the last three lines once we constructed the first. But any of the four does the trick.

Now, if you cannot construct a line where the conclusion is false and the premises are true, then the argument is valid. Consider the following example:

~(A v B); (D ⊃ (A v B)) /∴ ~D

In this argument the conclusion is complex, but it is easy enough to make false. Just label D as "true," and apply the negation operator:

~(A v B); (D ⊃ (A v B)) /∴ ~D
                             FT

Since the truth-value of D must remain consistent throughout the argument, label all other instances of D as "true" (don't accidentally label it "false"); it is only the negation operator that does that in the conclusion):

~(A v B); (D ⊃ (A v B)) /∴ ~D
         T   FT

Now, attempt to make the rest of the premises true, beginning with the major operator of each. The major operator in the first premise is the negation (~). In order to make a negation true, the operand, in this case (A v B), must be false. The major operator of this claim is a disjunction (v). The only way to make a disjunction false is to have two false disjuncts. Since nothing is preventing us from labeling them both "false," go ahead and do so:

~(A v B); (D ⊃ (A v B)) /.: ~D
T F FF   T   FT

So, the first premise is true. Now attempt to make the second premise true. Since the second premise includes A and B, and since a claim's truth-value must remain consistent throughout a line, we are forced to label A and B as "false":

~(A v B); (D ⊃ (A v B)) /.: ~D
T F FF   T   F **F** F   FT

But now we have a conditional (the major operator of the second premise) with a true antecedent, D, and a false consequent, (A v B), which is false:

~(A v B); (D ⊃ (A v B)) /.: ~D
T F FF   T **F** F F F   FT

So, we can see that there is no way to make the premises true and the conclusion false. This argument is valid. Try working this one again, but this time, start by trying to make the second premise true, then move on to the first premise. Did you get the same results?

Arguments with complex conclusions are trickier. In those cases, you must construct every possible way the conclusion can be false, then see if the premises could all be true on each line. If the premises cannot all be made true on the first line, move to the next. If the premises can all be made true on the first line, you can stop; the argument is invalid. We'll work three of these together, then we'll list five more for you to work on your own.

((P ⊃ ~Q) & (R & W)) ; (R v W) ; (P & R) /.: (P v W)

With the short method, we always begin by making the conclusion false. When the conclusion is a disjunction this is easy because there is only one way a conclusion can be false, that is, when both disjuncts are false:

((P ⊃ ~Q) & (R & W)) ; (R v W) ; (P & R) /.: (P v W)
                                            F F F

Remember, once you've stipulated that P and W are false, they must be labeled false in every other instance on the line:

<u>((P ⊃ ~Q) & (R & W)) ; (R v W) ; (P & R) /∴ (P v W)</u>
   F   F   F F   F F F

Now simply see if it's possible to make all the premises true. In this case, since one of the premises is a conjunction, and since one of its conjuncts is already false, then at least one of our premises cannot be true. Therefore, *this argument is valid*:

<u>((P ⊃ ~Q) & (R & W)) ; (R v W) ; (P & R) /∴ (P v W)</u>
   F   F   F F(F)?   F F F

Consider another argument:

(P ≡ Q) ; W ; (~R & W) /∴ ((P v W) ⊃ Q)

Since this argument has a conditional as a conclusion, we know there is only one way it can be false, that is, with the antecedent true and the consequent false. But in this case, the antecedent is a disjunction, and a disjunction can be true in three different ways. You will need to represent all three of these ways to fully evaluate the argument:

<u>(P ≡ Q) ; W ; (~R & W) /∴ ((P v W) ⊃ Q)</u>
                       T T T F F
                       T T F F F
                       F T T F F

Now, label the other simple claims, letting the stipulations we made in the conclusion determine the truth-values of the simple claims in the premises:

<u>(P ≡ Q) ; W ; (~R & W) /∴ ((P v W) ⊃ Q)</u>
T F T   T   T T T F F
T F F   F   T T F F F
F F T   T   F T T F F

Now see if it's possible to make all the premises true. Since we already know the second premise is false on line two, we only have to consider lines 1 and 3:

<u>(P ≡ Q) ; W ; (~R & W) /∴ ((P v W) ⊃ Q)</u>
T F T   T   T T T F F
~~T~~ ~~F~~ (F)   ~~F~~   ~~T T F~~ ~~F F~~
F F T   T   F T T F F

Looking at line 1, we see that, since the truth-values for P and Q were determined by the conclusion, and since a bi-conditional ($\equiv$) is true if and only if either both sides are true or both sides are false, we cannot make all the premises on line 1 true:

<u>(P $\equiv$ Q) ; W ; (~R & W) /.: ((P v W) $\supset$ Q)</u>
T (F) F T   T   T T T F F
T F F   F   T T F F F
F F T   T   F T T F F

Looking, then, at line 3, we see that the first premise is true and the second premise is true:

<u>(P $\equiv$ Q) ; W ; (~R & W) /.: ((P v W) $\supset$ Q)</u>
T F F T   T   T T T F F
T F F   F   T T F F F
F (T) F (T)   T   F T T F F

Whether this argument is valid depends on whether we can make the third premise true. The third premise is a conjunction (&) and the only way a conjunction can be true is if both conjuncts are true. We already know the right conjunct is true. Can we make the left conjunct true? Since the truth-value is not determined by the conclusion, we are free to stipulate whatever truth-value we wish. Therefore, in order to make the conjunction true we only have to make "R" false, so that "~R" will be true:

<u>(P $\equiv$ Q) ; W ; (~R & W) /.: ((P v W) $\supset$ Q)</u>
T F F T   T   T T T F F
T F F   F   T T F F F
| F T F T T (F) T T   F T T F F | ◄——

Since there is at least one line where all the premises are true and the conclusion is false, *the argument is invalid.*

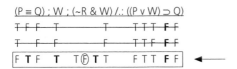

(A v B) ; (A & (C v D)) ; ~D ; (B $\supset$ C) /.: ~((C v D) & (D $\supset$ B))

5.5. More exercises:

Exercises 5.c.

Test each of the following arguments for validity using the short method:

1. (P v ~Q) ; (R ⊃ ~Q) /.: (~P ⊃ R)
2. (A v B) ; (A ⊃ B) /.: (B ⊃ ~A)
3. (~(Y & O) v W) /.: Y ⊃ W
4. (Y ≡ Z) ; (~Y v ~W) ; W /.: Z
5. (A & B) ; (~A v C) ; (~D ⊃ ~C) /.: (D & B)
6. (P ⊃ A) ; (Q ⊃ B) ; (P v Q) /.: (A v B)
7. (P ⊃Q) ; (Q ⊃ R) ; (R ⊃ S) /.: ((P ⊃ S) v W)
8. (~A v ~B) ; (C v D) ; ~(~A v C) /.: (~B & D)
9. (((P & Q) v W) ⊃ R) ; (~R & ~W) ; ~Q /.: (P & Q)

Exercises 5.d.

Translate each of the following arguments into propositional logic, then test for validity using the short method:

1. All the elves were sleeping. If all the elves were sleeping, then the caves were silent. If the caves were silent, the air would be thick like mud. Therefore, the air was thick like mud.
2. You should step lightly only if you don't want to be taken seriously. But if you know what's good for you, you want to be taken seriously. You know what's good for you, therefore you should step lightly.
3. If you take that particular Jenga piece, the whole stack will fall. If the whole stack does not fall, you did not take that piece. The whole stack fell, so you took that piece.
4. The wind blows heavily only if the night is most wicked. If the full moon is out, the night is most wicked. The night is not very wicked. So, the moon is not full.
5. Vinnie takes money from Frankie only if Frankie doubles his money on the ponies. If Frankie doubles his money on the ponies, he has to give half to his ex-wife. Hence, if Frankie gives half to his ex-wife, Vinnie takes money from Frankie.
6. It's a long way to the top if you want to rock and roll. It's not very far to the top. Therefore, you really don't want to rock and roll.
7. It's a long way to the top only if you want to rock and roll. It's a really long way to the top. Hence, you wanna rock and roll.
8. If you have a headache and take aspirin, your headache will go away and you will feel better. Your headache went away but you didn't feel better. Therefore, you didn't take aspirin.
9. If it is a cat, then it is a mammal. If it is a mammal, then it is warm-blooded. If it is warm-blooded, then it reproduces sexually. If it reproduces sexually, its reproduction can be explained by genetics. If its reproduction can be explained by genetics, then Johnny can explain its reproduction. Therefore, if it is a cat, Johnny can explain its reproduction
10. If it rains outside and the awning is broken, the sidewalk gets wet and becomes slippery. If the temperature never gets lower than seventy degrees, the sidewalk is slippery if and only if it is wet. We live in Florida and the temperature never gets lower than seventy degrees. Therefore, if the awning is broken, the sidewalk is becoming slippery.

⇨

11. You must stop at the intersection if and only if the traffic light is not green unless an emergency vehicle is coming through. If an emergency vehicle is coming through, you must stop at the intersection or you will be cited for reckless driving. Therefore, if you are cited for reckless driving and the traffic light is green, an emergency vehicle is coming through.

Real-Life Examples:

No matter how abstract logic can be, we're never more than a few steps away from the real world. **(1) Read the following two simple Real Life arguments**, **(2) translate them into symbolic logic**, then **(3) test them for validity**. Remember, an argument can be good without being valid (all inductive arguments are invalid). But, if an argument is not valid, then you have eliminated one way that it can be successful.

Real-Life Example 1: Former Illinois Governor Rob Blagojevich

The following argument is excerpted from a speech given by then-Illinois Governor Rob Blagojevich in response to allegations of misconduct on January 29, 2009:

"The evidence is the four tapes. You heard those four tapes. I don't have to tell you what they say. You guys are in politics, you know what we have to do to go out and run elections.

"There was no criminal activity on those four tapes. You can express things in a free country, but those four tapes speak for themselves. Take those four tapes as they are and you will, I believe, in fairness, recognize and acknowledge, those are conversations relating to the things all of us in politics do in order to run campaigns and try to win elections."

Don't forget to remove extraneous material:

"The evidence is the four tapes. <u>You heard those four tapes. I don't have to tell you what they say</u>. You guys are in politics, you know what we have to do to go out and run and run elections.

"There was no criminal activity on those four tapes. You can express things in a free country, <u>but those four tapes speak for themselves. Take those four tapes as they are and you will, I believe, in fairness, recognize and acknowledge</u>, those are conversations relating to the things all of us in politics do in order to run campaigns and try to win elections."

Real-Life Example 2: Political Pundit Rush Limbaugh

The following is an excerpt from a Wall Street Journal article written by conservative political pundit Rush Limbaugh about newly elected President Barak Obama. Be careful: some of the premises are implicit and the conclusion is sarcastic, meaning the opposite of what Limbaugh intends to convey.

> "He [Obama] explained that there was no use trying to tighten lending laws because, in Congress, quote, you have 534 massive egos up there. He, of course, built himself a seven million dollar auditorium and cafeteria in his office building and also had a personal tax-payer funded chef hired. There's no ego involved in that."[1]

Rules of Inference

6

Chapter Outline

6.1. Deductive inference

Since propositional logic is a *formal* language, as long as we reason according to a valid argument form, there is no loss of meaning or truth-value when we draw *appropriate inferences* from premises to conclusions. But what counts as an "appropriate" inference?

Thankfully, there are a set of rules to guide us in determining when a conclusion follows with certainty. Logicians have discovered a handful of rules that, if followed strictly, will always preserve truth-value from premises to conclusion. Rules that preserve truth-value are called *valid* for the same reasons that a good deductive argument is valid: it is impossible for the premises to be true and the conclusion false. If the premises are true, that truth is preserved through the inference to the conclusion.

In this chapter, we will introduce you to seven rules of valid inference and two methods of valid proof. Remember, the term "validity" applies exclusively to deductive arguments. As we will see in part III of this book, all inductive arguments are invalid, that is, it is always possible for the premises to be true and the conclusion false. Therefore, we will need a different set of criteria for evaluating the relationship between the premises and conclusion in inductive arguments. We'll begin with four basic rules of inference, then increase the complexity as we go through the chapter.

6.2. Four basic rules

Simplification
Conjunction
modus ponens
modus tollens

6.2.1. Simplification

Recall from Chapter 5 the truth table for a conjunction (&):

P & Q
T T T
T F F
F F T
F F F

A conjunction is true *if and only if* both conjuncts are true. In order to test whether an argument is valid, we assume the premises are true and then determine whether the conclusion could possibly be false. Therefore, if we come across a conjunction and assume it is true (for the sake of evaluating its validity and because we don't always not know its English equivalent), we can assume both conjuncts are true.

Because of this, we are permitted to reason as follows:

A.

P1: (P & Q)   or

C: P

B.

P1: (P & Q)

C: Q   1, simplification

From a conjunction, we can conclude/derive/infer either of its conjuncts. The rule that permits this inference is called **simplification**. When you apply a rule, note the premise number and the name of the rule off to the side, so others can see (and check) your reasoning. It may help to see a couple of English examples:

I.

P1: It is snowing and it is cold.

C: Therefore, it is cold.

II.

P1: He's a lawyer and he's a jerk.

C: Thus, he's a lawyer

Regardless of how complicated a claim is, if its major operator is a conjunction, you can derive either of the conjuncts. Here are a few more examples:

C.

P1: ((A ⊃ B) & (C v D))

C: (A⊃B)   P1, simplification

D.

P1: (P v Q)

P2: C

P3: (D & E)

C: E   P3, simplification

E.

P1: (((A v B) ⊃ C) & (P ⊃ Q))

P2: ((B & C) ⊃ Q)

C: (P ⊃ Q)   P1, simplification

F.

P1: (P v Q)

P2: (P & ~B)

P3: (A v B)

C: ~B   P2, simplification

* Notice that you cannot derive B or C from these premises. In premise 2, the major operator is a conditional, not a conjunction. You would need a different rule to break up the conditional before you could apply simplification.

6.2.2. Conjunction

Since a true conjunction is a conjunction with true conjuncts, we can also *construct* conjunctions from true claims. For instance, if we already know that some claim, S, is true and that some claim B is true, it seems fairly obvious that (S & B) is true. Therefore, we can reason as follows:

A.
P1: A
P2: B
C: (A & B)   P1, P2 conjunction

B.
P1: P
P2: Q
C: (P & Q)   P1, P2 conjunction

From true claims, we can conclude/derive/infer their conjunction. The rule that permits this is, therefore, aptly named **conjunction**. When you apply conjunction to a set of premises, note off to the side both or all the premises you use to derive the conjunction. Here are two English examples:

I.
P1: It is cloudy.
P2: It is cold.
C: Hence, it is cloudy and it is cold.

II.
P1: The president is a man.
P2: The president lives in the capital city.
C: The president is a man and lives in the capital city.

Here are a few more examples:

C.
P1: A
P2: (P v Q)
C: (A & (P v Q)) P1, P2 conjunction

D.
P1: X
P2: Y
P3: Z
C1: (X & Z) P1, P3 conjunction
C2: (Y & (X & Z)) P2, C1 conjunction

E.
P1: ((Y v W) ⊃ (A & B))
P2: (Z v X)
C: (((Y v W) ⊃ (A & B)) & (Z v X)) P1, P2 conjunction

6.2.2.1. Aside: A change of notation

Now that you have a clear grasp of premises and conclusions and recognize the roles they play in an argument, it is time to introduce some new notation. Look back at example D from the previous section. Notice how we derived a second conclusion from one of the premises and our first conclusion. Now the first conclusion is *playing the role of* a premise. As arguments become more complicated, this notation can become pretty cumbersome. Therefore, instead of writing "P" in front of every premise and "C" in front of every conclusion, we will simply number each line. We will still have the derivation line under our starting premises, but afterward we will just number the claims we derive, noting the rules by which we derive them.

For instance, example D above will now look like this:

D.
1. X
2. Y
3. Z
4. (X & Z)   1, 3 conjunction
5. (Y & (X & Z))   2, 4 conjunction

1, 2, and 3 are still premises (also called **assumptions** in deductive reasoning). 4 and 5 will play different roles depending on what we are doing at the moment. At some point, each line below the derivation line will be a conclusion—a claim derived from the premises. After each has been derived, we are free to use it as a further premise in the argument. This notation will help keep our inferences clear.

6.2.3. *modus ponens*

Recall our truth-table for the conditional ($\supset$):

P $\supset$ Q
T T T
T F F
F T T
F T F

A conditional is false only if the antecedent is true and the consequent is false. Remember that when we find a conditional in a set of premises, we assume it is true (for the sake of evaluating the argument). Therefore, whatever conditional we find, on the assumption it is true, will have either (a) a true antecedent and true consequent or (b) a false antecedent and either a true or false consequent. But now, if we assume a conditional, (P $\supset$ Q), is true and *also* discover that the antecedent (P) is true, there is only one possible truth value for the consequent (Q), namely, true. Here it is in standard form:

A.
1. (P $\supset$ Q)
2. P
3. Q   1, 2 *modus ponens*

The rule that permits us to draw this inference is called ***modus ponens***, which is short for *modus ponendo ponens*, and is Latin for "mode (or method) that affirms by affirming." Again, note to the side all the premises you use to apply the rule. Here are some English examples using our new notation:

I.	II.
1. If it snows, the roof will collapse.	1. If God exists, there is no unnecessary suffering
2. It is snowing.	2. God exists.
3. Therefore, the roof will collapse.	3. Thus, there is no unnecessary suffering.

Here are some further examples:

B.
1. A
2. (C v D)
3. (A ⊃ (E & F))
4. (E & F)   **1, 3 *modus ponens***

C.
1. (B & C)
2. D
3. (D ⊃ E)
4. E   **2, 3 *modus ponens***

---

* Notice that it doesn't matter what order the premises are in. In example B, we find the conditional on line 3 and the simple claim is on line 1. Neverthe***less***, we can still infer the consequent of line 3 using *modus ponens*.

D.
1. ~(X v Y)
2. ~Z
3. (~(X v Y) ⊃ (Z v W))
4. (Z v W   **1, 3 *modus ponens***

E.
1. (D & B)
2. (B v ~H)
3. A
4. ((B v ~H) ⊃ ~E)
5. ~E   **2, 5 *modus ponens***

6.2.4. *modus tollens*

Again, look at our truth-table for the conditional:

P ⊃ Q
T T T
T F F
F T T
F T F

Notice that there are only two lines where the consequent is false. Notice also that, only one of these two expresses a true conditional. If the consequent of a conditional is *denied*, that is, if we discover that the consequent is false (expressed by adding a negation: ~Q), there is only one line that expresses a true conditional, and that is line 4. If Q is false and P is true, the conditional is false. But if Q is false (~Q is true) and P is false (~P is true), the conditional, (P ⊃ Q), is true.

Therefore, if we come across a conditional (assuming, as we have been, that it is true) and discover also that its consequent is false, we can conclude that its antecedent is false, too. The inference looks like this:

A.
1. (P ⊃ Q)
2. ~Q
3. ~P   1, 2 *modus tollens*

The rule that allows us to draw this inference is called ***modus tollens***, which is short for the Latin, *modus tollendo tollens*, which means, "mode (method) of denying by denying." An English example helps make this inference clear:

I.
1. If you are caught stealing, you are going to jail.
2. You are not going to jail.
3. Therefore, you are not caught stealing.

II.
1. We'll call the police only if there's a riot.
2. But there won't be a riot.
3. Therefore, we won't call the police.

Notice that there may be many reasons for going to jail and stealing is just one. So, if you're not going to jail, then you are definitely not caught stealing. Similarly, we may do many things if there is a riot, and the first premise tells us that calling the police is one. But if there won't be a riot, we won't call the police. Here are a few more examples:

B.
1. (A ⊃ B)
2. (C v D)
3. ~B
4. ~A   1, 3 *modus tollens*

C.
1. P
2. ~Q
3. (R ⊃ Q)
4. ~R   2, 3 *modus tollens*

D.
1. ((R v V) & W)
2. ((W v P) ⊃ (R v S))
3. ~(R v S)
4. ~(W v P)   2, 3 *modus tollens*

E.
1. (~P & ~Q)
2. ((R v W) ⊃ P)
3. ~P   1, simplification
4. ~(R v W)   2, 3 *modus tollens*

---

*Notice in example E that we combined two rules. Applying simplification first makes it possible for us to use *modus tollens*.

6.3. Basic inference exercises 1

Exercises 6.a.

For each of the following set of premises, use simplification, conjunction, *modus ponens*, and/or *modus tollens* to derive the indicated conclusion:

1.
1. ((P &Q) & W)
2. R   derive W

2.
1. ((A v B) ⊃ C)
2. (F & D)
3. (A v B)   derive (F & C)

> * From now on we'll use the symbol "/∴" to mean "derive."
> So, exercises 1 and 2 would now look like this:
>
>   /∴ W   and   /∴ (F & C)

3.
1. A
2. (B v C)
3. ((A & (B v C)) ⊃ D)   /∴ D

4.
1. (B & D)
2. (D ⊃ (E ⊃ F))
3. ~F   /∴ (~E & B)

5.
1. ((P v Q) ⊃ (W & ~Y))
2. (~Q & W)
3. (X ⊃ Y)
4. (P v Q)   /∴ (~X & ~Q)

6.
1. P
2. (P ⊃ Q)
3. (Q ⊃ R)
4. (R ⊃ S)   /∴ S

7.
1. ~P
2. (S ⊃ R)
3. (R ⊃ Q)
4. (Q ⊃ P)   /∴ ~S

8.
1. A
2. B
3. ((A & B) ⊃ ~(C v D))
4. ((E v F) ⊃ (C v D))   /∴ ~(E v F)

9.
1. ~(B v D)
2. (A ⊃ (B v D))
3. (H ⊃ ((E & F) & G))
4. H   /∴ (~A & E)

10.
1. ~~P
2. (Q ⊃ ~P)
3. ~R   /∴ (~R & ~Q)

6.4. Three more rules

> Disjunctive Syllogism
> Addition
> Hypothetical Syllogism

6.4.1. Disjunctive syllogism

As we saw in Chapter 3, a syllogism is a valid deductive argument with two premises. The syllogisms we evaluated in that chapter were "categorical" meaning they had a quantifier such as "all," "none," or "some." A disjunctive syllogism is not necessarily categorical, and in this chapter, because we are not yet ready for propositional quantifiers, none will be explicitly categorical.

As you might expect, a disjunctive syllogism includes at least one premise that is a disjunction. We also know that, for a disjunction to be true, at least one disjunct must be true. Therefore, if we find a disjunction in the premises, we can assume that at least one disjunct is true. If, in addition, we discover that one of the disjuncts is false, we can conclude that the other disjunct must be true. For example:

A.		B.	
1. (P v Q)		1. (P v Q)	
2. ~P	or	2. ~Q	
3. Q		3. P	1, 2 disjunctive syllogism

Notice that things aren't so simple if we were simply to discover one of the disjuncts (rather than its negation):

1. (P v Q)		1. (P v Q)
2. P	or	2. Q
3. ?		3. ?

We cannot draw any conclusion using disjunctive syllogism from these premises. Why? Remember in Chapter 5, we said that in logic we interpret the "or" *inclusively*, meaning that at least one disjunct must be true and *both might be*. For instance, Rob might say, "He's either a lawyer or he's a nice guy." To which, Jamie might respond, "And in some cases, he may be both." To be sure, there are cases where disjunctions contain disjuncts that cannot possibly both be true, for example: "That toy is either round or square," "It's either raining or it is not," "The person singing is either Lady Gaga or it's not." But if we treat all disjunctions inclusively, we won't run into any trouble; though we may need extra information to know when it is exclusive.

To show you how it works out, here are two examples of disjunctive syllogism on an exclusive "or":

C.
1. (P v ~P)
2. ~P
3. ~P

or

D.
1. (Q v ~Q)
2. ~~Q
3. Q   1, 2 disjunctive syllogism

Notice that, in both C and D, premise 2 means exactly the same thing as the conclusion. This is a consequence of denying one side in an exclusive disjunction; the result is simply the only other possibility, namely, the other disjunct. So, if it's either raining or it's not, and you learn that it is not raining (~~R), then you learn, by definition, that it is raining. Therefore, treating all disjunctions inclusively works perfectly well even when the disjunction turns out to be exclusive.

Here are two English examples and four more symbolic examples:

I.
1. You're aunt is either married to your uncle or she's married to someone else.
2. Since she divorced your uncle, she's not married to him.
3. Therefore, she must be married to someone else.

II.
1. The progress of evolution is either the product of chance or intelligent design.
2. Chance could not produce events as complex as human thought.
3. Therefore, evolution is a product of intelligent design.

E.
1. ((A v B) v D)
2. ~D
3. (A v B)   1, 2 disjunctive syllogism

F.
1. ((A v B) v D)
2. ~D
3. ~A
4. (A v B) 1, 2 disjunctive syllogism
5. B   3, 4 disjunctive syllogism

G.
1. ~(P & Q)
2. ((P & Q) v (R ⊃ S))
3. (R ⊃ S)   1, 2 disjunctive syllogism

H.
1. (((X ⊃ Y) & (Z v Q)) v (R & W))
2. ~((X ⊃ Y) & (Z v Q))
3. (R & W) 1, 2 disjunctive syllogism

6.4.2. Addition

This next rule may be one of the easiest to perform, though it is often one of the most difficult to understand—at least, when you first see it. Recall that the truth table for disjunction shows that a disjunction is true as long as one disjunct is true, that is, the only false disjunction is one where both disjuncts are false:

P	v	Q
T	T	T
T	T	F
F	T	T
F	F	F

Given this truth table, as long as we know one disjunct is true, then regardless of what claim is disjoined to it, we know the disjunction will be true. Therefore, if we have a claim we know to be true (or that we are assuming is true), then we can disjoin anything to it and the resulting disjunction will be true. For instance, if we know it is true that, "Grass is green," then we also know it is true that, "Either grass is green or the moon is made of green cheese." Similarly, if we know that, "Humans need oxygen to survive," then we know that, "Either humans need oxygen to survive or Martians control my camera."

So, for any claim you know (or assume) to be true, you may legitimately disjoin any other claim to it by a rule called **addition** (not to be confused with conjunction).

A.
1. A
2. (A v B)   1 addition

B.
1. (A & B)
2. ((A & B) v C)   1 addition

This rule is sometimes helpful when attempting to derive a more complicated conclusion. For example, consider the following argument:

1. (P & Y)
2. ~R
3. (W v R)   /.: ((P & W) v Y)

You can derive this conclusion using only the rules we've covered so far. Start by using simplification to isolate P, then use disjunctive syllogism to isolate W. And then use conjunction to conjoin P and W:

```
1. (P & Y)
2. ~R
3. (W v R)          /.: ((P & W) v Y)
4. P                1 simplification
5. W                2, 3 disjunctive syllogism
6. (P & W)          4, 5 conjunction
```

Now the question becomes: how do I disjoin Y to 6? Notice that, in this argument, there is a Y in premise 1 that could be simplified:

```
1. (P & Y)
2. ~R
3. (W v R)          /.: ((P & W) v Y)
4. P                1 simplification
5. W                2, 3 disjunctive syllogism
6. (P & W)          4, 5 conjunction
7. Y                1 simplification
8. ?
```

Unfortunately, however, this won't help with our conclusion, which is a disjunction. The only way to reach our conclusion is to ignore the Y in premise 1 and simply use our addition rule to "add" (or disjoin) Y. Since we already know (P & W) is true, it doesn't matter what Y is or whether we already have one in the premises:

```
1. (P & Y)
2. ~R
3. (W v R)          /.: ((P & W) v Y)
4. P                1 simplification
5. W                2, 3 disjunctive syllogism
6. (P & W)          4, 5 conjunction
7. ((P & W) v Y)    6 addition
```

Since this rule is a more technical tool of logic, English examples do not tend to make the rule clearer. But just in case, here are two English examples and three more symbolic examples:

I.	II.
1. He's a Republican.	1. Tom is a state representative.
2. So, he's either a Republican or a Libertarian.	2. Thus, he's either a state representative or a farmer.

C.
1. P
2. ((P v Q) ⊃ Y)
3. (P v Q)   1 addition
4. Y   2, 3 *modus ponens*

D.
1. ((A v B) ⊃ C)
2. (D ⊃ E)
3. A
4. (A v B)   3 addition
5. C   1, 4 *modus ponens*
6. (C v (D ⊃ E))   5 addition

E.
1. P
2. (P v Q)   1 addition
3. ((P v Q) v (V v W))   2 addition
4. (P v ((Q v (V v W)))   1 addition

> Notice in example E that line 3 cannot be derived without first deriving line 2. Notice also that line 4 can be derived from line 1 without reference to line 2 or 3.

6.4.3. Hypothetical syllogism

Our next rule allows us to derive a conditional claim from premises that are conditionals. This one is fairly intuitive. Consider the following two premises:

1. If it is a cat, then it is a mammal.
2. If it is a mammal, then it is warm-blooded.

From these two premises, regardless of whether "it" is actually a cat or a mammal or warm-blooded, we can, nevertheless, conclude:

3. If it is a cat, then it is warm-blooded.

We can't conclude that "it" is warm-blooded because we don't yet know whether "it" is a cat. We don't know what it is. But one thing is for sure: if it turns out to be a cat, given these premises, it will also be warm-blooded.

The rule that allows you to draw this inference is called **hypothetical syllogism**. To help you remember how this one goes, think about when someone says, "Hypothetically speaking, if I were to ask you to go out to dinner, what would you say?" An adequate response would not be, "Yes (or, sadly, no), I will go with you," because, technically, the question is not, "Will you go out to dinner," but, "*If* I were to ask, what *would* you say?" So, an adequate answer would be, "If you were to ask, I would say yes (or no)."

For any two conditionals, if the antecedent of one is the consequent of the other, you can use hypothetical syllogism to derive a conditional:

A.
1. (P ⊃ Q)
2. (Q ⊃ R)
3. (P ⊃ R)

B.
1. (A ⊃ B)
2. (B ⊃ C)
3. (A ⊃ C)   **1, 2 hypothetical syllogism**

Notice in argument A, the claim Q is the consequent of premise 1 and the antecedent of premise 2. Similarly, in argument B, the claim B is the consequent of premise 1 and the antecedent of premise 2. Here are two more English examples and four more symbolic examples:

I.
1. If the levies break, the town will flood.

2. If the town floods, we will have to evacuate.

3. If the levies break, we will have to evacuate.

II.
1. If the dog barks, there is something in the yard.

2. If there is something in the yard, I need to get out of bed.

3. If the dog barks, I need to get out of bed.

C.
1. ((A v B) ⊃ (D & E))
2. ((D & E) ⊃ B)
3. ((A v B) ⊃ B)   **1, 2 hypothetical syllogism**

D.
1. (A ⊃ (D v F))
2. (B ⊃ A)
3. (B ⊃ (D v F))   **1, 2 disjunctive syllogism**

E.
1. ~P
2. (P v (R ⊃ S))
3. (S ⊃ (X v Y))
4. (R ⊃ S)   **1, 2 disjunctive syllogism**
5. (R ⊃ (X v Y))   **3, 4 hypothetical syllogism**

F.
1. ((X v Y) & ((W v Q) ⊃ Z))
2. (Z ⊃ (P v Q))
3. ((W v Q) ⊃ Z)   **1 simplification**
4. ((W v Q) ⊃ (P v Q))   **2, 3 hypothetical syllogism**

6.5. Basic inference exercises 2

Exercises 6.b.

For each of the following set of premises, use disjunctive syllogism, addition, and/or hypothetical syllogism to derive the indicated conclusion:

1.
1. ((A v B) ⊃ C)
2. (F & D)
3. (C ⊃ (E v H))   / ∴ ((A v B) ⊃ (E v H))

2.
1. (H v P)
2. ((H v A) ⊃ C)
3. ~P   / ∴ (H v A)

3.
1. (~P v (D v Z))
2. (~(D v Z) v B)
3. ~B   / ∴ (~P)

4.
1. (~S ⊃ R)
2. (R ⊃ B)
3. (B ⊃ ~Q)   / ∴ (~S ⊃ ~Q)

5.
1. ((P v Q) v (~R v ~S))
2. ~(P v Q)
3. ~~S   / ∴ ~R

6.
1. (M v N)
2. (A & R)
3. (B v S) / ∴ (((M v N) v (O & P)) v (Q v R))

7.
1. (((P v Q) & (R & S)) & (T v U))
2. B / ∴ (B v P)

8.
1. (R ⊃ Q)
2. (Q ⊃ (W v X)) / ∴ ((R ⊃ (W v X)) v P)

9.
1. A
2. ((A v B) ⊃ ~C)
3. (~C ⊃ F)   / ∴ ((A v B) ⊃ F)

10.
1. ((X v Y) v ~Z)
2. (W v ~~Z)
3. ~Y
4. ~W   / ∴ X

6.6. Two special rules

Conditional Proof
reductio ad absurdum / indirect proof

6.6.1. Conditional proof

One of the advantages of deductive logic is that it allows us to construct **proofs** for claims, much like we do in mathematics. So far, we have seen how valid rules of inference allow us to derive conclusions from premises in a way that preserves truth. That is, if we use a rule properly, we know that, if our premises are true, so is our conclusion. Proofs are powerful tools that extend this truth-preserving feature of our valid rules. We will introduce you to two common proof methods of propositional logic: the conditional proof and the *reductio ad absurdum* (reduction to absurdity).

A **conditional proof** allows us to construct a conditional from a set of premises that may or may not include a conditional. Here's the trick: since one sufficient condition for a true conditional is that it has a true consequent (every conditional with a true consequent is true), then, for any claim we know to be true, we can construct a conditional with that claim as the consequent.

For instance, if we know "B" to be true, we can construct the following true conditional: (A ⊃ B). This is because, regardless whether A is true or false, the conditional is true. This is more clearly seen by recalling the truth-table for a conditional:

$$
\begin{array}{c}
\underline{P \supset Q} \\
\longrightarrow\ \text{T T T} \\
\text{T F F} \\
\longrightarrow\ \text{F T T} \\
\text{F T F}
\end{array}
$$

Now, consider the following argument:

A.
1. (A & B)
2. C   /.: (F ⊃ A)

We are supposed to derive a conditional claim. To do this, we have to make an assumption, namely, that our antecedent, F, is true. We do this by adding what is known as a derivation line, to indicate that F is only an assumption and, therefore, may or may not be true. We also note that it is an assumption off to the side:

A.
1. (A & B)
2. C   /.: (F ⊃ A)
3.⎸F   assumption for conditional proof

Now, on the assumption that F is true, can we derive A using valid rules of inference? If we can, then we can conclude that the conditional claim (F ⊃ A) is true. And it turns out that we can derive A:

A.
1. (A & B)
2. C   /.: (F ⊃ A)
3. | F   assumption for conditional proof
4. | A   **1 simplification**

To complete this proof, close off the derivation line as shown below. Write your conclusion, then indicate to the right all the lines involved in the proof:

A.
1. (A & B)
2. C   /.: (F ⊃ A)
3. | F   assumption for conditional proof
4. | A   1 simplification
5. (F ⊃ A)   **3–4 conditional proof**

Here's a more complicated example:

B.
1. ((~P v ~Z) & (X v Y))
2. ~~Z
3. (W v P)   /.: (X ⊃ W)

Consider, first, whether there is any way to derive the conditional using only your rules of inference. In this case, there is not. X is in premise 1, but it is not obviously connected with W. Therefore, you will need to construct a conditional proof, assuming X is true:

B.
1. ((~P v ~Z) & (X v Y))
2. ~~Z
3. (W v P)   /.: (X ⊃ W)
4. | X   assumption for conditional proof

Now consider whether you can derive W from the premises given. As it turns out we can:

B.
1. ((~P v ~Z) & (X v Y))
2. ~~Z
3. (W v P)   /.: (X ⊃ W)

4.	X	assumption for conditional proof
5.	(~P v ~Z)	**1 simplification**
6.	~P	**2, 5 disjunctive syllogism**
7.	W	**3, 6 disjunctive syllogism**

Now we see that, on the assumption that X, we can derive W. Now we are ready to close off our derivation line, and draw our conclusion:

B.
1. ((~P v ~Z) & (X v Y))
2. ~~Z
3. <u>(W v P)</u>   /∴ (X ⊃ W)

4.	X	assumption for conditional proof
5.	(~P v ~Z)	1 simplification
6.	~P	2, 5 disjunctive syllogism
7.	<u>W</u>	3, 6 disjunctive syllogism
8.	**(X ⊃ W)**	**4–7 conditional proof**

Here are two English examples and two more symbolic examples:

I.
1. If Henry was at the station, the alarm would sound.
2. This is because, if the alarm sounded, then either the guard saw him or he threatened someone.
3. The alarm sounded and we have no reports that he threatened someone.
4. <u>And if the guard saw him, he can give us a description.</u> /∴ If Henry was at the station, the guard can describe him.

5.	Henry was at the station.	assumption for conditional proof
6.	The alarm sounded.	1, 5 *modus ponens*
7.	Either the guard saw him or he threatened someone.	2, 6 *modus ponens*
8.	We have no reports that he threatened someone.	3 simplification
9.	The guard saw him.	7, 8 disjunctive syllogism
10.	<u>The guard can give us a description.</u>	4, 9 *modus ponens*
11.	If Henry was at the station, the guard can describe him.	5–11 conditional proof

II.
1. If it is raining, the sidewalks are wet.
2. If the sidewalks are wet, they are uncovered.
3. <u>If those awnings are five feet wide, they cover the sidewalk.</u>
   /∴ If it is raining, those awnings are not five feet wide.

4.	It is raining.	assumption for conditional proof
5.	The sidewalks are wet.	1, 4 modus ponens
6.	The sidewalks are uncovered.	2, 5 modus ponens
7.	<u>Those awnings are not five feet wide.</u>	3, 6 modus tollens
8.	If it is raining, those awnings are not five feet wide.	4–8 conditional proof

C.
1. $((A \lor B) \supset C)$
2. $(F \& D)$
3. A
4. $\underline{(C \supset (E \lor H))}$ $/.: ((A \lor B) \supset (E \lor H))$
5. $(A \lor B)$ assumption for conditional proof
6. C 1, 5 modus ponens
7. $(E \lor H)$ 4, 6 modus ponens
8. $((A \lor B) \supset (E \lor H))$ 5–8 conditional proof

D.
1. $((S \& K) \supset R)$
2. $\underline{K}$ $/.: (S \supset R)$
3. S assumption for conditional proof
4. $(S \& K)$ 2, 3 conjunction
5. R 1, 4 *modus ponens*
6. $(S \supset R)$ 3–5 conditional proof

6.6.2. *reductio ad absurdum* / indirect proof

For some arguments, our first eight rules of inference will be inconclusive. You may apply rule after rule and see no clear way to derive a conclusion. When you run into this problem, it is time to try our next proof method, **reductio ad absurdum** (reduction to absurdity), or *indirect proof*.

You may have heard the phrase, "Let's assume, for the sake of argument, that X," only to discover that the arguer is really trying to prove that X is false. One way to do this is to show that X entails some sort of absurdity, like a contradiction. This is precisely what a *reductio ad absurdum* attempts to show. If some proposition, P, entails a contradiction, P is false. For example, consider the following argument for the claim, "There are no married bachelors":

I.
1. If someone is a bachelor, that person is   premise (definition of "bachelor")
    unmarried.
2. There is at least one person who is married   assumption for indirect proof
    and a bachelor.
3. Someone, X, is a bachelor.   2 simplification
4. X is unmarried.   1, 3 *modus ponens*
5. X is married.   2 simplification
6. X is both married and unmarried.   4, 5 conjunction
7. Therefore, there are no married bachelors.   2–6 indirect proof

From the definition of "bachelor" and the assumption that there is at least one person who is married and a bachelor, we can derive the contradiction that someone is both married and unmarried. Since our assumption entails a contradiction, we must conclude that it is false.

How do we know that a claim that entails a contradiction is false? There are two reasons, one that is generally intuitive and one that is more rigorous. First, logically we may derive the truth of any claim from a contradiction. For instance, from the contradiction, "God exists and doesn't exist" (G & ~G), we can derive anything we want, including farfetched claims like, "Satan rocks" (S) and "Def Leppard is the greatest band of all time" (D). Here's how:

A.

1. (G & ~G)	assumption
2. G	1 simplification
3. (G v S)	2 addition
4. ~G	1 simplification
5. S	3, 4 disjunctive syllogism

So, if God both exists and doesn't exist, we may derive that Satan rocks. And we may continue:

6. (G v D)	1 simplification
7. D	4, 6 disjunctive syllogism

And we could just keep going. Contradictions entail the truth of every claim. But surely this is wrong. Every claim cannot be true. Therefore, any claim that entails a contradiction must be false.

The second, more rigorous, reason to think claims that entail contradictions are false is that our definition of truth entails that contradictions are false. A claim is true if and only if its negation is false. This is evident from our truth table for the conjunction. If one or both sides of a conjunction are false, the conjunction is false:

P & Q	P & ~P
T T T	T F FT
T F F	F F TF
F F T	
F F F	

Therefore, any claim that entails a contradiction necessarily entails a false claim. But why also say that the claim that entailed it must be false? Remember, valid arguments preserve truth, so that if some premise is true, anything it validly entails is true. If, on the assumption that a claim, *P*, is true, we validly derive a contradiction (a false claim), it follows that *P* is false.

We can see this clearly using *modus tollens*. Assume that P entails a contradiction:

      1. (P ⊃ (Q & ~Q))   assumption

The truth table for conjunction entails that the consequent is false:

      2. ~(Q & ~Q)   premise (definition of truth)

Therefore, by *modus tollens*, the antecedent is false.

      3. ~P   1, 2 *modus tollens*

Here is another English example and two symbolic examples:

II.

1. If Goering was a Nazi, then either he was evil or he was an idiot.
2. If he was evil, then he should be punished.
3. Goering was not an idiot (had an IQ of 138).
4. Goering was a Nazi.
5. If someone should be punished, that person is morally responsible for his actions.
6. | No one is morally responsible for his actions.   assumption for indirect proof
7. | Goering was either evil or an idiot.   1, 4 *modus ponens*
8. | Goering was evil.   3, 7 disjunctive syllogism
9. | Goering should not be punished.   5, 6 *modus tollens*
10. | Goering was not evil.   2, 9 *modus tollens*
11. | Goering was and was not evil.   8, 10 conjunction
12. It is not the case that no one is morally   6–11 indirect proof
      responsible for his actions

B.

1. ((G & R) ⊃ (I & D))
2. (R ⊃ ~D)   /.: ~(G & R)
3. | (G & R)   assumption for indirect proof
4. | (I & D)   1, 3 modus ponens
5. | D   4 simplification
6. | R   3 simplification
7. | ~D   2, 6 modus ponens
8. | (D & ~D) 5, 7 conjunction
9. ~(G & R)   3–8 indirect proof

C.

1. (S ⊃ (P ⊃ B))
2. (S ⊃ P)
3. (C ⊃ (S v B))   /.: ~(C & ~B)
4. | (C & ~B) assumption for indirect proof
5. | C   4 simplification
6. | (S v B)   3, 5 *modus ponens*
7. | ~B   4 simplification
8. | S   6, 7 disjunctive syllogism
9. | P   2, 8 *modus ponens*

10.	(P ⊃ B)	1, 8 *modus ponens*
11.	B	9, 10 *modus ponens*
12.	(~B & B)	7, 11 conjunction
13.	~(C & ~B)	4–12 indirect proof

6.7. More complicated inference exercises

Exercises 6.c.

For each of the following arguments, use the rules from this chapter to derive the indicated conclusion:

1.
1. ((A v B) ⊃ C)
2. (F & D)
3. A
4. (C ⊃ (E v H))   /.: ((A v B) ⊃ (E v H))

2.
1. (H & P)
2. ((H v A) ⊃ C)
3. D   /.: (C & D)

3.
1. (~P v D)
2. (~D & B)
3. ((Z ⊃ P) & A)   /.: (~Z & A)

4.
1. (~S ⊃ R)
2. (~R v Q)
3. ~Q   /.: ~~S

5.
1. ((A v B) v (~C v ~D))
2. ~(A v B)
3. ~~D   /.: ~C

6.
1. (M v N)
2. (O & P)
3. (Q v R)   /.: (((M v N) & (O & P)) & (Q v R))

7.
1. (((M v N) & (O & P)) & (Q v R))
2. (A & B)   /.: (P & B)

8.
1. ((R & S) ⊃ Q)
2. (Q ⊃ (P v R)) /.: (((R & S) ⊃ (P v R)) v Z)

9.
1. A
2. ((A v B) ⊃ ~C)
3. (D ⊃ ~~C)   /.: ~D

10.
1. ((X & Y) v ~Z)
2. (W ⊃ ~~Z)
3. (W & V)   /.: X

11.
1. B
2. ((B v D) ⊃ ~H)
3. (H v F)   /.: (C ⊃ F)

12.
1. (~P & Q)
2. (Q ⊃ R)
3. (P v ~R)   /.: Y

13.
1. ((M ⊃ O) v S)
2. ((~S & N) & M)
3. M
4. (P & ~O)   /.: (S v B)

14.
1. (A ⊃ (D v F))
2. ((D v F) ⊃ H)
3. ((A ⊃ H) ⊃ B)   /.: (F ⊃ B)

15.
1. (X v Y)
2. ((X & W) ⊃ (Z ⊃ Y))
3. (~Y & W)
4. Z   /.: R

16.
1. (B & C)
2. (C ⊃ E))
3. ((E v F) ⊃ H)   /.: H

17.
1. X
2. ((~S v Y) ⊃ Z)
3. (~Z & ~S)   /.: (W ⊃ (Y v R))

18.
1. (P & (Q v R))
2. ((P v R) ⊃ (~S & ~T))
3. ((~S v ~T) ⊃ ~(P & Q))   /.: (Q ⊃ ~(P & Q))

19.
1. (A ⊃ (~A v F))
2. ~F   /.: ~A

20.
1. ((B & P) ⊃ D)
2. ((P ⊃ D) ⊃ H)
3. (~A & B)   /.: (H & ~A)

6.8. Three mistakes to avoid

Affirming the Consequent
Denying the Antecedent
Affirming the Disjunct

Even after you get the hang of applying valid rules of inference, you may be tempted to draw inappropriate inferences. The most efficient way to avoid this is to be aware of the most common mistakes. A mistake in reasoning is called a **fallacy**. We will discuss fallacies in more detail in Chapter 10, but in this chapter we will explain three very common mistakes in deductive reasoning.

6.8.1. Affirming the consequent

We have seen that, when reasoning from a conditional claim (P ⊃ Q), if we know the antecedent, P, we can derive the consequent, Q, using *modus ponens*. But what happens when, instead of learning that the antecedent, P, is true, we learn that the consequent, Q, is true? For instance:

1. (P ⊃ Q)
2. Q
3. ?

Any inference from these premises would be invalid. An argument of this form commits a fallacy called **affirming the consequent**, because, instead of claiming/asserting/*affirming* the antecedent of a conditional in premise 2, as in *modus ponens*, we are *affirming* the consequent. Nevertheless, because of *modus ponens*, we may be tempted to infer the antecedent of premise 1:

modus ponens (valid)	affirming the consequent (invalid)
1. $(P \supset Q)$	1. $(P \supset Q)$
2. P	2. Q
3. Q	3. P

This is a mistake if we are attempting to construct a *valid* argument. From 1 and 2, we cannot know anything conclusively about *P*. An English example shows why:

I.
1. If it is raining, then the sidewalk is wet.
2. The sidewalk is wet.
3.

Now, what might we conclude about the claim, "It is raining"? That the sidewalks are wet makes it more likely that it is raining than no wet-sidewalk-making event. But we cannot rule out other wet-sidewalk-making events, such as a sprinkler system, someone with a water hose, melting snow, a busted water pipe, a water balloon fight, etc. Since "It is raining" does not follow necessarily from the premises, the argument is invalid.

It is important to remember that an invalid argument is not necessarily a bad argument. All inductive arguments are invalid and we rely heavily on those in many fields of great importance, including every scientific discipline. Therefore, affirming the consequent is a *formal* fallacy in that, its *form* does not preserve truth from premises to conclusion, and so must not be employed in deductive arguments. Nevertheless, it is a useful tool in scientific reasoning, as we will see in Chapter 8.

Here are two more English examples:

II.
1. If it rained before midnight, the bridge is icy this morning.
2. The bridge is icy this morning.
3. Therefore, it rained before midnight. [Not necessarily. Even if the premises are true, it might have rained *after* midnight to the same effect. Or perhaps it snowed before midnight, melted, and then became icy in the early morning hours.]

III.
1. If he's coming with us, I'll get sick.
2. I'm getting sick.
3. Therefore, he's with us.   [Not necessarily. Even if the premises are true, he might not be coming with us. This is because there are many other reasons to be sick: bad sushi, a Leonardo DiCaprio film, the flu, etc.]

6.8.2. Denying the antecedent

Just as we cannot derive the antecedent, *P*, of a conditional, $(P \supset Q)$, from its consequent, *Q*, we cannot derive the *denial* of the consequent, ~*Q*, of a conditional from a *denial* of its antecedent, ~*P*. We may be tempted to do so because *modus tollens* tells us we can derive the denial of the antecedent, ~*P*, from the denial of the consequent, ~*Q*; but it is important to see that the implication does not move validly in the other direction:

modus tollens (valid)   denying the antecedent (invalid)
1. $(P \supset Q)$ 1. $(P \supset Q)$
2. ~Q   2. ~P
3. ~P   3. ~Q

Premise 1 of both arguments tells us that, if *P* is true, *Q* is also true. So if *Q* turns out to be false, we can be sure that *P* is, too. However, if *P* turns out to be false, what could we know about *Q*? Is *P* the only reason *Q* is true? Premise 1 doesn't tell us this.

For instance, if you graduate college, then you have taken at least some number of credit hours; let's say 120 credits are required in order to graduate. From this claim, we know that if you haven't taken 120 hours, then there's no chance you have graduated. But does the inference go the other way: you haven't graduated, so you haven't taken at least 120 credit hours? Surely not. You may have taken some strange combination of courses that guarantees you *won't* graduate.

Therefore, learning the denial of the antecedent of a conditional does not allow us to draw any *valid* conclusion about the consequent. Here are two more English examples to clarify:

I.
1. If she's going to the party, Jeff will not be there.
2. She's not going to the party.
3. Thus, Jeff will be there.   [Not necessarily. Even if she's not going, Jeff might have gotten sick or crashed his car, etc. There are lots of reasons Jeff might not be there even if the premises are true.]

II.
1. If the bulbs are lit, they are getting electricity.
2. The lights aren't lit.
3. Hence, they are not getting electricity. [Not necessarily. The bulbs might be burned out. Even though they are getting electricity, they would not be lit.]

6.8.3. Affirming the disjunct

Our first two fallacies highlight ways that reasoning from conditionals can be tricky. Our third common fallacy highlights a way that reasoning from a disjunction can be tricky. Disjunctive syllogism tells us that, if we know that a disjunction is true, (P v Q), and we know that one of the disjuncts is true, say ~Q, we can infer the other disjunct, P. But there are times when, instead of knowing the negation of one of the disjuncts, we know the affirmation of one of the disjuncts:

1. (P v Q)
2. Q
3. ?

In this case, we cannot infer anything about the other disjunct. This is because, in a true disjunction, at least one disjunct is true and both might be true. So, knowing that one disjunct is true isn't sufficient for inferring the truth or falsity of the other disjunct.

Because of disjunctive syllogism and because we often think of disjunctions as expressing an *exclusive* "or" (either P or Q, and not both), we might be tempted to infer the negation of the other disjunct:

disjunctive syllogism (valid)
1. (P v Q)
2. ~Q
3. P

affirming the disjunct (invalid)
1. (P v Q)
2. Q
3. ~P

Replacing P and Q with English sentences helps to show why affirming the disjunct is invalid:

I.
1. Either London is the capital of England or Madrid is the capital of Spain.
2. London is the capital of England.
3. Therefore, Madrid is not the capital of Spain. [Premise 1 is true because at least one disjunct is true. Remember, in logic, we interpret disjunctive claims "inclusively"; both sides can be true. Therefore,

learning that London is, in fact, the capital of England does not provide reasons to conclude anything about whether Spain is the capital of Madrid.]

II.
1. Toyota is a Japanese company or the earth is not flat.
2. The earth is certainly not flat.
3. Hence, Toyota is not a Japanese company.   [Again, both disjuncts in premise 1 are true, so it is impossible to conclusively derive any claim about Toyota.]

Jamie can relate a personal example of how tempting it can be to affirm the disjunct. One night he walked into the kitchen one night and noticed one pan near the stove with warm food in it and two eyes, each of which could have been hot. Since there was only one pan, he assumed that only one eye was likely to be hot. He held his hand above one eye and felt that it was warm. And then, to his dismay, he reasoned as follows:

III.
1. Either the left eye is hot or the right eye is hot.
2. The left eye is hot.
3. Therefore, the right eye is not hot.

On the basis of this fallacious inference, he sat a plate on the right eye and severely burned his finger. The problem, of which he is now painfully aware (literally), is that both sides of a disjunction can be true, and, in this case, both were true. (As it turns out, his wife had used two pans and both eyes.)

6.9. Formal fallacy exercises

Exercises 6.d.

For each of the following fallacious arguments, identify which formal fallacy has been committed and explain your answer:

1.
1. He's the president of the company or I'm a monkey's uncle.
2. Here is the memo announcing that he is president.
3. So, I'm obviously not a monkey's uncle.

2.
1. If I flip this switch, the light will come on.
2. I'm not flipping the switch.
3. Therefore, the light will not come on.

3.
1. It is either raining or storming.
2. It is certainly raining.
3. Thus, it is not storming.

4.
1. If you flip this switch, the light will come on.
2. The light is coming on.
3. Hence, you must be flipping the switch.

5.
1. If it drops below 0°C, either the roads will become icy or the water line will freeze.
2. It is –5°C (below 0°).
3. So, either the roads will become icy or the water line will freeze.
4. The roads are icy.
5. Therefore, the water line is probably not frozen.

6.
1. If the stars are out, you can either see Orion (a winter constellation) or Aquarius (a summer constellation).
2. You can see either Orion or Aquarius (because you can see Orion).
3. Therefore, the stars are out.

7.
1. We'll see you this Christmas if God's willing and the creek don't rise.
2. It is not the case that God is willing and the creek don't rise (because of the huge flood this year).
3. Therefore, we won't see you at Christmas.

8.
1. There will be a labor strike unless the company changes its benefits plan.
2. I just saw all the factory workers on strike.
3. Hence, the company will change its benefits plan.

9.
1. If things don't change, it will either be bad for us or good for your family.
2. But things seem to be changing.
3. Thus, it will either be bad for us or good for your family.
4. These changes are looking good for your family.
5. Therefore, they aren't looking good for us.

10.
1. Unless Nintendo does something fast, the Wii will be outdated or at least cease to be comptetitive.
2. Nintendo has announced no immediate plans.
3. So, either the Wii will be outdated or cease to be competitive.
4. The Wii's design is no longer competitive.
5. So, it will be outdated.

Exercises 6.e.

For each of the following arguments, construct the formal fallacy indicated by filling in the missing premise and conclusion:

1. Affirming the disjunct
1. Either the Bulls will win or the Suns will.
2. _____
3.

2. Affirming the consequent
1. If the road is wet, your tires won't have as much traction.
2. _____
3.

3. Denying the antecedent
1. If the bar is close, it will be safer to drive home.
2. _____
3.

4. Affirming the consequent
1. We will win only if we strengthen our defense.
2. _____
3.

5. Affirming the disjunct
1. They will break up unless she is honest.
2. _____
3.

6. Denying the antecedent
1. They will break up if she doesn't tell him the truth.
2. _____
3.

7. Affirming the disjunct
1. Don't spoil it for everyone unless you like being ostracized.
2. _____
3.

8. Affirming the consequent
1. Toyota trucks will outsell Ford trucks only if Ford makes bad financial decisions.
2. _____
3.

9. Affirming the consequent
1. We'll starve if we don't get something to eat.
2. _____
3.

10. Denying the antecedent
1. If we win, we're going to the state championships.
2. _____
3.

Real-Life Example: Former Illinois Governor Rob Blagojevich's Resignation Speech

Below we have pasted some selections from Governor Blagojevich's resignation speech. When you find what seems like a deductive argument, reconstruct it in propositional logic, then identify whether Blagojevich has used or implies modus ponens, modus tollens, or disjunctive syllogism, or whether he has committed a formal fallacy (you should be able to identify at least three valid arguments and at least one formal fallacy):

In the first term, they were successful in saving over $500 million for taxpayers because they found creative ways to do it. And in this particular case, on this issue with the auditor general, they found a way to save some money in someplace and then what they wanted to do was allow us to be able to use that money in the general revenue fund to invest in health care and education and in other general revenue items. But then the auditor general got involved and said, stop, don't do it.

Now, I have a recollection of actually remembering this, because I remember I was in Washington, D.C., when the head of CMS and that Mr. Holland, the auditor general, got into a little bit of a verbal fight. I remember being amused by that, thinking you had a couple of accountants kind of scrapping over the issue of whether or not some money should be spent a certain way or not. When the inspector general, Mr. Holland, told us, you can't do it, guess what we did? We didn't do it.

How can you impeach me and throw me out of office? The chief accountant of the state comes in and says, you can't do that. We hear you. We're not doing it. And we didn't do it. How can that be an impeachable offense?

And here, too, like on prescription drugs for seniors and flu vaccines for the elderly and for infants, here, too, this was an issue that took place in the first term, not the second term. This was something, if it was so bad, you should have impeached me on before and not now. And in spite of it, the people of Illinois elected me a second time.

[. . .]

We hired a former United States attorney as our first inspector general. This report from the inspector general alleges that some people perhaps may have — it's an allegation, nothing proven, nothing shown yet to be true — but an allegation that some people who worked for me may have violated some of the hiring rules. In that very report by the inspector general, there's never an allegation that I ever knew anything about it. How can I possibly be thrown out of office on something that the inspector general doesn't even claim I knew anything about? And, incidentally, something that still has not been resolved.

So I ask you to remember, too, that that issue was one that took place in the first term, not the second term. And if it was so bad then, then perhaps I should have been impeached over that. But, yet again, the inspector general doesn't say that I knew anything about it. There hasn't been any finding that anybody did anything wrong. And I've got to tell you, the fact that we have an inspector general was something that I pushed very hard for. And, yes, it gets embarrassing sometimes when your own inspector general finds that some people who work for you may not have done something right. But the greater good is served because you're policing the system and making sure that people don't do things they shouldn't do and have a better understanding on some of the things they shouldn't be in a position to be able to do.

Rules of Valid Inference:	English Examples:

1. Simplification

1. (A & B)
2. A

1. It is raining and it is windy.
2. So, it's raining.

2. Conjunction

1. A
2. B
3. (A & B)

1. The field is overgrown.
2. The field attracts lots of birds.
3. The field is overgrown and attracts lots of birds.

3. Modus Ponens

1. (A ⊃ B)
2. A
3. B

1. If you jump in a pool, then you get wet.
2. You jump in a pool.
3. So, you get wet.

4. Modus Tollens

1. (A ⊃ B)
2. ~B
3. ~A

1. If you open the wine, then you pop the cork.
2. You do not pop the cork.
3. Hence, you do not open the wine.

5. Disjunctive Syllogism

1. (A v B)
2. ~A (or, ~B)
3. B (or A)

1. Either we go or she comes.
2. We do not go (or, she does not come).
3. So, she comes (or, we go).

6. Addition

1. P
2. (P v Q)

1. She's a good swimmer.
2. Either she's a good swimmer or I'm a poached egg.

7. Hypothetical Syllogism

1. (A ⊃ B)
2. (B ⊃ C)
3. (A ⊃ C)

1. If I exercise, then I burn calories.
2. If I burn calories, then I lose weight.
3. Thus, if I exercise, then I lose weight.

8. Conditional Proof

1. (A & B)
2. C   assumption for conditional proof
3. A   1 simplification
4. (C ⊃ A)   2-3 conditional proof

1. It is hot and it is raining.
2. It is summer.   assumption for conditional proof
3. It is hot.   1 simplification
4. If it is summer, then it is hot.   2-3 conditional proof

9. *reductio ad absurdum* / **indirect proof**

1. P		1. If it is raining, then the sidewalks are wet.	
2. ~P		2. It is raining and the sidewalks are not wet.	
3. ~X	assumption for indirect proof	3. It is not the case that the Earth is square.	assumption for indirect proof
4. (P & ~P)	1, 2 conjunction	4. It is raining.	2 simplification
5. X	3-4 indirect proof	5. The sidewalks are wet.	1, 4 *modus ponens*
		6. The sidewalks are not wet.	2 simplification
		7. The sidewalks are wet. and not wet	5, 6 conjunction
		8. The Earth is square.	3-8 indirect proof

Part Three
INDUCTIVE REASONING

Probability and Induction

7

Chapter Outline

7.1. Inductive strength

In Chapter 2, we explained that a good inductive argument must meet two conditions: (1) the relationship between the premises and the conclusion must be strong, and (2) the premises must be true. If both conditions are met, the argument is cogent. We explained that the strength of an inductive argument is indicted by the likelihood or probability that a conclusion is true given a set of premises. Consider the following two examples:

A.
1. Most Americans are communists.
2. Osama Bin Laden is an American.
3. Osama Bin Laden is probably a communist.

B.
1. Some Americans are communists.
2. Osama Bin Laden is an American.
3. Osama Bin Laden is probably a communist.

Intuitively, the conclusion of argument A is more likely to be true given the premises than the conclusion of argument B. The difference between A and B is the quantifier in the first premise. "Most" indicates more than 50% of the American population, whereas "some" could indicate anything from 1 American to 99.99999% of all Americans. The vagueness of "some" prevents the premises from granting strength to the conclusion.

We can roughly evaluate the strength of an inductive argument by noting whether the quantifier is strong or weak. Recall our list of strong and weak quantifiers from Chapter 2:

Strong Quantifiers:	Weak Quantifiers:
Most	Some
Almost all	A few
It is likely that	It is possible that
Most likely	Somewhat likely
The majority	A percentage
Almost definitely	Could be
Highly probable	Many
More often than not	A significant percentage

This is a good short-hand for evaluating strength. But how do we evaluate these quantifiers? How do we know when to use "most likely" instead of "somewhat likely," or "could be" instead of "almost definitely"? A precise way, and perhaps the most common, is to evaluate the **probability** that a premise is true.

The probability that a claim is true is a function of the evidence we have for that claim given everything else we know about the claim. So, for instance, if we have a two-sided coin (heads and tails) and some background conditions are held constant (e.g., the coin couldn't land on its edge, the coin is not weighted on one side, the coin is flipped fairly), then the *probability* that the coin will land on heads is 50%. Probability measurements are expressed as *chances*—in this case, 1 in 2, or 1/2—or as *percentages*—50%, as we just noted—or as *decimals*—the decimal of 50% is .5, so we write this: P(.5). Chances and probabilities are related, as we will see later in this chapter.

When calculating probabilities, decimals are the most common expression. When expressed as a decimal, a probability will always be either equal to 0 or 1 or fall somewhere between them:

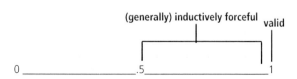

Where a probability falls in relation to P(.5) is a good short-hand way of determining whether an argument in which a probabilistic claim is found as a premise is strong or weak.

Be careful, though. Different probabilistic claims can refer to different sets of conditions on which the probability depends. For instance, the best evidence we have suggests that the universe began to exist about 13 billion years ago. The probability we are correct about the age of the universe given our evidence is fairly high. However, the probability that a universe like ours would come into existence when it did is fairly low (all one-time events have a low probability). We'll say more about this in 7.2. The important thing to remember is not to infer more from a probabilistic claim than is warranted.

Notice that probabilities are *forward-looking*, that is, they predict some state of affairs. This distinguishes them from *statistics*, which are always *backward-looking*. Statistics describe relationships among current or former states of affairs. For instance, a statistic for a school system in Georgia might be that 53% of students in the eighth grade are female. This statistic tells us what is the case, *not* what is *likely* to be the case. In order to determine what will likely be the case, we must draw an inference from statistical data.

To reiterate, statistical data are not predictions, but claims about what was or is the case. We can, however, make predictions *on the basis of* statistics. For instance, imagine we learn, from statistical data, that the percentage of females in the eighth grade has risen by one percent each year for the past five years. This data can be organized into a chart so we can more clearly see the relationship between female eighth-grade students and years. If the relationship expresses certain sorts of patterns, we say that the two pieces of data express a *statistical correlation*. Our chart might look like this:

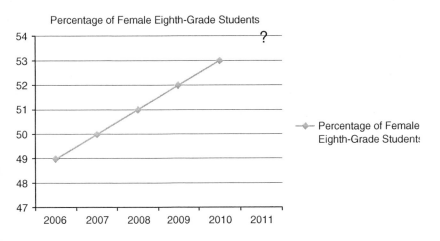

From this data we can infer a probabilistic claim. We can predict that, next year, the number of females in the eighth grade will *probably* be one percent higher than this year. But notice: the claim that the number of females will be one percent higher *is not a statistic*; it is a *prediction*. How do we measure the likelihood of this prediction? We turn to probabilities.

7.2. Types of probability

Probability is a measure of the plausibility or likelihood that some event will occur given some set of conditions. The three primary sets of conditions that probabilities express are (i) the way the world is (i.e., sets of facts), (ii) the evidence we have that the event in question will occur (i.e., sets of data), or (iii) our personal assessment of the event's occurrence given the conditions we are aware of and our best judgment. Our goal in this chapter is not to explain in any depth how to calculate probabilities, but to simply explain what sorts of claims they express and how to use and evaluate probabilistic claims in arguments.

If we are interested in the probabilities associated with (i), we are interested in the chances or **objective probability** of an event. For instance, the way the world is determines the chances that a normal quarter will land on heads when flipped. If the quarter has a rounded edge and is landing on a flat surface and gravity remains constant (all of which prevent it from landing on its edge or not landing at all), then we say the chances of it landing on heads is 1 out of 2, or 50%. This *doesn't* mean that every other time I flip a fair coin it will land on heads. The objective probability is simply the chances the coin will land on heads for any single toss. Similarly, if we draw a card from a deck of 52 cards, something about the distribution of faces and suits objectively determines the chances of drawing an ace, namely, 4 out of 52, or 7.69%.

Alternatively, if we are dealt with a card from a deck of 52 cards, the world determines the chances the card in our hand is an ace, namely, 1 in 1 or 0 in 1, 100% or 0%. This is because the card either is an ace or it isn't. Once the card is in our hand, the world dictates that we have the card or we don't. You may now wonder: if this is the case, why do we bet about the *chances* of a card turned face down making a good hand (as in Texas Hold 'Em)? Well, we don't. In this case, we bet, not on chances, but on *the evidence we have* about the cards already in play. We call this type of probability: **epistemic probability**.

Epistemic probability corresponds to condition (ii), the evidence we have that an event will occur. It is a measure of the likelihood of an event given our current evidence. Let's begin simply, by imagining drawing a playing card from a deck of 52 cards. Imagine you draw an ace:

What is the likelihood that the *second* card you draw will be an ace? The objective probability that it is an ace is either 1 or 0. The order of the cards in the deck has already been determined by shuffling the cards, so the next card is either an ace, P(1), or it isn't, P(0). But, since you do not know the order of the cards, you have to make our decision about the likelihood the next card is an ace on the evidence you have about the deck of cards and the card in your hand.

You know there are four aces in the deck (an ace for every suit), so, given that you have one in your hand, three are left. You also know that there are fifty-two cards in the deck, which, minus the one in your hand, leaves fifty-one. So, the epistemic probability that the next card is an ace is 3/51, or roughly 5.8%.

Let's try a more complicated example. Take, for example, a game of Texas Hold 'Em, where you have two cards in your hand, three cards face up on the table, and two cards face down:

The goal of Texas Hold 'Em is to make the best five card hand you can using the two cards in your hand (which can be used only by you) and three of the five cards on the table (which are shared by everyone playing the game).

To keep things simple, let's say that, in your hand you have two 9s:

In dealing the cards, the world (the order of the cards in the deck) has already determined the number and suit of the face-down cards. But, in order to survive the game without going broke, you need to figure out the likelihood that the cards on the table will give you the hand you need to beat the other players.

Now, one way to draw a really good hand given the cards on the table and that you were dealt these 9s is to draw another 9 for three-of-a-kind. What is the likelihood that there is another 9 lurking in the two cards that are face down? The probability of any one of those cards being a 9 is precisely 2 out of 47, or around 4.2%. This is because you have two in your hand, so only two 9s remain in the deck, there are no 9s face up on the table, and there are 47 cards left in the deck.

This probability is helpful, but you actually want to know something more interesting. The epistemic probability of winning the hand with three 9s doesn't just depend on the probability that one of the cards is a 9; it depends on whether there is a 9 among in the two face-down cards. You want to know the probability that one of *those two* cards is a 9 given that there are only two 9s left in the deck.

To calculate this probability, you take the likelihood that any one card is a 9, given that there are two left (2/47 or 4.2%) and multiply that by 2 (since the two cards were drawn at random, this gives us the probability that any two cards drawn randomly from the deck contains a 9). So, if any one draw is 4.2% likely to be a 9, the likelihood that any two draws is a 9 increases your chances to 8.4%.

Remember, 8.4% is not the *objective* probability that one of those two cards is a 9. The objective probability has been settled by the world independently of what we know about it. Each of those cards is a 9 or it isn't. In this case, 8.4% expresses an *epistemic* probability. And how you bet depends on it.

So 8.4% is the probability that one of the two cards on the table is a 9. You should treat them just like random draws from the deck (since, if you're at a fair casino, that's what they were). So, given the probability, what should your first bet be? Whether you should bet on an epistemic probability depends partially on our third type of probability, credence. We will discuss this in detail very shortly. For the moment, imagine you decided to bet (however much) and stayed in the game.

As it turns out, the first round reveals a 3 of diamonds:

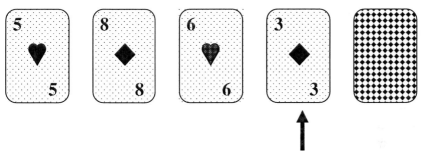

Now there are only 46 possible cards in the deck that could be a 9. And since you know the remaining card came from the deck, the epistemic probability that any one of the three cards is a 9 drops to the probability of drawing a 9 randomly from a deck of 46 cards, that is, 2/46 or 4.3%.

Should you bet on *this* round? Whether you should depends on the third major type of probability: **credence** or, **subjective probability**, which corresponds to condition (iii). A subjective probability is a measure of how likely you *think or feel* the event will happen—it is similar to a gut-level judgment. For instance, you can determine the objective probability of the cards on the table by looking at them (don't try this in a game). You can determine the epistemic probability of the cards on the table by drawing an inference from the number of cards on the table and those in your hand. But this information alone cannot tell you whether to bet. Your belief that the card you need is the one face down on the table is determined by epistemic probabilities plus a variety of other factors, including the likelihood that three 9s is a better hand than your opponents', the amount of money you will lose if you are wrong compared to the amount of money you might win, and your willingness to take a risk.

For example, if after the 4 is turned over, one of your opponents at the table bets a very large sum of money, this might affect your beliefs. She may be bluffing, but she may also already have a good hand. For instance, she might have two Jacks in her hand. Or she might have one of the other 9s and is hoping the last card is a 7 for a straight. If she does, then even if the last card is a 9, you still lose.

There is little evidence on which to calculate this type of probability (unless your opponent has an obvious tell), but you cannot rely solely on epistemic probabilities. Nonetheless, you can form a legitimate probabilistic judgment worthy of consideration, since many of your decisions are made under this sort of uncertainty. You may rely on your beliefs about the tendency of your opponent to bluff (which may involve some epistemic probabilities), or about your own desire not to lose the money you have put in. Other examples of credences include: "It looks like it will be a cold winter," "I think it will rain tomorrow," "You are likely to need the four-wheel-drive to the cabin," "It is *highly* likely that they'll get married," "It seems more likely that God exists than that this universe came about simply by chance."

It is worth noting that, with betting games, there is at least one widely-accepted systematic method of calculating credences. Simply compare what are called the "pot odds" (the amount you might win versus the amount you have to bet) with the "card odds" (the likelihood that you will *not* get the card you need versus the likelihood that you will). If the pot odds are higher than the card odds, you have a reason to bet. The idea is that, if the payoff odds are better than the odds you will lose, it is better to play out the hand than to fold. (Some say, you are "more likely to win," but the "likely" here cannot refer to either objective or epistemic probabilities for reasons that will soon become clear.)

So, let's say the pot odds are 10 to 1, written: 10:1 (for example, you have to pay $1 to win $10). In addition, let's say that your cards are the cards from above. In this case, the card odds are 22:1 (2/46 reduces to 1/23; there is one chance in 23 that you will get your card and 22 that you won't, thus 22 to 1 against). Since the pot odds (10:1) are lower than the card odds (22:1), you shouldn't bet.

On the other hand, there are other ways to get a winning hand from this set of cards. Since you have three hearts, then, instead of trying for three 9s, you might instead try for two more hearts to make a flush. What is the likelihood that the two face-down cards are hearts? With three hearts in your hand, ten are left in the deck. The likelihood of getting one heart is 10/47, or 21.2% (37:10 odds, roughly, 4:1, 37 chances you won't get a heart, 10 that you will). Things are different now than before with the 9s. With the 9s, you only needed to know the probability that *one* of two randomly drawn cards is a 9. In this case, you need to know the likelihood that *both* of two randomly drawn cards are hearts. Therefore, instead of multiplying 21.2% by 2 (for two chances at one card), we would need to multiply the likelihood of drawing one heart (10/47) by the likelihood of then drawing a second heart (9/46), which is 90/2162, which reduces to about 1/24. 1/24 translates to 23:1 odds. Again, you should probably fold this hand. Of course, things are much more complicated at a real card table, since you must calculate (and pretty quickly) the odds of getting both the 9 and the two hearts (about 12:1, by the way), since either will increase your chances of winning.

You might ask why this method of calculating probability is categorized as a *credence* instead of an *epistemic probability*. The answer is simple: this calculation tells you nothing more about your chances of winning than the card odds alone. The likelihood that you will get a certain set of cards remains fixed given the organization of the deck regardless of how much money is at stake. Nevertheless, whether this method tells you to bet changes dramatically depending on how much money is at stake. With the card odds, you have already calculated the epistemic probability. So, whether I give you 10:1 pots odds or 1000:1 pot odds on a coin flip, your chance of getting either a heads or a tails is still 50%. Comparing card odds with pot odds has proven useful to many gamblers, but it ultimately does not affect your likelihood of winning.

For the purposes of constructing and evaluating arguments, and unless you find yourself in a casino, it is helpful to focus only on epistemic probabilities. Credences, as important as they are, are difficult to assess rationally. You may bet me $1 that the next flip of this coin won't be tails. If I reason that, because the last five flips have been heads, I will take your bet, my reasoning would be fallacious, though it "seems" right "in my gut." To consider this a worthy bet, my credence in the coin's likelihood of being tails must be different from yours. In this case, my credence can be traced to poor reasoning (called the gambler's fallacy). But what accounts for *your* credence? Credences are notoriously difficult to evaluate and are often fallacious, so, where we can, our best *bet* is to reason closely with our epistemic probabilities.

Similarly, when scientists evaluate the laws and events of nature, they are investigating what they hope are *objective* probabilities—they want to know what the world is like. Unfortunately, even scientists are limited to their evidence. Scientists depend on evidence to learn about nature, so that every probability they express depends solely on the evidence they have for that claim. We would love to have objective probabilities, but we are stuck, most of the time, with epistemic probabilities.

7.3. Conditional probabilities

In one sense, all probabilities are conditional; the truth of a probabilistic claim depends on its relationship to a set of conditions (we've described those conditions as objective, epistemic, or subjective). But the phrase **conditional probability** is reserved for probabilities that are conditional on other probabilities. For example, we can figure the probability of rolling a 6 on a six-sided die just by counting the sides and the number of 6s: 1 in 6. But what if we want to know the probability of rolling two sixes in a row? Or, what if we want to know the probability of rolling a 6 *given that* we just rolled a 6?

In this section, we will explain the main concepts required for understanding what a conditional probability expresses. We will leave a full explanation of calculating probabilities to more advanced texts.

An event's probability either depends on another event's probability or it does not. An event that depends on another's probability is called a *dependent event*. For instance, imagine drawing a playing card from a deck of 52 cards. The probability that that card is an ace is 4 in 52, or 7.69%. Let's say you've drawn the ace of hearts and you lay it aside. Now, what are the chances that the next card you draw will be an ace? 3 in 51, or 5.88%. So, the probability of the second event is dependent on the first event.

What if we want to know the probability of drawing two aces in a row without replacement and before we look at the first? We take the probability of drawing one of four aces from 52 cards (4/52) and multiply that by the probability of drawing one of three aces from 51 cards (3/51). (4/52) = 7.69%; (3/51) = 5.88%; multiplied = roughly .452%. It is *really* unlikely that you will randomly draw exactly two aces from a deck of 52 cards.

Now, imagine that, instead of laying the ace aside, we slide it back into the deck and reshuffle. What are the chances that the second card we draw will be an ace? They will, again, be 7.69%. Putting the first card back eliminates the dependence of the second card's probability on the first draw, so we call it an *independent event*. Since we replaced the first card, the probability of the second event is independent of the first.

Whether an event's probability is dependent or independent of another event determines how we calculate conditional probabilities. The probability of two independent events occurring is calculated by multiplying the probabilities together. The probability of drawing an ace is 7.69%. The probability of drawing two aces in a row (after replacing the first) is 7.69% x 7.69%, which is more easily calculated as decimals: P(.0769) x P(.0769) = P(.0059), or around .6%.

Similarly, individual die throws are independent events. Consider our second question from above: what is the probability of rolling a 6 *given that* we just rolled a 6? This case is just like our playing card case where we replaced the ace after drawing it. Since the rolling events are independent, the probability of rolling a 6 given that we just rolled a 6 is no different than simply rolling a 6, or that rolling a 6 given that we just rolled a 3 or a 4.

Nevertheless, to figure out the probability of multiple die throws before you have thrown any, you calculate them as dependent events. Consider our first question from above: what is the probability of rolling two 6s in a row? Since each roll has about a 16% probability of landing on 6, the formula for answering the question is: 16% x 16%, or P(.166) x P(.166), which comes out to P(.0275), or around 2.7%. Knowing whether two events are dependent or independent is crucial for calculating probabilities accurately.

7.4. Using probability to guide decisions: The cost/benefit analysis

A common use of probability in reasoning is to calculate the expected value of an action. Economists and business professionals often refer to this calculation as a *cost/benefit analysis*. The idea is to subtract the cost from the benefit of an action, and if the outcome is positive, the option is a live one. If more than one option has a positive outcome, the rational choice is the choice with the highest positive outcome.

For example, let's say I am desperately trying to lose weight. I've been working out and cutting calories for weeks, and I've recently begun to see some results. In addition, tonight, a friend has just brought over a large container of fresh, moist, warm, double-chocolate brownies just for the two of us. To decide whether to stick to my diet or indulge, I can employ a cost/benefit analysis.

To begin, I identify my options and the possible outcomes associated with those options:

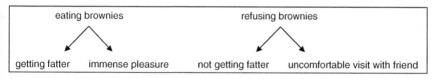

I then assign a probability and a value to each event. Probabilities are expressed: P(x), where x is a decimal expressing the likelihood of the event. Values are expressed: V(y), where y is the cost or benefit of the event.

These assignments can be *objective*, for instance, some scientific data about the likelihood of an event, or money as a measure of value; or they can be *subjective*, for instance, my credence in an event's likelihood or how much an heirloom means to me, regardless of its market value. In this case, I have pretty good evidence that one night of brownie indulgence probably won't hinder my weight-loss severely, so I will assign it a relatively low probability. What about the likelihood of pleasure? Probably pretty close to 1 (unless my friend butchered the recipe or I just don't like her very much). Similarly, I assign values to the outcomes. I don't want to gain weight, so it gets a pretty high negative score. But I love brownies and spending time with my friend, so it gets a very high positive score. After I have assigned all probabilities and values, I have a chart that looks something like this:

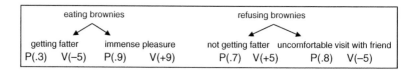

Are these probabilities and values arbitrary? To some extent, yes. But I am the only one who knows how much I value eating brownies or disvalue an uncomfortable visit with a friend, and I can assign rough, relative values to those events. As long as I am honest with myself and the grounds for my probability assignments are realistic, the calculation should come out roughly right.

To calculate the expected value of my decisions, I simply multiply the probability of each outcome by its value, then add the two results for each outcome:

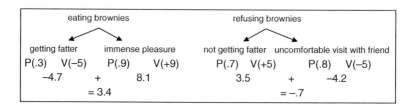

As it turns out, though I disvalue the prospect of getting fat, the probability is fairly low that I will, plus the pleasure of brownies and time with my friend is very high. So, the expected value of my decision to eat brownies is considerably higher than refusing the brownies and risking an uncomfortable evening with a friend.

The formula for calculating expected value on a cost-benefit analysis looks like this:

$$((((P(o_1) \times V(o_1)) + (P(o_2) \times V(o_2))) + (P(o_3) \times V(o_3))) + \ldots (P(o_n) \times V(o_n)))$$

where "o" refers to the possible "outcome" of a decision. The ellipses [. . .] indicate that you can evaluate as many different outcomes as you want, or as you find realistic.

You probably wouldn't take the time to run a cost-benefit analysis in the case of the brownies, so let's look at a more realistic example, where it might be a good idea. Let's say you're looking to open a restaurant. You figure your costs (rent, insurance, remodeling, employees, overhead, etc.) at around $50,000 for the first year. You figure your benefits (profit) at around $35,000 for the first year. If you don't open the restaurant, you will stay at your $35,000/year job, clearing around $2,000 after expenses. So, chart the outcomes:

Option 1: Open the restaurant

O_1: Lose $50,000 in costs. $P(O_1) = 1$ $V(O_1) = -\$50,000$
(Notice that these costs have a probability of 1. This is because the prices of most goods are fixed by the producers. If the costs were negotiable, such as with real estate, the probability might be different.)

O_2: Gain $35,000 in profits. $P(O_2) = .9$ $V(O_2) = \$35,000$

Option 2: Stay at your regular job

O_3: Lose $33,000 in expenses. $P(O_3) = 1$ $V(O_3) = -\$33,000$
O_4: Gain $35,000 in income. $P(O_4) = .9$ $V(O_4) = +\$35,000$

Plugging these figures into our cost/benefit analysis, we get the following results:

Option 1: Open the restaurant

$P(1)$ x $V(-\$50,000) = -\$50,000$
$P(.9)$ x $V(+\$35,000) = \$31,500$ $= -\$18,500$

Option 2: Stay at your regular job

$P(1)$ x $V(-\$33,000) = -\$33,000$
$P(.9)$ x $V(+\$38,000) = \$34,200$ $= +\$1,200$

As a one-year projection, it looks like you're better off staying at your job. But statistical data tells us that restaurant owners often lose money the first two years of operation, so if we recalculate over a longer period of time, taking into account that you won't have many of your start-up expenses during the second and third years, the restaurant may be the more profitable option.

These examples show the role that probabilities play in one of the most common decision-making procedures. As long as any one of the probability claims in the cost-benefit analysis is less than P(1), the analysis is an inductive argument. The outcome cannot be guaranteed, even if it is highly likely.

7.5. An obstacle: The problem of induction

Despite its usefulness in almost every area of our lives, induction faces a serious philosophical objection. The **problem of induction** is a classical philosophical problem that, to this day, has no widely-accepted solution. The rough idea is that, evidence about the past or a sample of a population does not constitute evidence for the future or for the whole population.

In his classic example, David Hume (1711–1776) asks us to consider: What reason do you have that the sun will rise tomorrow? Any argument for this claim will be either deductive or inductive. Evidence about the past or a sample doesn't logically entail any particular thing about the future (by definition, it includes only information about the way the world *was*). Therefore there is no deductive argument for claims about the future. Any inductive evidence simply restates the problem: What is the likelihood that the sun will rise tomorrow, *given that* it already has repeatedly risen in the past? If you answer, "high likelihood," you are assuming that past states of affairs are connected or related in some important way to future states of affairs, so that the truth of claims about the past somehow imply or suggest the truth of some claims about the future. But what sort of connection could this be and how do we know there is one?

There is certainly nothing about a connection mentioned in the claim: The sun has always risen in the past. So, we must be introducing (implicitly) some principle or connection that seems to explain why the sun has always risen in the past. Many of us, for instance, assume that there are a set of natural laws that accounts for this uniformity of nature. But natural laws are not things that we can see or feel or hear; they are descriptions of past couplings of events.

For instance, the series: I let go of the pen; the pen falls; I let go of the pen; the pen falls; I let go of the pen; etc, may be described using the laws of gravity and inertia. But these laws simply describe events that have happened in the past; they do not tell us something about the way pens will behave when dropped unless we are sure that those laws govern future instances of dropping pens as well. Why believe these laws *will* govern future events? We need, again, some principle or connection to explain the past behavior of laws with the future behavior of laws. And, of course, descriptions of the way laws *have behaved* are no different than descriptions of how the sun *has behaved* in the past; no connection is mentioned in these descriptions. Therefore, laws of nature cannot account for our beliefs about future states of affairs any better than the sun's past rising can account for our belief that it will rise tomorrow.

The problem seems to be that, in any argument from past states of affairs (e.g., the sun has always risen; the pen has always fallen when dropped) to future states of affairs (e.g., the sun will rise tomorrow; the pen will fall ifI let it go), we will need, at some point, a premise stating that the future will look like the past. But since the argument is an attempt to prove that the future will look like the past, including a premise that the future will look like the past makes our argument **circular**; we are assuming the very claim we need to prove.

Consider the argument in standard form:

A.
1. Every morning humans have observed, the sun has risen.
2. Therefore, the sun will rise tomorrow morning.

The conclusion of A follows from the premise only if we assume that something connects these past states of affairs with the future. We can introduce this premise as follows:

B.
1. Every morning humans have observed, the sun has risen.
3. The laws of nature guarantee that the future will look like the past.
2. Therefore, the sun will rise tomorrow morning.

The conclusion of B follows validly from the premises, but we need some reason to think premise 3 is true. We might do this with the following argument:

C.
4. The laws of nature have always governed past events.
3. Therefore, the laws of nature guarantee that the future will look like the past.

Like A, the conclusion of C does not follow from the premises without assuming there is some reason to think there is a connection between the way the laws have behaved and the way they will behave. We might make this assumption explicit with another premise:

> D.
> 4. The laws of nature have always governed past event.
> 5. The future will look like the past, or nature is uniform.
> 3. Therefore, the laws of nature guarantee that the future will look like the past.

But now, as with B, though the conclusion of D follows from the premises, we need some reason to believe that 5 is true. How might we justify 5? Unfortunately, only by assuming that something like 5 is true:

> E.
> 6. The future will look like the past.
> 5. Therefore, the future will look like the past.

And of course, an argument like this leaves us no better off than where we began.

Taking stock, here is the problem: You seem clearly justified in believing the sun will rise tomorrow. You should be as sure of this as almost anything. Yet, we do not directly experience that the sun will rise tomorrow (we are not yet there), and any deductive argument for the claim that the sun will rise tomorrow is circular (the past does not entail anything about the future; and adding any premise to that effect assumes what we are trying to prove). So, where do we go from here?

The type of circularity involved in the above deductive arguments is called **premise-circularity**, which means that there will always be a premise that explicitly restates the conclusion. A simpler example of a premise-circular argument would be a child attempting to justify the claim, "I need candy," by simply stating "Because I need it."

But what if we could construct an argument that does not require an explicit premise about the past's connection to the future? Philosopher of science Wesley Salmon (1925–2001) offers an insightful example of this sort of argument:

> A crystal gazer claims that his method is the appropriate method for making predictions. When we question his claim he says, "Wait a moment; I will find out whether the method of crystal gazing is the best method for making predictions."

He looks into the crystal ball and announces that future cases of crystal ball gazing will yield predictive success. If we protest [arguing from induction] that his method has not been especially successful in the past, he might well make certain remarks about parity of reasoning. "Since you have used your method to justify your method, why shouldn't I use my method to justify my method? . . . By the way, I note by gazing into my crystal ball that the scientific method is now in for a very bad run of luck."[1]

In this case, the crystal-ball-gazer does not explicitly identify any connection between crystal ball gazing and the truth of claims derived from crystal ball gazing. He simply uses the crystal ball to justify a claim about crystal ball gazing. Instead of attempting to validly derive the reliability of crystal ball gazing, the gazer appeals to crystal ball gazing to justify the future reliability of crystal ball gazing. The rule here is not induction, but crystal-ball-gazing. Nevertheless, there is a worry that, if I assume the reasoning principle, or rule, that I am trying to prove (crystal ball gazing is reliable because crystal ball gazing tells me so), my conclusion is no more justified for me than before I constructed the argument. This type of circularity is called "**rule-circularity**," because, though the rule is not explicitly stated in the argument, it is assumed in order to prove it.

Is rule-circularity any less worrisome than premise-circularity? It would seem not. This is because any rule-circular argument can be made premise-circular by adding a premise about the reliability of the method being used; and it seems that this sort of premise is already implicitly assumed in rule-circular arguments. Therefore, the same worry seems to attach to induction:

F.	G.
7. <u>Crystal ball gazing tells me crystal ball gazing is reliable.</u>	9. <u>Induction tells me induction is reliable.</u>
8. Therefore, crystal ball gazing is reliable.	10. Therefore, induction is reliable.

Taking stock once again, we find that, direct experience does not justify induction, deductive arguments for induction are premise-circular, and inductive arguments for induction are rule-circular. Therefore, induction is an unjustified form of reasoning. If this argument is sound, science and all other inductive reasoning processes aimed at justifying the truth of claims (as opposed to, say, their usefulness) are in serious trouble.

Philosophers have offered a variety of solutions to the problem of induction, but none are widely accepted. For example, American philosopher Laurence BonJour (1943—) argues that there is a way of justifying induction that is not considered by Hume, namely, **inference to the best explanation**. We will take a closer look at inference to the best explanation in Chapter 9, but for now it is enough to note that BonJour argues that, among competing explanations, the best explanation for induction's past success is that nature is uniform. Inference to the best explanation is a complicated form of reasoning, and BonJour argues that it is justified *a priori*, that is, independently of experiential evidence. We need no experience, either directly of the future, or of the past, or of any connection between the past and the future to justify induction. We may rely on our *a priori* evidence that inferences to the best explanation are justified. And from this, we may justify our belief in induction. To motivate this conclusion, we would need to explain BonJour's account of *a priori* justification, and how inference to the best explanation is justified on non-experiential evidence. Do not quickly dismiss it on account of our brief discussion. Many philosophers argue (Jamie included) that our beliefs about the rules of mathematics and logic are similarly justified.

American philosopher John Hospers (1918—) offers a defense of induction very different from BonJour's. Hospers concedes that arguments for induction are circular, but argues that, in this case, circularity does not constitute sufficient reason to reject induction. In fact, he argues, most of our deductive rules suffer the same fate:

H.[2]	I.
11. If snow is white, *modus ponens* is valid.	14. Either *modus ponens* is valid or $2+2=5$.
12. Snow is white.	15. It is not the case that $2 + 2 = 5$
13. Therefore, *modus ponens* is valid.	16. Therefore, *modus ponens* is valid.

There is no way to prove that a rule is valid without appealing to a valid rule. But we certainly do not think we should reject *modus ponens* or disjunctive syllogism as unjustified. We could not perform logical or mathematical calculations without them; they are *indispensable* to our reasoning process. Induction is similarly indispensable. John Hospers explains:

> It would seem . . . that to demand a logical basis for the principle [of induction] is as unreasonable as to demand it in the case of the principles of logic them-selves. . . . In the case of the principles of logic it was the impossibility of any coherent discourse without the use of them; in the present case the situation is not quite so radical: it is the fruitlessness of any scientific procedure without the adoption of the Principle of the Uniformity of Nature, which alone enables us to make inferences from the past to the future. . . . the laws of nature are the only sound basis for such prediction. It is these or nothing.[3]

Hospers admits that indispensability arguments are pragmatic rather than epistemic, that is, they do not guarantee or necessarily track the truth of claims they justify. Nevertheless, we are stuck with them for many of our most fundamental reasoning processes. If we are not willing to give up valid arguments despite their circularity, similarly we should not be willing to give up induction.

As we discuss inductive argument forms in the next chapter, it is important to keep worries about induction in the back of our minds. BonJour's and Hospers' responses to the problem are merely two among dozens, none of which are widely accepted solutions. Therefore, unless you find one of these responses convincing, every inductive conclusion should probably be qualified with, "given that there is a satisfactory solution to the problem of induction."

7.6. Exercises

Exercises 7.a.

For each of the following, explain whether the claim expresses a statistic or whether it expresses a probability (note: some probabilistic claims will contain statistical data and some statistical data will be represented as percentages):

1. 74% of men interviewed say they would prefer not to have a male tend to them in a hospital. (Men's Health Magazine, April 2010, Kyle Western.)
2. Male smokers had more than a 30% increase in risk of dying from [colon cancer] compared to men who never had smoked.
   ("Cigarette Smoking and Colorectal Cancer Mortality in the Cancer Prevention Study II," *Journal of the National Cancer Institute*, Vol. 92, No. 23, 1888–1896, December 6, 2000, Oxford University Press.)
3. Male smokers have more than a 30% increase in risk of dying from colon cancer compared to men who never have smoked.
4. In 2003 about 45,000 Americans died in motor accidents out of population of 291,000,000. So, according to the National Safety Council this means your one-year odds of dying in a car accident is about one out of 6500. Therefore your lifetime probability (6500 ÷ 78 years life expectancy) of dying in a motor accident are about one in 83. (www.reason.com)
5. Scientists find that 10 out of 10 people have mothers.
6. Most people do not die on an airplane. Therefore, you will probably not die on your upcoming flight.
7. The probability of rolling two 6s with two dice is $(1/6) \times (1/6)$.
8. The odds of a mother having twins are 90:1.
9. Out of 100 coin flips, 57% were heads and 43% were tails.
10. The Cubs have a 10:1 shot this season.

Exercises 7.b.

For each of the following claim, identify which type of probability is being expressed: objective probability (chance), epistemic probability, or subjective probability (credence):

1. "They've only been on three dates. I bet they'll break up before next week."
2. "The card in your hand is either a 2 of hearts or it isn't."
3. "It feels like rain."
4. "He's giving you 4:1 odds on a ten dollar bet? You should definitely take it."
5. "Given what we know about the chimp, showing him a red cloth will likely make him angry."
6. "The data indicates that trans fats are bad for your health."
7. "The radioactive isotope thorium-234 decays at a rate of half every 24 days."
8. "The likelihood of drawing the ace of spades is 1 in 52."
9. "I just don't think our economy is in that bad of shape."
10. "Given that a pen has fallen every time I have dropped it in the past, it is likely that it will fall the next time I drop it."

Exercises 7.c.

For each of the following arguments, explain whether the probability claims in the premises make it inductively strong, inductively weak, or valid:

1.
1. Many Muslims are Sunni.
2. Janet is a Muslim.
3. Therefore, Janet is a Sunni.

2.
1. Most violent criminals are recidivists.
2. Joe is a violent criminal.
3. Therefore, Joe is likely a recidivist.

3.
1. At least a few lawyers are honest.
2. Sarah is a lawyer.
3. So, Sarah might be honest.

4.
1. Aces can be played high or low in Blackjack.
2. In this game of Blackjack, you were just dealt the ace of spades.
3. Therefore, you can play it high or low.

5.
1. In most cases, weddings are nauseating affairs.
2. This wedding we're invited to, will likely be a nauseating affair.

⇨

6.
1. Some politicians are trustworthy.
2. Jake is trustworthy.
3. Hence, he might be a politician.

7.
1. The islands are nice this time of year.
2. You're going to Fiji?
3. It should be great!

8.
1. This restaurant has a reputation for bad service.
2. I don't suspect this visit will be any different.

9.
1. All the watches I've worn break easily.
2. I can't imagine this one will be different.

10.
1. Every swan scientists have studied have been white.
2. Scientists are on their way to study swans in Australia.
3. They will probably find only white swans there, too.

Exercises 7.d.

For each argument in C that is inductively weak, restate the one or more of the premises to make it inductively strong.

Exercises 7.e.

For each of the following decisions, construct a cost/benefit analysis to justify one of the options:

1. After you graduate, do you go to college or go to work?
2. After college, do you settle down immediately (get a family) or spend time travelling and building your career?
3. Your boss offers you a promotion that comes with a hefty raise. The catch is that it is a job you despise. Do you take it?
4. You've just been dumped by your significant other. Tonight the roommate comes knocking at your door asking to go out. Do you accept?
5. You recently found out that your boss is lying to clients and cheating them out of small amounts of money, though they are not aware of it. She has recently put you in a position where you have to corroborate the lie. If anyone finds out, you will both be fired. Do you stay on?

Exercises 7.f.

To the best of your ability, explain the problem of induction in your own words.

Real-Life Example: The Teleological Argument for God's Existence

Consider the following excerpt of an argument from philosopher Robin Collins (also some footnotes have been removed). Collins uses probability measures to argue that the probability that a being like God exists is greater than the probability that a being like God doesn't. Write a short essay explaining how Collins uses probabilities in the premises and then how these probabilities are supposed to lend strength to the conclusion that something like God exists.

The remainder of this argument, and a more technical version of it, can be found at Professor Collins' website: http://home.messiah.edu/~rcollins/

General Principle of Reasoning Used

The Principle Explained

We will formulate the fine-tuning argument against the atheistic single- universe hypothesis is in terms of what I will call the **prime principle of confirmation**. The prime principle of confirmation is a general principle of reasoning which tells us when some observation counts as evidence in favor of one hypothesis over another. **Simply put, the principle says that whenever we are considering two competing hypotheses, an observation counts as evidence in favor of the hypothesis under which the observation has the highest probability (or is the least improbable).** (Or, put slightly differently, the principle says that whenever we are considering two competing hypotheses, H_1 and H_2, an observation, O, counts as evidence in favor of H_1 over H_2 if O is more probable under H_1 than it is under H_2.) Moreover, the degree to which the evidence counts in favor of one hypothesis over another is proportional to the degree to which the observation is more probable under the one hypothesis than the other. For example, the fine-tuning is much, much more probable under the theism than under the atheistic single-universe hypothesis, so it counts as strong evidence for theism over this atheistic hypothesis. In the next major subsection, we will present a more formal and elaborated rendition of the fine-tuning argument in terms of the prime principle. First, however, let's look at a couple of illustrations of the principle and then present some support for it.

Additional Illustrations of the Principle

For our first illustration, suppose that I went hiking in the mountains, and found underneath a certain cliff a group of rocks arranged in a formation that clearly formed the pattern "Welcome to the mountains Robin Collins." One hypothesis is that, by chance, the rocks just happened to be arranged in that pattern—ultimately, perhaps, because of certain initial conditions of the universe. Suppose the only viable alternative hypothesis is that my brother, who was in the mountains before me, arranged the rocks in this way. Most of us would immediately take the arrangements of rocks to be strong evidence in favor of the "brother" hypothesis over the "chance" hypothesis. Why? Because it strikes us as extremely improbable that the rocks would be arranged that way by chance, but not improbable at all that my brother would place them in that configuration. Thus, by the prime principle of confirmation we would conclude that the arrangement of rocks strongly supports the "brother" hypothesis over the chance hypothesis.

⇨

Or consider another case, that of finding the defendant's fingerprints on the murder weapon. Normally, we would take such a finding as strong evidence that the defendant was guilty. Why? Because we judge that it would be unlikely for these fingerprints to be on the murder weapon if the defendant was innocent, but not unlikely if the defendant was guilty. That is, we would go through the same sort of reasoning as in the above case.

Support for the Principle

Several things can be said in favor of the prime principle of confirmation. First, many philosophers think that this principle can be derived from what is known as the probability calculus, the set of mathematical rules that are typically assumed to govern probability. Second, there does not appear to be any case of recognizably good reasoning that violates this principle. Finally, the principle appears to have a wide range of applicability, undergirding much of our reasoning in science and everyday life, as the examples above illustrate. Indeed, some have even claimed that a slightly more general version of this principle undergirds all scientific reasoning. Because of all these reasons in favor of the principle, we can be very confident in it.

Further Development of Argument

To further develop the core version of the fine-tuning argument, we will summarize the argument by explicitly listing its two premises and its conclusion:

Premise 1. The existence of the fine-tuning is not improbable under theism.

Premise 2. The existence of the fine-tuning is very improbable under the atheistic single-universe hypothesis.

Conclusion: From premises (1) and (2) and the prime principle of confirmation, it follows that the fine-tuning data provides strong evidence to favor of the design hypothesis over the atheistic single-universe hypothesis.

At this point, we should pause to note two features of this argument. First, the argument does not say that the fine-tuning evidence proves that the universe was designed, or even that it is likely that the universe was designed. In order to justify these sorts of claims, we would have to look at the full range of evidence both for and against the design hypothesis, something we are not doing in this chapter. Rather, the argument merely concludes that the fine-tuning strongly supports theism over the atheistic single-universe hypothesis.

In this way, the evidence of fine-tuning argument is much like fingerprints found on the gun: although they can provide strong evidence that the defendant committed the murder, one could not conclude merely from them alone that the defendant is guilty; one would also have to look at all the other evidence offered. Perhaps, for instance, ten reliable witnesses claimed to see the defendant at a party at the time of the shooting. In this case, the fingerprints would still count as significant evidence of guilt, but this evidence would be counterbalanced by the testimony of the witnesses. Similarly the evidence of fine-tuning strongly supports theism over the atheistic single-universe hypothesis, though it does not itself show that everything considered theism is the most plausible explanation of the world. Nonetheless, as I argue in the conclusion of this chapter, the evidence of fine-tuning

⇨

provides a much stronger and more objective argument for theism (over the atheistic single-universe hypothesis) than the strongest atheistic argument does against theism.

The second feature of the argument we should note is that, given the truth of the prime principle of confirmation, the conclusion of the argument follows from the premises. Specifically, if the premises of the argument are true, then we are guaranteed that the conclusion is true: that is, the argument is what philosophers call valid. Thus, insofar as we can show that the premises of the argument are true, we will have sh own that the conclusion is true. Our next task, therefore, is to attempt to show that the premises are true, or at least that we have strong reasons to believe them.

Inductive Arguments

8

Chapter Outline

8.1. Types of inductive argument

Inductive arguments come in a variety of forms. In this chapter, we will explain four popular forms: enumerative induction, generalization, argument from analogy, and causal argument. Inductive forms are determined by the way the premises of an inductive argument lead you to draw a conclusion. As we noted in the previous chapter, no inductive arguments are valid. This means that the conclusion will only follow from the premises with some degree of probability between zero and 99.9999%. Classically, it is said that an inductive argument is **ampliative** (think, "amplify"), that is, something is added or new in the conclusion that is not included in the premises. In contrast, deductive arguments are **non-ampliative**; their conclusions do not include anything that is not already in the premises. To be sure, deductive conclusions may be surprising and lead to new discoveries, but the point is that everything we discover is true just because the premises are true.

Consider these two examples:

Deductive Argument	**Inductive Argument**
1. All men are mortal.	1. Most men are mortal.
2. Socrates was a man.	2. Socrates was a man.
3. Thus, Socrates was mortal.	3. Thus, Socrates was probably a mortal.

In the argument on the left, the conclusion does not include any information beyond what can be understood from the premises. We can use a Venn diagram to see this more precisely (see Chapter 3 for more on Venn diagrams):

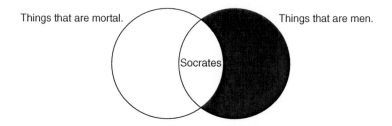

All the things that are men are within the scope of all the things that are mortal, and all the things that are Socrates are within the scope of things that are men. Because of these premises, we know exactly where Socrates fits. In order to draw this conclusion, *we do not have to add anything* to the premises. Therefore, we call this a non-ampliative inference.

In the argument on the right, on the other hand, there is more information in the conclusion than is strictly expressed in the premises. A Venn diagram also makes this clear:

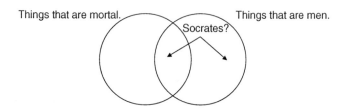

In this case, it is isn't clear which side of the line Socrates belongs on. Nevertheless, since most of the things that are men are found in the category of things that are mortal, we can, with some confidence, draw the conclusion that Socrates is *probably* in the overlapping section. However, in order to draw this conclusion, *we have to add something* to the premises, namely, a decision about the side of the line on which Socrates is likely to fall. Therefore, we call this an ampliative inference.

So, as we have said before, a good (cogent) inductive argument is strong and has true premises. But how do we determine whether a conclusion follows *strongly* from a set of premises? Probability—whether objective, epistemic, or subjective (see Chapter 7)—is the most important measure of inductive strength. The differences in inductive forms dictate how we evaluate the probability that a conclusion follows from a set of premises, and therefore, the strength of that argument. For instance, in an inductive generalization, a conclusion follows with high probability if the conditions for a good generalization are met, for instance, a sample is representative of a population.

For each argument form, we will discuss the form itself, some strengths and weaknesses, give some examples, and then offer some exercises to help you become adept at using each form. At the end of this chapter, we will offer further exercises to help you distinguish each inductive form, as well as a real-life example.

8.2. Enumerative induction

In an **enumerative induction**, a conclusion about a particular object or event is inferred from premises about previous instances of that object or event. For instance, you probably have no fear of your next airplane flight because most airplanes make their destinations safely. Similarly, you probably have no fear that the next soft drink you drink will be poisonous because most soft drinks aren't poisonous. And recall our discussion from the last chapter about whether the sun will rise tomorrow morning. The inference that it will rise from premises about how many times it has risen in the past is an enumerative induction.

Enumerative inductions typically have one of the following forms:

Form I:
1. Most (almost all, more than 50% of) X are Y.
2. Z is an X.
3. Therefore, Z is probably a Y.

Form II:
1. All/most of the Xs we observed turned out to be Y.
2. We are observing an X (not a member of our sample).
3. Therefore, we are probably observing a Y.

The differences are subtle but important. In Form I, if we had used the quantifier "all" instead of "most" or "almost all" in the first premise, the argument would be deductive. But in Form II, even if we used "all" in the first premise, the argument may still be inductive. This is because, in Form II, the quantifier is restricted to what we have observed. Even if all the Xs we have observed are Ys, there may be lots of Xs we have not observed, therefore, an inference to objects beyond what we have observed is still ampliative. So, whereas premise 1 of Form I quantifies over an unrestricted category (Xs in general), premise 1 of Form II quantifies only over a restricted category (Xs we have observed).

Here are some examples:

Form I Examples:

A.
1. Most Republicans are conservative.
2. <u>Senator Lindsey Graham is a Republican.</u>
3. Therefore, Graham is probably a conservative.

B.
1. Almost all ducks float.
2. <u>That is a duck.</u>
3. Hence, it probably floats.

C.
1. 85% of U.S. congress voted to invade Iraq in 2002.
2. <u>Senator John Kerry is a member of congress.</u>
3. Thus, it is likely that Kerry voted to invade Iraq.

Form II Examples:

D.
1. Almost all the swans we have observed are white.
2. <u>There are 200 swans on the island we haven't observed.</u>
3. Thus, those are probably almost all white, as well.

E.
1. All 300 cats in the sample get hairballs.
2. <u>We found this cat behind the dumpster.</u>
3. It probably gets hairballs.

F.
1. All 50 patients we surveyed have strep throat.
2. <u>You have five patients in the waiting room.</u>
3. They probably have strep throat, too.

Notice example *C*. As it turns out, the conclusion is false. Kerry was one of the 15% who voted against invading Iraq. Nevertheless, this is a good inductive argument. If we were drawing senators out of a hat, given these premises, we would be more likely to draw a supporter of the war than a dissenter. The fact that we happened to draw a dissenter doesn't change this.

Consider example *D*. In this case, even if the conclusion is true, the inference is weak. We don't know how many swans were observed, so just learning that all the observed ones were white doesn't tell us much. It might have only been two or three. Therefore, even though it has the quantifier "almost all," it is a weak inductive argument.

Enumerative inductions can be a useful way to reason inductively from past experience. But how do we justify unrestricted claims such as premise 1 of Form I? In order to justify very general claims ("All *X*s are *Y*s") we turn to our next inductive argument form.

8.3. Exercises with enumerative induction

Exercises 8.a.

Complete each of the following enumerative inductions by supplying the conclusion:

1.
1. You haven't liked anything you've tried at that restaurant.
2. Therefore, this time . . .

2.
1. Most of the philosophers we met at the conference were arrogant.
2. And those two we met at the bar weren't any better.
3. Oh no, here comes another. I bet . . .

3.
1. Every time you have pulled the lever on the slot machine, you've lost.
2. So, . . .

4.
1. Every girl I met at the bar last night snubbed me.
2. Every girl I met at the bar so far tonight has snubbed me.
3. Therefore, . . .

5.
1. All the politicians at the convention last year were jerks.
2. All the politicians we've met at the convention this year were jerks.
3. Hence, probably, . . .

Exercises 8.b.

Construct an enumerative induction for each of the following claims (that is, consider each of the following claims the conclusion of an argument; come up with premises to support these claims):

1. "The next mallard we see will have a white stripe on its neck."
2. "I bet the next car we see will be blue."
3. "That cop will probably hassle us."
4. "That shirt is not likely to fit you."
5. "This car won't be better than any of the others."

8.4. Inductive generalization, or reasoning from a sample

We often hear reports of new experiments on drugs, or suggestions that will purportedly make our lives better:

> **"CRESTOR can lower LDL cholesterol up to 52% (at the 10-mg dose versus 7% with placebo)"** (www.crestor.com).

> **"Research has shown that regular aspirin use is associated with a marked reduction from death due to all causes, particularly among the elderly, people with heart disease, and people who are physically unfit"** ("Heart Disease and Aspirin Therapy," www.webmd.com).

> **"A U.S. Department of Transportation study released today estimates that 1,652 lives could be saved and 22,372 serious injuries avoided each year on America's roadways if seat belt use rates rose to 90 percent in every state"** (www.nhtsa.gov).

How do researchers draw these sorts of conclusions? How do they know what their drug might do for *you*? We assume you weren't one of their test subjects. We also assume they don't have access to your medical records or lifestyle. Nevertheless, something connects their research to your body—a member of the population that *wasn't* part of the study.

The most common way to extend an experiment's results beyond the laboratory results is to use an inductive generalization. An inductive generalization is an inference from one group of things—a sample of some population (e.g., 486 registered voters, 2,500 citizens of the United Kingdom, 30 known felons)—to every member of that population (e.g., all registered voters, all citizens of the United Kingdom, all known felons). If the sample meets the right conditions, then an inference about the population will be strong, that is, we can legitimately infer from this sample something about the whole population.

Inductive generalizations tend to have the following form:

1. <u>Most (almost all, more than 50%) of a sample of X is Y.</u>
2. All Xs are Ys.

Here are some examples:

G.
1. <u>Most of our 35-year-old male test subjects reacted positively to drug X.</u>
2. Therefore, probably most 35-year-old males will react positively to it.

H.
1. Almost all the sixth-graders we interviewed loved Harry Potter.
2. Therefore, Harry Potter probably appeals to most sixth-graders.

I.
1. 75% of 300 Labour Party members said they approve of Bill X.
2. Therefore, probably most Labour Party members approve of Bill X.

Notice that, in each of these examples, a sample of a population is identified in the premises (a particular set of 35-year-old males, sixth-graders, etc.), and from this sample, a generalization is drawn to the whole population (all 35-year-olds, all sixth-graders, etc.). What conditions constitute a good sample? There tend to be four agreed-upon criteria:

1. A sample must be random.
2. A sample must be proportionate.
3. A sample must be obtained using a valid instrument.
4. A sample must be obtained using a reliable instrument.

1. A sample must be *random.*

If we are concerned with public perception of a liberal politician's job performance, we do not want our sample taken only from the conservative population, or only from the liberal population, or only from the rich population, or only from the religious population. These niche groups do not necessarily represent the whole population, and therefore, **bias** the sample. A **random** sampling takes information from all relevant portions of the population. If a sample is not random, it is biased.

This point depends on the information we are looking for. For instance, if instead of the public perception of a politician's job performance, we are interested in the *male* perspective on that performance, we want to be sure not to include any female perspectives. But we also do not want to restrict our sampling to the teenage male population or the elderly male population. Of the population we are concerned with, even if narrow—in this case, males—our sample must still be random.

The methods used by surveyors are a primary cause of bias. For instance, if surveyors call participants on the telephone between 7 and 9 PM on weekdays, they will miss significant portions of the population, including: many younger people who no longer have land-line phones, college students who work retail jobs in the evenings, people who work swing shift, and professionals who have better things to do than answer phone questions during prime time.

Similarly, surveys such as radio call-ins, questionnaires found in newspapers or magazines that must be sent-in or submitted online, and on-line opinion polls tend to be biased toward a certain type of participant, namely, participants whose interests overlap with those of the media in which the poll is offered. In these surveys, researchers do not ask or select participants, but participants choose to participate. The sample selects itself, so we call such surveys *self-selecting*. One way to mitigate self-selecting bias is to include a demographic questionnaire: age, race, occupation, gender, etc. This way, if your primary participant pool turns out to be, for example, elderly women, at least your conclusion can reflect that. Nevertheless, self-selecting samples are generally considered biased and therefore cannot support a strong inductive argument.

When you evaluate survey data, check the method used to obtain the data. Ask: Does this method leave out significant portions of the population? Does the conclusion reflect the population likely to have participated in the survey? If a survey method is likely to lead to bias, a conclusion will not follow strongly from the data.

2. A sample must be *proportionate*.

Samples that are too small are not a good indication of the whole population. In the United States, there are roughly 100,000,000 registered voters. Therefore, if we want to know the public's perception of the president's job performance, a survey of 200 people will not proportionate to the population of registered voters. Similarly, in a college of 2,000 students, a survey of one student will not be representative of the student body.

If a sample is too small, a strong inductive inference cannot be drawn. A generalization that draws a conclusion about a population from a disproportionate sample size commits the fallacy of **hasty generalization**. (For more on the fallacy of hasty generalization, see Chapter 11.) The problem is that such an inference includes too little information in the premises to grant a high degree of probability to the conclusion.

There is some difficulty in determining when a sample is proportionate. Is 1% enough? Is 10%? Clearly, the larger the percentage, the better the sample will be. But in cases like the president's job performance in the United States, we are not likely to have the money or the time to survey even 1% of the population.

For very large populations, we (the authors) like to use the 1% rule. If a survey or experiment sampled 1% of the population (1 out of every 100 people in that particular population), the results are likely representative. Of course, it is much easier to get a 1% sample in very small, well-known populations, e.g., eighth-graders in your county, females in the state of Georgia between the ages of 18 and 22, CEOs in Atlanta, etc. It is much more difficult when the actual population size is unknown, e.g., dolphins in the Atlantic, illegal immigrants in the United States, pine trees in Virginia, etc.

There are some ways to mitigate the weakening effects of small sample sizes. If more than one research group is studying the same feature of a population (and are asking the relevant questions in the right way; see "validity" and "reliability" below), the results can be combined for a much larger sample size. For instance, if the question is: "Is the governor doing a good job?" and if three research groups ask this exact question to different samples of the population, you can average the results for a new generalization that is stronger than any one of the three. Imagine that each group randomly samples 900 voters in the state of Georgia and get the result: *Yes*, 55%, 57%, 51% of the time, respectively. Now your sample size is 2,700 and your percentage of "Yes" answers is 54.3%. Of course, since the population of Georgia is just over 9 million, you are nowhere close to the 1% rule, but the conclusion that more than 50% of Georgians are happy with the governor is at least stronger than before.

Is it objectively strong? Probably not, especially since just 300 additional "No"s would drop the approval rating below 50%. On the other hand, if you surveyed 1% of Georgians, roughly 90,000, and the results were 54.3%, it would take over 7,000 "No"s to drop the approval rating below 50%. This is a much more stable statistic. The conclusion (that the job approval is over 50%) is still derived inductively, and may be false given accurate survey techniques. But now, at least, the conclusion follows strongly from the premises.

When evaluating survey data, check the sample size. Use your best judgment to determine whether the sample size is large enough to represent the population. If the sample size is considerably small (many national political surveys in the United States include only 900 participants), the conclusion will not follow strongly from the premises.

3. A sample must be obtained using *a valid instrument*.
Here we must be careful because the word "valid" has a different meaning from the term we use to describe the relationship between premises and a conclusion. A *valid deductive argument* is an argument in which the conclusion follows from the premises with certainty. A **valid scientific instrument**

(survey or experiment) is an instrument that yields the relevant information we are looking for, that is, it measures what it claims to measure.

For instance, we might survey college students voting for their student government president whether they like Bud Buffman for the position. But if our survey simply asked, "Do you like Bud?" our results might be overwhelmingly, "Yes," but only because the students thought we were asking about Budweiser beer. While we want to know how students feel about Bud Buffman, we may be getting their opinion on Budweiser. In this case, the survey does not yield the relevant information, and is therefore, invalid.

Similarly, in the 1930s, psychologist Lewis Terman discovered that intelligence test scores differed in unexpected ways between children who were raised in the country and those raised in urban areas. The IQ of country children dropped over time after entering school, while the IQ of urban children rose over time after entering school. Late researchers have shown that Terman's intelligence tests were not calibrated for cultural bias. This means that the tests were tracking factors other than intelligence, rendering them invalid. Similar studies were conducted with Wechsler intelligence scales given to groups of American Indian children, some of whom were more "acculturated" than others. The less acculturated groups performed more poorly than the more acculturated groups. Researchers argue that this discrepancy reflects a bias in the test.

If at all possible, make sure whoever constructed the instrument you use has tested the instrument for validity. Otherwise, you will not know whether your results are representative.

4. A sample must be obtained using *a reliable instrument.*
In addition to validity, a scientific instrument must be structured so that it measures the relevant information *accurately*. Imagine a tire gauge that gives you dramatically different readings despite little change in your tire. The gauge is measuring what it claims to measure (air pressure), so it is valid. But it is not measuring it accurately, so the gauge is not reliable.

Many factors affect the reliability of an instrument. For instance, psychologists have learned that, in some cases, the order in which certain questions are asked on surveys affects responses—a phenomenon known as **ordering bias**. Imagine you were given a survey with the following two questions:

1. Do you reject abortion in all circumstances?
2. Is it permissible to abort if both the mother and fetus will die unless the fetus is aborted?

It is easy to think that a pro-life advocate might answer "yes" to both questions when presented in this order. But it is also easy to see how the same pro-life advocate might give different answers if the question order were reversed:

1. **Is it permissible to abort if both the mother and fetus will die unless the fetus is aborted?**
2. **Do you reject abortion in all circumstances?**

In this case, when the survey participant gets to question 2, he has just considered the case in question 1. Because of this, he might answer question 2 differently than if he had not considered the case. He might not reject abortion in *every conceivable case.*

To overcome ordering bias, researchers construct a series of different surveys, where the questions are presented in different orders. If the sample is large enough, the ordering bias will cancel out. There are a number of biases that affect testing, including, but not limited to: **confirmation bias** (unintentionally choosing data that favors the result you want); **cultural bias** (wording questions so that only native speakers or members of a certain economic class can respond accurately); and the **framing bias** (asking questions too narrowly or in a closed-ended way, e.g., "Have you stopped beating your wife?").

If at all possible, make sure whoever constructed the instrument you use has taken measures to mitigate these biases. Otherwise, you will not know whether your results are representative.

One further warning: Notice in examples *G* through *I* that the conclusion does not claim more for the population than the premises do for the sample. For example, the premise "most 35-year-old test subjects" implies something about "*most* 35-year-old males," not about "*all* 35-year-old males." Similarly, the premise "75% of 300 Labour Party members" implies something about "75% of all Labour Party members," not about "*all* Labour Party members." A conclusion that generalizes beyond what is permitted in the premises also commits the fallacy of hasty generalization.

8.5. Statistical errors

Often you will see a statistic followed by "±3%" or "±1.5%" or the words "plus or minus x percentage points":

> Percentage of Americans who approve of Congress's decision on the latest bill: 52%, ±3.2.

Interviews with 1,030 adult Americans, including 953 registered voters, conducted by telephone by Opinion Research Corporation on March 19–21, 2010. The margin of sampling error for results

based on the total sample is plus or minus 3 percentage points and for registered voters is plus or minus 3 percentage points (CNN Opinion Research Poll).

This percentage is called the **margin of error**, or **random sampling error**, in the sample data. It is important to understand what this percentage represents so we are not misled when evaluating arguments.

A margin of error is a mathematical function of the size of a sample. It is an estimate of the possible variation within the population, *given that* the sample is representative. But, of course, sample size is one condition that determines whether a sample is representative. So, if you already know that your sample is proportionate, random, obtained validly and reliably, the margin of error will be meaningful. But if you know this, you already know that your inference will be strong. So, margins of error do not inform your evaluation of an inductive generalization.

Knowing only the sample size, we can calculate the margin of error in a statistic. Here are some standard margins of error:

sample size	margin of error
2,401	2%
1,067	3%
600	4%
384	5%
96	10%

Beyond two-thousand test subjects, margins of error do not change dramatically. A sample of 10,000 has a margin of error of 1%.

But it is important to reiterate that the margin of error reflects the degree of potential variation among the population *if* you already know that the sample is representative, and even then it is only an estimate. It is *not*, contrary to popular website explanations, an indicator of how likely this sample is *representative* of a population. Here is an example to show why. Imagine you want to know how citizens of Tennessee feel about their governor. Tennessee is divided into 95 counties and has around 5.9 million residents. We want a random sample of Tennesseans, so we randomly survey 11 people from each county (for a sample size of 1,045). From the chart above, we can see that this sample has a margin of error of roughly 3%. If we take this as an indicator of the degree of variation in the *population* (rather than the sample), then we should expect a 3% variation in the final job approval of the governor among all the citizens of Tennessee. Now, imagine the counties that house the largest cities (Nashville, Memphis, and Knoxville) double in size, raising the population to roughly 7.3 million. Should we expect the potential variation in public opinion to change?

Consider that it only takes 40 people to move into Tennessee (or better, to disagree with those polled) to change the approval rating more than 3%. 40 people that might have been polled could change a 52% approval rating to 55.7% or 48.1%. So, would a dramatic increase in population affect the representativeness of our sample? It would seem so. Yet, even if the whole population of Tennessee doubles, the margin of error for a random sample of 1,045 is about 3%. This tells us that margins of error are a function of sample sizes and not necessarily population diversity.

Therefore, margins of error tell us something about populations only after we have determined that the sample is representative of the population. But after we have determined this, the margin of error doesn't tell us much. If we already know our sample is representative, we have already eliminated the relevant worries about drawing an inference from this sample.

The strange result of this formula is that it becomes counterintuitive once the sample becomes very small. For instance, a sample of ten people should have a very large margin of error. Yet, if we have ten people, it should be very obvious how to root out any error.

Another type of error mentioned in statistics is called **sampling error**, or **non-random sampling error**. Sampling error is a function of your method of sampling and *does* have implications for the population. A sampling error results from sampling methods that undermine one of the four conditions of a good sample, that is, from having a sample that's too small or biased, or from using an invalid or unreliable instrument. Sampling errors can sometimes be discovered by comparing the results of the same test on similar populations. If the same test yields dramatically different results on similar populations, it is likely that something is going wrong (like a bathroom scale or a thermometer that varies with each successive measurement). Rooting out the source of this difficulty can be costly and time-consuming. The cheapest way to avoid sampling error is to control for the conditions of a good sample.

Some researchers are fairly up-front about the limitations of their studies. A recent Gallup Poll (www.gallup.com) included this block of info:

> **Survey Methods**
>
> Results are based on telephone interviews with 1,033 national adults, aged 18 and older, conducted March 26–28, 2010. For results based on the total sample of national adults, one can say with 95% confidence that the maximum margin of sampling error is ±4 percentage points.
>
> Interviews are conducted with respondents on landline telephones (for respondents with a landline telephone) and cellular phones (for respondents who are cell phone only).
>
> In addition to sampling error, question wording and practical difficulties in conducting surveys can introduce error or bias into the findings of public opinion polls.

The phrase, "margin of sampling error" can be misleading, since margins of error are functions of sample sizes, and sampling errors, as we have defined them, are a function of survey methods. But non-random sampling errors are not calculable in percentages, so we can safely assume this phrase simply refers to "random sampling error," or "margin of error," as we have defined it. "Confidence," often called a "confidence interval," is a parameter used to calculate margins of error. The confidence interval affects slightly the margin of error relative to the sample size. In the chart above, the confidence interval is set at 95%.

In this Gallup poll, researchers remind readers that some biasing factors are always possible. "Question wording" may refer to the possibility of cultural, framing, or ordering bias, and "practical difficulties" may refer to confirmation bias, difficulties guaranteeing randomness, and variation among members of the population. This reminder is helpful to us all; even those of us who teach this material, since it is easy to take statistics at face value.

How does all this help critical thinkers? In order to effectively evaluate statistical data, we should first determine the degree to which they meet the conditions of a good sample (random; proportionate; valid; reliable). We should believe inferences drawn from this data only to the degree they meet these conditions.

8.6. Exercises with inductive generalizations

Exercises 8.c.

Complete each of the following generalizations by supplying the conclusion:

1.
1. We watched videos of 100 politicians.
2. Every one told at least one lie.
3. Hence, . . .

2.
1. We surveyed 80% of the school, and 75% agreed with the class president.
2. Therefore, . . .

3.
1. In the first experiment, sugar turned black when heated.
2. In experiments two through fifty, sugar turned black when heated.
3. Therefore, probably . . .

4.
1. We surveyed 90% of the city, and only 35% approve of the mayor's proposal.
2. Thus, most people probably . . .

5.
1. 65% of the citizens we polled are married.
2. We polled 10% of the city.
3. Hence, . . .

Exercises 8.d.

Construct an inductive generalization for each of the following claims:

1. "All politicians are the same."
2. "Probably all rock musicians use drugs."
3. "I think all professors grade too hard."
4. "You know as well as I do that frat boys cheat on their girlfriends."
5. "Everyone lies."

Exercises 8.e.

For each of the following generalizations, *explain* whether it is non-random, rendering the sample *biased*, or whether it is disproportionate, rendering the generalization *hasty*:

1.
1. We interviewed 1% of Londoners, and the vast majority approve of the prime minister's job performance.
2. Therefore, probably all England approves.

⇨

2.
1. Both students I asked said they would rather have a different lunch menu.
2. I agree with them.
3. Therefore, probably the whole school would agree.

3.
1. Almost everyone I know believes smoking cigarettes is unhealthy.
2. Also, the editors of this magazine say it is unhealthy.
3. Thus, almost everyone nowadays believes smoking is unhealthy.

4.
1. We gave our product to 150 fraternity houses across the nation.
2. 85% said they like it and would use it again.
3. Therefore, probably 85% of people would like our product.

5.
1. This whole grove of ponderosa pine trees has developed disease _X_.
2. Probably, all ponderosas are susceptible.

8.7. Argument from analogy

There are some claims for which statistical data are either irrelevant or difficult or impossible to gather. This sort of claim would answer questions like these:

How do doctors distinguish your illness from the patient's down the hall?
How does an archaeologist determine that a piece of stone is a _tool_ and not simply a _rock_?
How does a historian determine that two texts were written by the same author?

In each case, the investigator relies heavily on **argument from analogy**. In an argument from analogy, a comparison is made between two states of affairs (usually an object or event), one of which is better understood than the other. Then, on the basis of the similarities, new information is inferred about the lesser known object. For example, imagine you have a Dell laptop computer. Your Dell laptop has a 16" screen, 185 gigs of memory, and 3 gigs of RAM. In addition, your Dell has the Microsoft Office Suite software. Now imagine you are looking to buy another laptop and, on EBay, you discover a Dell like yours, with a 16" screen, 185 gigs of memory, and 3 gigs of RAM. Simply given these similarities with your laptop, it seems that you may infer that the EBay laptop also has the Microsoft Office Suite. *You don't even have to understand what these features mean.* From the similarities between the laptops, you infer something about a new laptop from something you already know about your old laptop.

Doctors often do the same thing when diagnosing an illness. Imagine you are a doctor and a patient comes to you with the following symptoms:

- A sudden, severe sore throat.
- Pain when swallowing.
- Body temperature over 101F.
- Swollen tonsils or lymph nodes.
- White or yellow spots on the back of the throat.

Imagine, also, that you have had five other patients with the same symptoms this week and each of these other patients had strep throat. What can you conclude? Given the similarities in the symptoms, it seems safe to conclude this patient also has strep throat.

How do doctors distinguish one disease from another? Imagine that you just diagnosed this patient with strep throat, when another patient comes in with all these symptoms, minus the white or yellow spots on the back of the throat? Do you conclude that the patient *does not* have strep throat based on this one dissimilarity? It can be difficult to tell, because the symptom that really sets strep throat apart from a cold or the flu is the spots on the throat. In this case, you may want to perform a strep test.

Arguments from analogy typically have the following form:

1. Object A has features v, w, x, y, and z.
2. <u>Object B has features v, w, x, and y.</u>
3. Therefore, object B probably also has feature z.

Here are three more examples:

J.
1. Watches are highly organized machines with many interrelated parts that all work together for a specific purpose, and they were designed by an intelligent person.
2. <u>The mammalian eye is an organized machine with many interrelated parts that all work together for a specific purpose.</u>
3. Therefore, it is likely that the mammalian eye was also designed by an intelligent person.

K.
1. This instrument fits well in a human hand, has a sharp blade, a hilt to protect the hand, and was designed by humans to cut things.
2. This rock fits well in a human hand, has what appears to be a blade, and what appears to be a hilt to protect the hand.
3. Therefore, this rock was probably designed by humans to cut things.

L.
1. My old Ford had a 4.6 liter, V8 engine, four-wheel drive, a towing package, and ran well for many years.
2. This new Ford has a 4.6 liter, V8 engine, four-wheel drive, and a towing package.
3. Hence, it will probably also run for many years.

It is not always easy to use this method to diagnose illnesses. Some diseases are too similar. For instance, colds, the flu, swine flu, and allergic rhinitis all exhibit the same symptoms, but to greater or lesser degrees. And there is no test to distinguish them until they get much worse. This is why it is important to monitor a cold carefully, even if it starts mildly. So, how do we know when an analogy is a *strong* analogy?

8.8. Strengths and weaknesses of analogies

Unfortunately, arguments from analogy, without proper qualification, are *notoriously weak*. There are often more dissimilarities than similarities. Even if you can identify 185 similarities between two objects, if there are 250 dissimilarities, it is not clear what sort of inference you can draw. For instance, bears and humans are alike in many ways. Both are mammals (which means both are warm-blooded, give birth to live young, have hair, and have milk-producing mammary glands), both are omnivores, both play important roles in their environments, both are protective of their young, and both are unpredictable when they encounter strangers. Nevertheless, there are hundreds of differences between bears and humans, so it is not clear what sort of inference we could draw about one from the other given these similarities. We shouldn't conclude that bears are moral or rational creatures, and we shouldn't conclude that humans are amoral or irrational creatures.

In addition, despite enormous similarities, two objects may be very different. Chimpanzees are humans' closest genetic ancestor. Our DNA is 98% similar. Nevertheless, we should not conclude from this similarity that humans are chimpanzees, or that chimpanzees are humans. Consider our laptop case again, Dell computers do not often come with software, so despite enormous similarities, we are not justified in inferring that the EBay laptop comes with Microsoft Office Suite. We can see this more clearly if, instead of considering that your computer has a certain software, you consider the fact that it was once owned by your brother. Surely, despite enormous similarities, you should not conclude that the Dell on EBay was probably owned by your brother.

These examples show that some serious weaknesses threaten the strength of arguments from analogy. Two widely-acknowledged weaknesses are that: (1) There are often more dissimilarities than similarities between the compared objects or events, and (2) the similarities noted are often irrelevant to the feature inferred in the argument.

1. There are often more dissimilarities than similarities.

Consider example *J* above, comparing watches and cells. There are many more dissimilarities between watches and cells than similarities. For example: watches are made of metal and glass, are designed to tell time, have hands or digital displays, have buttons or winding stems, have bands, are synthetic, etc. Cells have none of these features. In fact, many things are often different in as many ways as they are similar. Consider two baseballs. Even though they share all the same physical properties (shape, size, weight, color, brand, thread, etc.), they may be dissimilar in dozens of other ways:

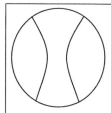 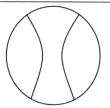

– Was made in China.
– Was sold in a local retail store.
– Is owned by Jimmy Smith of Scranton, PA.
– Was recently used in a neighborhood pick-up game.
– Once broke Mrs. O'Leary's window.

– Was made in Indonesia.
– Was sold wholesale to a professional team.
– Was the winning homerun ball of the 1993 World Series.
– Is now owned by Joe Carter.

Therefore, the key to constructing a good argument from analogy is not simply to amass a large number of similarities, but to identify a number of *relevant* similarities. This brings us to the second serious problem for arguments from analogy:

2. The similarities often are irrelevant to the feature inferred in the conclusion.
Not all features of an object are relevant indicators of the feature we are interested in inferring about a similar object. For instance, considering, again, the analogy between watches and cells, perhaps having a "purpose" or a "goal" more strongly implies an intelligent designer than having interrelated parts. If this is right, then noting that both watches and cells have a goal makes the argument for design stronger than noting that it has interrelated parts. In fact, having interrelated parts may be irrelevant to design.

How can we determine whether a feature of an object or event is relevant to the feature we are interested in? There is no widely-accepted answer to this question. But a promising strategy is to gather independent evidence that there is a *causal relationship* between certain features of an object or event and the feature being inferred.

Consider example *L* from above:

> L.
> 1. My old Ford had a 4.6 liter, V8 engine, four-wheel drive, a towing package, and ran well for many years.
> 2. This new Ford has a 4.6 liter, V8 engine, four-wheel drive, and a towing package.
> 3. Hence, it will probably also run will for many years.

That a vehicle has a 4.6 liter, V8 engine may be irrelevant to whether that vehicle will run for many years. We can imagine a wide variety of 4.6 liter, V8s that are very poor quality. It doesn't seem plausible to find independent evidence linking the features "4.6 liter, V8" with "will run for many years." But it does seem plausible to think that *certain* 4.6 liter, V8s, for instance those made by Ford, may run longer than others. We can imagine gathering evidence that the 4.6 liter, V8s made by Ford during the years 1980–1996 have an excellent track record of running for many years. From this evidence we could draw an analogy between the old Ford and the new Ford based on their relevant similarities, reformulating *L* as *L**:

> L*.
> 1. My old Ford had a 4.6 liter, V8 engine, was made in 1986, and ran well for many years.
> 2. Ford produced excellent motors between 1980 and 1996.
> 3. This new Ford has a 4.6 liter, V8 engine, and was made in 1996.
> 4. Hence, it will probably also run will for many years.

If an arguer attempts to draw an analogy in which there are more dissimilarities than similarities or the similarities are irrelevant to the conclusion, she has committed a fallacy known as **false analogy**. We will say more about false analogy in Chapter 11. Strong arguments from analogy avoid one or both weaknesses. One important way of avoiding these weaknesses is to include a well-supported causal claim in the premises or conclusion. In example L^*, premise 2 is a causal claim; Ford produced (caused, brought about) excellent motors. A second important way is to reformulate the argument from analogy as a causal argument, that is, so that its conclusion is a causal claim. How do we evaluate causal claims? That is the subject of the next section.

8.9. Exercises with arguments from analogy

Exercises 8.f.

Complete each of the following arguments from analogy by supplying the conclusion:

1.
1. Bear paw prints have five toe marks, five claw marks, and an oblong-shaped pad mark.
2. This paw print has five toe marks, five claw marks, and an oblong-shaped pad mark.
3. Thus, . . .

2.
1. *My* mug is red with "Starbucks" written on it, and a chip on the handle.
2. This mug is red with "Starbucks" written on it, and has a chip on the handle.
3. So, this is . . .

3.
1. The jeans I'm wearing are Gap brand, they are "classic fit," they were made in Indonesia, and they fit great.
2. This pair of jeans are Gap brand, "classic fit," and were made in Indonesia.
3. Therefore, . . .

4.
1. Alright, we have the same team and coach we won with last year against the same team.
2. We're even wearing the same uniforms.
3. It is likely that . . .

5.
1. At the first crime scene, the door was kicked in and a playing card was left on the victim.
2. At this crime scene, the door was kicked in and there is a playing card on the victim.
3. Therefore, . . .

Exercises 8.g.

Construct an argument from analogy for each of the following claims:

1. "You have a cold, just like everyone else in the dorm."
2. "I bet you'll have as many problems with this car as you did with your last."
3. "The new mp3 player from Mac will be better than the one that came out last year."
4. "You will look great in that dress, just like she does."
5. "You are going to have a terrible hangover."

Exercises 8.h.

Explain why each of the following arguments from analogy is weak, by explaining whether there are more dissimilarities than similarities between the compared objects or events, or whether the similarities are not relevant to the feature in the conclusion, or both:

1.
1. Our college has a basketball team, a sports arena, and two head coaches, and we're number 1 in the nation.
2. Your college has a basketball team, a sports arena, and two head coaches.
3. Therefore, your college is probably also number 1 in the nation.

2.
1. That guy is 6'1" tall, has brown hair, was born in Tennessee, and has cancer.
2. I am 6'1" tall, have brown hair, and was born in Tennessee.
3. So, I probably have cancer.

3.
1. That object is round, inflatable, white, and used for volleyball.
2. This object is round, inflatable, and striped. (weather balloon)
3. It follows that it is probably used for volleyball.

4.
1. Last semester I took a philosophy course with Dr. Arp in room 208 and it was super easy.
2. The philosophy class Dr. Arp is offering next semester is also in room 208.
3. This implies that that class will be super easy, as well.

5.
1. The last book I read by that author had a male protagonist.
2. That book was over 600 pages and terribly boring.
3. Her new work also has a male protagonist and is at least as long.
4. Therefore, it will probably be terribly boring.

8.10. Causal arguments

You may have noticed that some arguments attempt to answer questions about *causes*:

> What causes paper to turn black when burned?
> What causes a cat's purring sound?
> What causes Canadian geese to fly south every winter?

The concepts of "cause" and "effect" are subjects of much philosophical strife. Because of this, reasoning about causes is one of the most difficult things philosophers and scientists do. **Causal arguments** are inductive arguments with causal claims in the conclusion, that is, one or more premises intended to support a causal claim. A **causal claim** is a claim expressing a causal relationship between two events. Examples of causal claims include:

a. The sun caused my car seats to fade. b. Pressing a button caused the television to turn on.
c. Texans elected the new governor. d. Penicillin cured my infection.

Notice that not all causal claims include the word "cause" in them. As long as a claim implies that one event brings about another, it is a causal claim. In examples *c* and *d*, the words "elected" and "cured" imply that the subject of the claim (respectively: Texans, penicillin) did something to bring about the object of the claim (the governor's appointment, the elimination of the infection).

It is also important to note that just because a claim has the word "because" in it does not make it a causal claim. For example, none of the following "because" claims are causal claims:

e. I'm going to the game because you f. The reason he is pitching is because the asked me. score is so low.
g. She failed because she is lazy. h. Don't cry because you're losing.

The word "because" has three meanings: (i) the cause of; (ii) the reason that; (iii) the fact that. In a claim, if "because" means (i), it is a causal claim. Meaning (ii) is not sufficient because not all reasons are causes. In example *g*, that she is lazy is *the reason that* she failed, but it is not the cause of her failing. If her failing was on a test, the cause may be that she answered the questions incorrectly. Meaning (iii) is not sufficient because it is an indirect way of expressing meaning (ii). In example *f*, the fact that the score is low is the reason that he is pitching. The cause may be the coach's decision to give a young player some experience. Thus, causal arguments are arguments with a causal conclusion, that is a conclusion expressing (implicitly or explicitly), meaning (i).

Once you have identified that an argument has a causal claim in the conclusion, you can begin to evaluate the argument. Causal arguments can take the form of any of the three types of inductive arguments we have discussed already: enumeration, generalization, or analogy. In fact, some of the arguments we considered earlier in this chapter can be re-formulated as causal arguments. Consider the patient with the symptoms of strep throat. Because five other patients had those symptoms and strep throat, we concluded that this patient must also have strep throat. If we think about it, we probably also think that the streptococcus bacteria (which causes strep throat) *causes* the patient to have the symptoms we noted. We could have formulated it as: streptococcus caused these symptoms in other patients; therefore, it is probably causing these symptoms in this patient. Nevertheless, our conclusion did not express this, implicitly or explicitly, so it is not, strictly speaking, a causal argument.

That causal arguments take the form of other inductive arguments raises an interesting question: Why single them out as a unique type of inductive argument? The primary reason is that causal relationships are special. Without noting the causal relationship between the symptoms and the bacteria, we could have easily inferred from the fact that five people had those symptoms plus strep throat, that someone who has strep throat must also have those symptoms. This would be a perfectly good argument from analogy. But we would not, in this case, want to say that *the symptoms caused the strep throat*. This confuses the cause with the effect, but without more information, there is no way to determine which event is the cause and which is the effect.

Causal relationships are special because they relate two things in one specific direction, from cause to effect. We call this one-directional relationship, "asymmetric." A **symmetric relationship** is a relationship that holds in both directions. For example, if I am a sibling to someone, that person is a sibling to me. Sibling relationships are symmetric. An **asymmetric relationship** is a relationship that holds only in one direction. For example, if I am a parent to someone, that person is not a parent to me. Parenting relationships are asymmetric.

Causal relationships are asymmetric; therefore, to evaluate a causal argument we must determine (i) whether it meets the conditions of a good inductive argument (of whatever form—enumeration, generalization, etc.), and (ii) whether the causal relationship is testable. Consider two cases.

First, imagine discovering strong evidence that people who write songs live longer than people who do not. Would you conclude that (i) writing more and more songs causes you to live longer, (ii) living longer causes you to write more and more songs, (iii) some independent factor leads to both long life and writing songs, or (iv) the connection is merely coincidental? How would you decide?

Imagine, second, discovering strong evidence that as coffee sales increase, allergy attacks decrease. Would you conclude that (i) coffee reduces allergy attacks, (ii) allergy attacks prevent coffee sales, (iii) some independent factor leads both to increased coffee sales and low allergy attacks, or (iv) the connection is merely coincidental? How would you decide?

Choosing appropriately involves avoiding four common mistakes that attend causal arguments. These mistakes can affect your conclusion even if all the other conditions for a good inductive argument are met. In this section, we will discuss these mistakes so you will be aware of them, and in the next section, we will discuss some reasoning strategies that will help you avoid them. The four common mistakes are:

1. Mistaking correlation for causation
2. Mistaking temporal order for causal order
3. Mistaking coincidence for causation
4. Mistaking indicators for causes

1. Mistaking correlation for causation

In both examples, you have discovered "strong evidence" connecting writing songs and life expectancy. Statisticians call this relationship a **correlation**. Data can be positively or negatively correlated. In a **positive correlation**, the frequency of one event increases as the frequency of another event increases, as in the songwriting/life expectancy example:

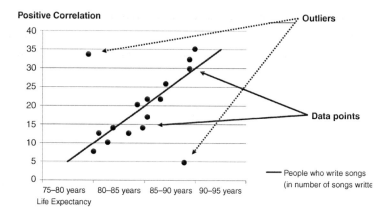

In this example, the data points represent people who write songs. They are placed in the graph according to the number of songs they wrote (vertical axis) and the number of years they lived (horizontal axis). If the data points fall roughly along a diagonal line that extends from the bottom left of the graph to the top right, there is a strong positive correlation between the events. The more tightly the points fall along this line, the stronger the correlation. Of course, even when you discover a strong correlation, there may be outliers. **Outliers** are data points that do not conform to the correlation line. If there are too many outliers, the correlation is not strong.

In a **negative correlation**, the frequency of one event decreases as the frequency of another event increases. Consider the case of increased coffee sales and reduced allergy attacks. If we compare how much coffee is sold each month with how many allergy attacks are reported during those months, we might get the following graph:

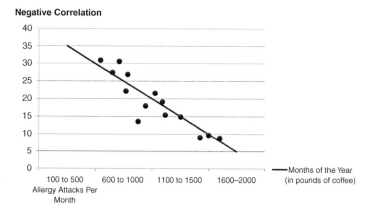

In this example, the data points represent months of the year. They are placed on the graph according to how many pounds of coffee are sold (vertical axis) and how many allergy attacks are reported (horizontal axis). If the data points fall roughly along a diagonal line slanting from the top left of the graph to the bottom right, there is a strong negative correlation between the events. Just as with positive correlations, the more tightly the points fall along this line, the stronger the correlation.

Now, the question is: Does correlation indicate anything with respect to causation, that is, does it help us answer the question about whether one of these events caused the other? Without further evidence, it would seem not. There is no obvious causal relationship between writing songs and long life or drinking coffee and allergic reactions. It certainly seems strange to think that allergic reactions might reduce coffee drinking.

The most that a strong correlation implies (absent any additional experimental conditions) is that the events are not coincidentally related. If a correlation is strong, it is unlikely that it is a function of chance. When we reason about causal events, we rely on a certain regularity in nature, attributed most often to natural laws. That regularity helps us predict and manipulate our reality: we avoid walking near cliffs, walking in front of buses, we press the brake pedal when we want to stop, we turn the steering wheel when we want to avoid a deer in the road, etc. The fact that this relationship seems to hold universally often leads us to believe that two events paired in increasing or decreasing intervals under similar conditions are related causally.

Notice we did not say "paired regularly," but "paired in increasing or decreasing intervals." This is because two events may occur regularly together, yet not imply any sort of causal relationship. The rising of the sun is paired regularly with my heart beating at that time, waking up is often followed by eating, certain lights turning green is often followed by moving cars, etc. But none of these events are causally related. My heart could stop without the slightest change in the sun's schedule, I could wake without eating, and sit still at a green light. Thus, causal relationships are better indicated by positive or negative correlations than simple regularities.

It is true that the problem of induction (see Chapter 7) raises an important problem for assuming the regularity of nature, but the assumption is so fundamental to the way we reason, it is difficult to ignore. For this reason, when we discover a strong correlation, like that stipulated in our two examples above, chance or coincidence (option iv in each case) is less plausible than a causal relationship of some sort. Nevertheless, that two events are correlated does not indicate which, if either, is the cause of the other. Event *A* may cause event *B*, *B* may cause *A*, or there may be some other event, *C*, that causes both. Therefore, a strong correlation simply indicates that we should investigate further the apparent causal relationship between *A* and *B*.

2. Mistaking temporal order for causal order

Temporal order is the order in which events occur in time. A two-o'clock event precedes a three-o'clock event in temporal order. It is true that a cause cannot occur after its effect in time. Rain today doesn't help crops last month, and a home run today won't win last week's game. It is also true that not all causes precede (or, come before) their effects; some are simultaneous with their effects. For instance, a baseball's hitting a window causes it to break, but the hitting and the breaking are practically simultaneous. However, it is sometimes tempting to think that because one event precedes another, the first event causes the second, especially if those events are paired often.

Consider classic superstitions: walking under a ladder gives you bad luck; letting a black cat cross your path gives you bad luck; wearing your lucky socks will help your team win; not forwarding those emails about love or friendship or God will give you bad luck. These superstitions often arise out of our desire to control reality. If I win a game, I might begin looking for some cause I can control to help me win the next game. "It just so happens that I wore my red socks today; that must be it." If I win the next game wearing the same socks, I will probably be tempted to think the superstition is confirmed and that wearing my red socks causes me to play better.

But it should be clear that just because one event regularly precedes another doesn't mean the first event causes the second. This is a fallacious inference known as *post hoc, ergo propter hoc* (after the fact, therefore because of the fact). For example, in typing this book, we regularly place consonants just before vowels. We do it quite often; perhaps more often than not. But even if we do, that is no indication that typing consonants is causally related to typing vowels. Similarly, traffic signals turning red are often followed by stopping cars. But surely no one would believe that red lights cause cars to stop. Therefore, that event *A* occurs before event *B* does not imply that *A* caused *B*.

3. Mistaking coincidence for causation

We just noted that we should not think that simply because one event precedes another that the first causes the second. But what about coincidences, events that seem to occur together in clusters? Many of us have learned a new word or have begun thinking about a vacation only to suddenly begin hearing the word or the destination very frequently. It seems an amazing coincidence that, after learning the word, "kibosh," Jamie began encountering it practically everywhere: on television, in a book, in a conversation at the next table in a restaurant. We have reason to believe that learning the word doesn't cause all these instances. But surely, there is *some* causal force at work. As it turns out, there is something at work, though experts disagree as to whether it is causal. This phenomenon of encountering something repeatedly after learning it or recognizing it for the first time is known in psychology as synchronicity.

Coincidences are a regular part of our lives, but there is little reason to believe that any particular causal force is at work to bring them about. The mistake is in thinking that because some events are really improbable (the probability that they will occur is very low—see Chapter 7), some independent causal force must be at work to bring them about. But it is not obvious that this is the case. Probabilities are calculated either by counting past occurrences of events (on average, boys have performed better in college than in high school) or by identifying the disposition of an object to act a certain way (a fair, two-sided coin will land heads about 50% of the time). These probabilities help us reason about objects, but they do not dictate precisely how an object will act. For example, imagine flipping a quarter fifty times and writing down the result each time. You might discover that one segment of your results looks like this:

H T H H T T H T H T H H H T T T T T T T T T T T T T T T T T H H T

Notice the long string of tails in the middle. Since the probability of a coin landing heads is around 50% every time you flip it, this result is unexpected and the probability that it would happen if we flipped another fifty times is very low. Nevertheless, there is no reason to believe there are any causal forces at work beyond the act of flipping the coin. Over time, any number of strings of coin flips will occur, each fairly improbably when compared with the tendency of a coin to land heads about 50% of the time. The same goes for drawing letters out of a bag of Scrabble letters. Drawing any *particular* long string:

a o e k p e n l d z e n r b d w p d i u m n y q n

is very improbable, though no causal forces need be introduced to explain them. If a highly improbable event can be explained without appealing to extra mechanisms, it is reasonable to do so. This is a reasoning principle known as "simplicity," or "Ockham's Razor," which we will discuss in more detail in Chapter 9. The basic idea is: do not introduce more explanations than are absolutely necessary.

How might we know when a highly improbable event needs an additional explanation? Causal factors become more plausible when low probability is combined with some other feature, say "specificity," that is, something that appears to serve a unique purpose. The following string of letters drawn from a Scrabble bag is no more or less probable than the above string (they have the same number of letters), but there is something unique about this string:

> f o u r s c o r e a n d s e v e n y e a r s a g o

In this case, the string appears to have a purpose that the former string does not, namely to communicate in English the first six words of the Gettysburg Address. If we drew these letters in this order from the Scrabble bag, we should probably suspect that something fishy has happened.

Mistaking coincidence for causation has been motivated a host of new age religious ideas that seek to explain coincidence in terms of supernatural causal forces. We found the following paragraph from www.crystalinks.com using a random online search for "synchronicity":

> We have all heard the expression, "There are no accidents." This is true. All that we experience is by design, and what we attract to our physical world. There are no accidents just synchronicity wheels, the wheels of time or karma, wheels within wheels, sacred geometry, the evolution of consciousness in the alchemy of time.

Unfortunately, this set of claims was not followed by a philosophical or scientific justification. The idea seems to be that just noticing the "coincidences" in nature will help you achieve some higher spiritual consciousness. However, if our arguments above are correct, and there is good evidence for thinking that coincidence does *not* imply causation, this paragraph is nonsense.

4. Mistaking indicators for causes
Finally, there is a mistake that even the most competent researcher can make. It is possible to find a feature of an event that does not seem an

arbitrary correlation, doesn't simply precede another, and isn't mere coincidence, but is still irrelevant to the effect in question. This means that, even if a feature of an event is an *indicator* of an effect, it is not a *cause* of the effect.

For example, imagine researchers develop a drug intended to lower blood pressure. Because the pill happens to be rather large, in producing this drug for experiment, the designers coat the drug with a material derived from apple skins in order to make the pill easier to swallow. Three months later, the results of the experiments reveal that taking the drug is strongly correlated with lower blood-pressure. Various measures were taken to narrow the causal process to the pill, so the results are not merely correlation; taking the drug does not merely precede low blood pressure, and the results are not merely coincidental. Yet, when produced, the drug's success is deplorable. Further investigation reveals that the only difference is that the new manufacturer used a different coating for the pill. As it turns out, the coating derived from apples, was the relevant causal feature of the pill, not the drug it was used to coat.

This is an extreme case, but the point is that, even under the best conditions, it is possible to fix on irrelevant features of events that are strong indicators of particular effects. Often these events have an independent common cause that, with a little effort, can be discovered. For instance, if we discover that, every year, ice cream sales increase as crime increases. Even if we identified a strong correlation between these events, it would seem odd to label one as the cause of the other. Perhaps it is an increase in temperature that sets off the criminal mind as well as the urge for Rocky Road. The best way to avoid this mistake is to control for as many features of an event as our resources will allow us. We will discuss how this is done in greater detail in the next chapter.

If any of these four mistakes are made, the arguer has committed a fallacy known as **false cause**. Though the conclusion is a causal claim, the premises are not sufficient to support that claim strongly. We'll say more about this fallacy in Chapter 11. In order to avoid making any of these mistakes, we need a systematic method of detecting causes. Thankfully, others have done the hard work for us, and there are a handful of tools we can use to test causal claims. We will explore the most common of these in the next chapter, beginning with a brief introduction to scientific explanation, then introducing formal and informal scientific experiments.

8.11. Exercises with causal arguments

Exercises 8.i.

Complete each of the following arguments by supplying a causal claim for the conclusion:

1.
1. I have released this pen 750 times.
2. Every time, it has fallen to the floor.
3. Thus, . . .

2.
1. As I press the gas pedal on my truck, it accelerates.
2. As I release the gas pedal, the truck decelerates.
3. Therefore, . . .

3.
1. In the past, when I thought about raising my arm, it raised.
2. So, . . .

4.
1. On the mornings I drink coffee, I am more awake than on the mornings I drink nothing.
2. Similarly, on the mornings I drink black tea, I am more awake than on the morning I drink nothing.
3. But on the mornings I drink milk, I am not more awake than drinking nothing.
4. Therefore, . . .

5.
1. The label says gingko biloba increases energy.
2. I have taken gingko biloba every day for two months.
3. I notice no increase in energy.
4. Thus, . . .

Exercises 8.j.

Construct a causal argument for each of the following claims. Come up with imaginary evidence if you need to, but make sure it is relevant to the conclusion. You may construct it as an enumerative induction, generalization, or analogy, but be sure there is a causal claim in the conclusion.

1. Turning the ignition on my car causes the engine to start.
2. Taking aspirin cures my headache.
3. Just seeing me causes my dog to get happy.
4. Drinking coffee makes my heart race.
5. As a bee moves from flower to flower, it pollinates the flowers.

Exercises 8.k.

Explain the mistake made in each of the following arguments, by explaining whether the argument:

1. **Mistakes correlation for causation**
2. **Mistakes temporal order for causal order**
3. **Mistakes coincidence for causation**
4. **Mistakes indicators for causes**

or any combination of the four.

1.
1. Every time I have worn this ring, my choir performances are excellent.
2. Therefore, this ring is responsible for my excellent performances.
(So, I'm definitely wearing this ring during the next performance.)

2.
1. I always get nervous just before I go on stage.
2. So, nervousness causes me to perform publically.
(In that case, I should definitely stop getting nervous, so I won't have to perform.)

3.
1. That girl is here at the library every time I come in.
2. She must be interested in me.

4.
1. The last three times I played golf, my knee has hurt.
2. And today, while playing golf, my knee is hurting.
3. Golf must cause knee problems.

5.
1. As it turns out, people who write a will tend to live longer.
2. Hence, writing a will leads to long life.
(So, if you want to live longer, you should probably write a will.)

6.
1. Acne increases significantly from age 10 to age 15.
2. So, aging must cause acne.

7.
1. Every time Dr. Watson teaches a class, someone fails.
2. Therefore, Dr. Watson's teaching leads to failures.

8.
1. I see the same woman at the traffic light on my way to work every morning.
2. Therefore, fate has determined that we should be together.

9.
1. Every time I let the dog out, he uses the bathroom.
2. So, maybe if I stop letting him out, he'll stop using the bathroom.

10.
1. Interestingly, religious belief seems to decline with the number of academic degrees a person has.
2. Thus, education causes atheism and agnosticism.

Real-Life Example 1: The Ouija Board

a. Consider the following case: Two girls, Brittany and Chloe, are playing with a Ouija board. Chloe asks whether she will get into a good college. The girls place their hands on the planchette and concentrate. Surprisingly, the planchette seems to move on its own, directing the girls' hands to "Yes" on the board. Chloe sighs with relief, concluding that she will, in fact, get into a good college.

- Give reasons for thinking this may not be a case of supernatural causation.

b. Consider this modification of the previous case: Instead of asking about colleges, Chloe asks the name of the boy she will marry. Again, they place their hands on the planchette and concentrate. The planchette begins moving over the letters on the board, spelling out B-R-A-D. Chloe blushes. As it turns out, there happens to be a boy in her school she likes named Brad. On this evidence, she begins thinking about how to ask him to take her to the prom.

- Give reasons for thinking this may not be a case of supernatural causation. What else might explain these eerie results?

Real-Life Example 2: Horoscopes

a. Consider the following case: Thomas, an Aquarius, read in his horoscope today that he will discover romance in an unexpected place at work. When Thomas got to work he suddenly realized how attractive his boss's secretary is. He thought, "I'd never considered her before. My horoscope must be right!"

- Explain the problem or problems with Thomas's causal argument.

b. Consider this modification of the previous case: After realizing his attraction for his boss's secretary, Thomas wants to gather a bit more evidence before he concludes his horoscope is correct. So, he conducts an informal survey of the people in his office building. He asks: "Has your horoscope ever accurately predicted a significant change in your life?" Of the 52 people he asked, only 40 read their horoscopes. Of these 40, 35% (14 people) said yes. Given that this is significantly less than 50%, Thomas concludes that horoscopes are an unreliable source of evidence.

- Explain the problem or problems with Thomas's generalization.

c. Consider one further modification: Thomas does not let this low percentage dissuade him. He goes back to each of the 14 yes's and asks a further question: "What significant change was predicted?" As it turns out, each answer had to do with a romantic relationship. Thomas then draws an analogy between these cases and his own and reasons: "Each of these accurate predictions was about a romantic relationship; my prediction was about a romantic relationship. Therefore, the horoscope is probably reliable when it comes to romance."

- Explain the problem or problems with Thomas's argument from analogy.

Experiment and Inference to the Best Explanation

9

9.1. Testing causal claims

Causal claims are often used to answer "why" questions about reality. Why does the sun appear to rise every morning? Why do chameleons change colors? etc. In the last chapter, we explained how causal claims can be supported using three forms of inductive argument: enumeration, generalization, and analogy. But we also highlighted an important problem for causal claims. Even if an inductive argument for a causal claim is strong, we may still mistake irrelevant factors (e.g., correlation, temporal order, coincidence, and indicators) for causal factors. Even good inductive arguments cannot always help us reliably identify relevant causes.

To remedy this problem, philosophers and scientists have devised a number of clever methods of identifying causes and distinguishing them from irrelevant events, and the foremost strategy is the "experiment." An **experiment** is a method of testing causal claims by holding certain features of an event fixed (the controls), observing any changes that might result from another feature of the event (the variable), and reasoning inductively from the results to a conclusion about the cause. Experiments may be scientific, conducted in labs, using a variety of physical instruments. They may also be philosophical, or "thought experiments," conducted using hypothetical examples and case-studies. The results of scientific experiments are evaluated using our sense faculties, while the results of thought experiments are evaluated using our intuitions about the rules of logic and mathematics to evaluate the possibility or impossibility of a particular claim. These results are then formulated into claims, to be used as evidence in an argument.

Both scientific and thought experiments can be "formal," in which extensive care is taken to control for and reduce bias. Both can also be "informal," in which, either because less evidence is available or because gathering evidence would be impractical, philosophers and scientists use a series of heuristics, or rules-of-thumb, to eliminate less plausible causal claims and to increase our confidence in either one causal claim or a small pool of causal claims.

9.2. The structure of an experiment

Imagine coming across some event you want to better understand. It may be the schedule of ocean tides, the phases of the moon, the changing colors of a chameleon, your little sister's choice in boyfriends, whatever. Let's label whatever it is, **O**, for "observation." In order to understand *why* O occurs, you will need to devise some claim or set of claims that, *if true*, would account for O (that is, it would tell us *why* O is true). We call a claim or set of claims that accounts for O an **explanation** of O.

There are a variety of discussions about the conditions necessary for a good explanation. Do explanations require premises about natural laws? Are all explanations "causal"? Must explanations be formulated as arguments? Are all explanations probabilistic or are some deductive? These and a host of other questions occupy many pages in philosophy journals. In this section, we will introduce you to the basics of explanation, offer a simple set of models for testing explanations, and then explain the most common types of formal and informal experiments that apply these models. In the following sections, we will highlight a problem that sometimes arises on this approach and a strategy for overcoming this problem known as "inference to the best explanation."

Because of the controversies over the nature of explanation, we will restrict our discussion to causal explanations, that is, to causal claims intended to explain some observation. In order to evaluate causal explanations, we need to set up an experiment.

A causal claim that acts as an explanation is called a **hypothesis**, which we'll label, **H**. A hypothesis, perhaps contrary to what you have heard, is not an "educated guess"—at least, it doesn't have to be. *A hypothesis is a claim that counts as a reason to expect some observation.* If H is true, we would expect to find O. It is *at least* an indicator of an effect, and it may be a cause. For example: why do we find that black bear sows protect their young when threatened? One hypothesis is that animals that protect their young have a better chance of transmitting their genetic makeup to future generations. If this hypothesis is correct, *we would expect to find* lots of animals protecting their young when threatened, including black bear sows. If this is right, the genetic make-up of a black bear is an indicator of our observation, and it also plays a causal role in bringing it about.

The only restriction on formulating a hypothesis is that it must be testable. A hypothesis can be about aliens or protons or hobbits, as long as there is something that could serve as evidence for its truth. So, is our explanation for a mother bear's protective behavior a *good* explanation? There is a classic method of testing hypotheses that will serve as a useful introduction to inference to the best explanation.

If a hypothesis explains an observation, then we can organize our hypothesis and observation in the following argument form:

The Simple Model of Confirmation	The Simple Model of Disconfirmation
1. If H, then O.	1. If H, then O.
2. O.	2. It's not the case that O.
3. Therefore, H.	3. Therefore, not H.

So, if H is the claim, "Animals that protect their young have a better chance of transmitting their genetic makeup to future generations," and O is the claim, "Black bear mothers will protect their young when threatened," then we can construct the following models of testing the hypothesis:

Confirmation
1. If animals that protect their young have a better chance of transmitting their genetic makeup to future generations, then black bear mothers will protect their young when threatened.
2. Black bear mothers will protect their young when threatened.
3. Thus, animals that protect their young have a better chance of transmitting their genetic makeup to future generations.

Disconfirmation

1. If animals that protect their young have a better chance of transmitting their genetic makeup to future generations, then black bear mothers will protect their young when threatened.
2. Black bear mothers will not protect their young when threatened.
3. Thus, animals that protect their young do not have a better chance of transmitting their genetic makeup to future generations.

If H is true, O is what we would expect to find. So, if we discover that O is true, H is confirmed, and if we discover that O is false, H is disconfirmed.

It is important to treat both models as probabilistic, and therefore, inductive. This is straightforward for the simple model of confirmation, since it is invalid. It commits the formal fallacy of "affirming the consequent" (see Chapter 6 for more on formal fallacies). However, this argument form is useful as an inductive form because it increases the probability that H is true, even if H doesn't follow with necessity. Recall the following clam from an earlier chapter: If it rains, then the sidewalk is wet. If we learn that the sidewalk is wet, we cannot draw any valid conclusion as to whether it is raining. Someone could have turned the sprinkler on, or have washed the sidewalk with a pressure washer. Nevertheless, learning that the sidewalk is wet increases (albeit very slightly) the probability that it is raining. This is because it is evidence that some wet-making event occurred. Since rain is a wet-making event, it is more likely that it is raining than if the sidewalk weren't wet.

Regarding the simple model of disconfirmation as inductive is less straightforward. This model expresses the deductive argument form, *"modus tollens"* (see Chapter 6 for more on *modus tollens*). If the premises are true, the conclusion must be. Nevertheless, there are a number of ways premise 1 (If H, then O) can be false that are independent of H, but affect it, nonetheless. For example, most of us are comfortable with the claim that Tylenol relieves pain, that is, we believe that the primary medicine in Tylenol, acetaminophen, *causes* a reduction in pain. Nevertheless, there are times when Tylenol just doesn't seem to work. In these cases, we would have model of disconfirmation that looks like this:

1. If (H) Tylenol relieves pain, then (O) taking Tylenol will cure my headache.
2. (Not O) Taking Tylenol did not relieve my headache.
3. Therefore, (not H) Tylenol does not relieve pain.

Both premises seem true and the argument is valid, and yet the conclusion seems false. What has happened?

The problem is that reality is often more complicated than our original hypothesis (or even our seventh or fifteenth). There are typically *hidden variables*, or features of reality we weren't originally aware of, that are relevant to our hypothesis. For instance, there may be conditions under which Tylenol just doesn't work. This, however, doesn't mean that it doesn't relieve pain in most instances. There are just a limited number of times that it doesn't, for instance, on particularly bad migraine headaches. Sometimes we can identify these cases and make our hypothesis more precise (e.g., If H under conditions C_1, C_2, and C_3, then O). Other times we must rest content with the probability that it will relieve pain given the vast number of times it has in the past. The problem of hidden variables explains why even disconfirmation must be treated inductively and why many experiments must be conducted before we are justified in claiming that a hypothesis is confirmed or disconfirmed with high probability.

In addition to the problem of hidden variables, there is another glaring problem with our models of confirmation and disconfirmation in the case of our black bear mother. We already knew that O is true. H was formulated for the express purpose of explaining O, so there is no possibility of disconfirming the hypothesis given that we began with the observation. H is not more probable given O just because we came up with it to explain O. Therefore, to increase the probability of H, we must test it *independently* of O. A hypothesis is independently testable if it is possible to confirm or disconfirm it independently of the observation for which it was developed.

How might we independently test our hypothesis about transmitting genetics to future generations? We formulate another observation that would be true if the hypothesis is, which is called a *test implication*, and is labeled I. A similar observation would be that, "Wolf mothers will protect their young when threatened," and another might be, "Opossum mothers will protect their young when threatened":

H
1. If animals that protect their young have a better chance of transmitting their genetic makeup to future generations,

I_1
then wolf mothers will protect their young when threatened.

H
1. If animals that protect their young have a better chance of transmitting their genetic makeup to future generations,

I_2
then opossum mothers will protect their young when threatened.

If the first test implication (I_1) is observed, the probability that H is true is increased. If the second implication (I_2) is also observed, the probability of H is increased even more. The need for multiple, independent tests highlights, again, why both confirmation and disconfirmation must be treated inductively, and why multiple experiments are required before we are justified in claiming that a hypothesis is confirmed or disconfirmed with high probability.

Now that we have identified the major components of an experiment and models for testing causal explanations, we will explain the most common types of experiments that employ these models. As we noted earlier, tests can be either *formal*, taking special care to control for bias, or *informal*, using heuristics (shortcuts) to reason efficiently.

9.3. Formal experiments

Because of their subject matter (and because they often receive more research money than philosophers!), scientists have the luxury of conducting formal experiments. Formal experiments are constructed on one of three models:

1. **Randomized Experimental Study**
2. **Prospective Study**
3. **Retrospective Study**

1. Randomized Experimental Study

A randomized experimental study is widely considered the best experiment for testing causal claims. This type of test gives researchers an enormous amount of control over the experimental process, and, with enough time and money, these experiments yield a lot of useful data.

Consider the following example. Imagine we want to discover the effects of taking Emaci-Great, a new experimental diet pill, over a 12-month period. Researchers decide that, if the pill works, participants should lose around 20 pounds over 12 months. In a randomized experimental study, researchers choose subjects that meet certain conditions to comprise the test population. In this case, they need participants who need to lose weight. In addition, they control for other factors that may affect weight loss by choosing participants from a range of demographics, such as varying lifestyles, diets, drug use (prescription and non-prescription), a range of ages, and genders.

To conduct the study, researchers divide the test population into an "experimental group" and a "control group." The supposed causal factor is introduced to the experimental group, and something innocuous is introduced into the control group. In this case, the experimental group is given two Emaci-Great per day, and the control group is given a placebo, typically a water pill. Neither the researchers nor the participants know which group gets which pill, only the lab assistants keep track.

This type of randomized study is called a *double-blind experiment*. The first blind is that the participants do not know who gets the drug and who gets the placebo. This helps to cancel the *placebo effect*, which is a psychological phenomena that affects some people who believe they are getting the real drug and will get results. In some cases, patients who are given a pill, regardless of what the pill is, experience (to a small degree) the effects they assume the experimental drug has. Administering a placebo to the control group cancels out this effect in the experimental group. The second blind is that the researchers evaluating the data do not know which participants received the drug and which the placebo. This helps to cancel *confirmation bias*, which is a psychological phenomenon in which researchers will conclude that some data set confirms their desired hypothesis, even though the data is quite ambiguous or inconclusive.

The hypothesis is: Emaci-Great causes weight loss. The test implication should be something specific and restricted to the practical constraints on gathering a population. So, researchers might formulate the test implication: subjects between the ages of 25 and 35, and who are at least 20 lbs overweight, will lose at least 10 lbs over a two month period. Plugging these into our simple models, we can see clearly how to confirm or disconfirm our hypothesis:

1. If (H) Emaci-Great causes weight loss, then (I) subjects between the ages of 25 and 35, and who are at least 20 lbs overweight, will lost at least 10 lbs over a two month period.

Either I . . .	**or not I . . .**
2. subjects between the ages of 25 and 35, and who are at least 20 lbs overweight, lose at least 10 lbs over a two month period	2. subjects between the ages of 25 and 35, do not lose at least 10 lbs over a two month period.
Therefore, either H is confirmed and . . .	**or H is disconfirmed and . . .**
3. Emaci-Great causes weight loss.	3. Emaci-Great does not cause weight loss.

The results of the double-blind experiment are then evaluated. If the experimental group lost significantly more weight than the control group, we have strong evidence that Emaci-Great is an effective diet drug. If the experimental group did not lose much weight, or the results are inconclusive, researchers either start over with a new test population, or move on to another drug.

So, in a **randomized experimental study**, researchers (i) begin with a relevant population (in this case, obese adults); (ii) randomly choose a control and experimental group; (iii) introduce X (the alleged cause, in this case, Emaci-Great) to the experimental group, and introduce a placebo to the control group; (iv) observe the groups over a specified time; and (v) compare the results with the relevant effect, Y.

Strengths and limitations of randomized studies

Unfortunately, this type of study requires a lot of resources, such as: lab space, expensive technology, the drug, placebos, researchers' time, lab assistants' time, and participants' time. And since formal experiments depend heavily on how much money a corporation is willing to contribute or how much grant money is available, some experiments are simply impractical.

In addition, it is illegal to conduct some experiments, irrespective of whether there are moral implications. For instance, experimental studies on the effects of marijuana (in most states), firing a gun in public, and running stop signs would violate civil laws even if they were conducted under morally permissible circumstances.

And finally, randomized experiments can raise controversial moral issues. If, instead of a diet pill, researchers wanted to investigate the effects of heroin, a randomized experiment would require that they inject participants with heroin. But there is independent evidence that heroin has damaging effects that can be permanent or life-threatening, and it seems immoral (not to mention illegal) to place participants at that much risk. The same goes for testing the effects of smoking, fast food, post-traumatic stress syndrome, and biological weapons. As with heroin, there are also many legal restrictions motivated by moral considerations, such as experiments that cause pain or trauma. For examples of experiments the moral implications of which led to legal restrictions on animal testing, Google "Seligman learned helplessness," on children, Google "little Albert experiment," on adults, Google "Milgram experiment." If practical, legal, or moral limitations apply, researchers typically choose a different type of experimental study.

2. Prospective Study

Let's say that Emaci-Great includes an ingredient that is controversial in the researchers' country, so the government agency in charge of such things would not approve tests on Emaci-Great. There is another country where the drug is legal and used regularly, but it would cost far too much to conduct a randomized study in that country. So, for practical reasons, researchers choose a prospective study.

Researchers begin by gathering a group of people that meet the control conditions for weight, diet, age, etc., and who also already use the main ingredient in Emaci-Great. This is the experimental group. They then match the experimental group with a group that is similar in control conditions (weight, diet, age, etc.), but that *does not* use the main ingredient in Emaci-Great. This is the control group. Researchers then watch the participants over a specified period of time and evaluate whether there is greater weight loss in the experimental group than in the control group.

In this type of experiment, participants obviously know whether they are taking the ingredient, so the placebo effect cannot be controlled for. However, researchers can let their assistants choose the groups and record the data so that the researchers can evaluate the results without knowing which participant was in which group. This is known as a *single-blind experiment.* The researchers are blind, even though the participants are not. In some cases, even single-blind experiments are impractical. For instance, some psychologists use prospective studies to track the effects of abortion on anxiety. In cases, it may be difficult to identify relevant control groups under single-blind conditions.

The hypothesis is the same as in the randomized study: Emaci-Great causes weight loss. The test implication is also the same: subjects between the ages of 25 and 35, and who are at least 20 lbs overweight, will lose at least 10 lbs over a two month period. If the experimental group loses significantly more weight than the control group, we have strong evidence that Emaci-Great is an effective diet drug. If the experimental group does not lose much weight, or the results are inconclusive, researchers either start over with a new test population, or move on to another drug.

So, in a **prospective study**, researchers (i) choose an experimental group with a relevant set of control factors (A, B, C, and D) plus the hypothesized cause, X; (ii) match this group with a control group that has the relevant set of control factors (A, B, C, and D), but *not* X; (iii) observe the groups over a specified time; and (iv) compare the results with respect to the relevant effect, Y.

Strengths and limitations of prospective studies

Prospective studies avoid worries about the morality of an experiment, since they do not require researchers to administer a hypothesized cause that might potentially harm participants. They also tend to require fewer resources than randomized experiments. Nevertheless, there are a handful of limitations of these studies.

Researchers have far less control over the test population (both control and experimental groups). Participants are not administered the hypothesized cause, so if they forget or take a different dosage or change one of their control conditions (e.g., start drinking heavily or taking other drugs), the results may be affected. In addition, we have hypothesized that X is the relevant causal factor, but there may always be others that researchers unintentionally ignore or just aren't clever enough to recognize that may affect the results of the test. Any conditions, causes, or events that researchers cannot control, but that might affect an experiment's results, are called *confounding factors*. The possibility of confounding factors limit the strength of conclusions drawn from prospective studies.

3. Retrospective Study

Imagine, now, that there are significant moral concerns about diet pills in general. Dozens of people taking a variety of diet pills, including participants in Emaci-Great studies, have developed severe stomach ulcers. Developers of Emaci-Great, concerned that the main ingredient of their product might be harming people, commission a study to determine the extent to which Emaci-Great is linked to the ulcers.

Researchers are commissioned to look back (hence "retrospective") over the lifestyles of people who developed ulcers and try to identify something they all have in common. In this type of experiment, the idea is to start from an *effect* instead of a cause, and, by controlling for a variety of factors, accurately identify the cause.

In this case, researchers choose an experimental group of subjects who both used to take diet pills and developed ulcers, controlling for various other factors, especially type of diet pill (along with weight, diet, age, etc.). They then match this group with a control group with similar control factors (type of diet pill, weight, diet, age, etc.) but *without* the ulcers. They then attempt to identify something present in the ulcer group not present in the non-ulcer group.

In this case, researchers begin with a test implication: many people who take diet pills develop ulcers. And instead of using their imaginations to develop a hypothesis, researchers begin looking for differences between the experimental group and the control group. If they discover an additional, non-diet-pill-related feature in the ulcer group (for instance, the experimental group also took large doses of ibuprofen), then diet pills, including Emaci-Great, would no longer be a moral concern. On the other hand, if researchers discovered a higher ulcer rate in participants who took diet pills with the main ingredient in Emaci-Great, then developers of Emaci-Great may need to pursue a different product line.

So, in a **retrospective study**, researchers (i) choose an experimental group with a relevant set of control factors (A, B, C, and D) plus an effect, Y, that needs an explanation; (ii) match this group with a control group that has the relevant control factors (A, B, C, and D), but *not* Y; and (iii) look for something, X, that appears in the experimental group but not the control group that might explain Y.

Strengths and limitations of retrospective studies

Like prospective studies, retrospective studies avoid the morality problem associated with randomized studies. In addition, retrospective studies are useful when there is no known cause or clear hypothesis, or when a disease or cause is rare. For instance, a person may exhibit symptoms similar to the flu, but also develop fainting spells. Researchers can then gather data from patients with these symptoms and compare them with patients who simply had flu-like symptoms, then investigate the difference in diagnosis or genetic make-up of the disease. In this way, researchers can begin to narrow the possible causes of these symptoms.

But also like prospective studies, retrospective studies suffer from the problem of confounding factors. Not only may there be additional causes that researchers do not consider, for whatever reason, with no clear hypothesis, it is easier to misidentify causes. So, the problem of confounding factors may be even more worrisome for retrospective studies.

9.4. Exercises with formal experiments

Exercises 9.a.

For each of the following causal claims, explain how you would set up a randomized experimental study. (i) Identify some relevant controls for your test group; (ii) explain a specific test implication; (iii) explain how you would conduct the experiment.

1. Eating a bag of potato chips every day leads to weight gain.
2. Regular exercise lowers blood pressure.
3. Taking large doses of vitamin C reduces the duration of a cold.
4. Yoga increases your overall sense of well-being.

Exercises 9.b.

For each of the following causal claims, explain how you would set up a prospective study. (i) Identify some relevant controls for your test group. (ii) Explain a specific test implication. (iii) Explain how you would conduct the experiment.

1. Smoking marijuana causes short-term memory loss.
2. Drinking soda raises cholesterol.
3. Chevy trucks are safer in accidents than other models.
4. Going to church makes you a better person.

Exercises 9.c.

For each of the following observations, explain how you would set up a retrospective study to discover a relevant cause. (i) Identify some relevant controls for your test group; (ii) explain how you would conduct the experiment.

1. My allergies increase when I'm at my parents' house.
2. Chronic headaches.
3. An overall sense of well-being.
4. Students at school *A* score higher, on average, on SATs than students at school *B*.

9.5. Informal experiments

When formal experiments are not practical for identifying causes and evaluating causal arguments (because non-scientists rarely receive funding for experiments), there are a handful of informal experiments at our disposal. Philosopher John Stuart Mill (1806–1873) discovered five simple informal tests for causes. Because of their widespread influence, they have become known as **Mill's Methods:**

1. The Method of Agreement
2. The Method of Difference
3. The Joint Method of Agreement and Difference
4. The Method of Residues
5. The Method of Concomitant Variation

1. The Method of Agreement

One way to explain why some event, *E*, occurs is to identify a set of conditions or events that preceded *E* in a variety of cases, and then to identify one event that is common to each set. If there are a number of events that occur before *E* in each case, but only one common to all cases, the one they have in common is probably the cause. This is an informal variation on the retrospective study;

we begin with a test implication and look back over previous cases in order to identify a cause.

For example, imagine there are ten friends that regularly hang out at one another's apartments. One of the friends, Jan, begins sneezing violently at four of the friends' apartments. To investigate the cause, one of the friends, Brad, sets up the following argument:

1. Brad's house: Jan ate hot dogs, sat on shag carpet, pet Brad's cat, then began sneezing.
2. Dean's house: Jan ate hamburgers, sat on mohair couch, pet Dean's cat, then began sneezing.
3. Rachel's house: Jan pet Rachel's cat, ate quiche, sat on a wooden chair, then began sneezing.
4. Brit's house: Jan ate a soufflé, pet Brit's cat, then began sneezing.
5. All cases of sneezing were preceded by Jan's petting a cat.
6. Therefore, Jan is probably allergic to cats.

In this case, there is only one feature common to all the cases, that is, there is only one event on which all cases *agree* (hence, the method of "agreement"), and that is Jan's petting the cat.

The method of agreement has the following general form, though the number of cases may vary:

1. Case 1. Features A, B, C, and D preceded event E.
2. Case 2. Features B and C preceded event E.
3. Case 3. Features A and C preceded event E.
4. Case 4. Features C and D preceded event E.
5. All cases of event E have feature C in common.
6. Therefore, it is likely that C is the cause of E.

The method of agreement is limited to cases where there is only one feature that agrees among all the cases. If more than one feature agrees, you will need to use method number 3, The Joint Method of Agreement and Difference, to identify the cause.

2. The Method of Difference

Another way to explain some event, *E*, is to identify a set of conditions or events that preceded *E* and a similar set of events that did not precede *E*, and if there is only one feature present in the case where *E* occurs that is not present in the case where it doesn't, that feature is likely to be the cause. The Method of Difference is also similar to the retrospective study; we begin with an implication and look back over cases to identify a cause.

Consider Jan's sneezing, again. Imagine Brad had set up the experiment in the following way:

1. Brad's house on Monday: Jan ate hot dogs, sat on the shag carpet, pet Brad's cat, then began sneezing.
2. Brad's house on Friday: Jan ate hot dogs, sat on the shag carpet, but did not begin sneezing.
3. <u>Jan began sneezing only after she pet the cat.</u>
4. Therefore, it is likely that Jan is allergic to cats.

In the case, there is only one feature different between the days Jan visited Brad, that is, there is only one feature on which the cases disagree (hence, the method of "disagreement"), and that is her petting his cat. Therefore, petting the cat is probably the cause.

The method of disagreement has the following general form, though, again, the number of cases may vary:

1. Case 1. Features A, B, and C preceded event E.
2. Case 2. Features A and B did not precede event E.
3. <u>Event E occurred only when C was present.</u>
4. Therefore, it is likely that C is the cause of E.

Like the Method of Agreement, the Method of Difference is limited to arguments where, when *E* is absent, there is only one feature that disagrees with cases where *E* is present. If more than one feature disagrees, you will need to use method number 3, to which we now turn.

3. The Joint Method of Agreement and Difference

When more than one feature of a case agrees or disagrees prior to some event *E*, it is helpful to combine the methods of agreement and disagreement. In order to explain some event, *E*, identify a set of cases in which multiple conditions or events precede *E*. If one event is present in cases where *E* occurs and absent in cases where E does not occur, that event is probably the cause of *E*.

Imagine things had happened slightly differently with Jan's sneezing. Let's say she began sneezing at the first two apartments, but not at the second two, and that the meals were similar. Brad could have set up the following informal experiment:

1. Brad's house: Jan ate hot dogs, sat on shag carpet, pet Brad's cat, then began sneezing.
2. Dean's house: Jan ate hot dogs, sat on mohair couch, pet Dean's cat, then began sneezing.
3. Rachel's house: Jan ate quiche, sat on a wooden chair, and didn't sneeze.
4. Brit's house: Jan ate hot dogs, sat on shag carpet, and didn't sneeze.
5. All cases of sneezing were preceded by Jan's petting a cat.
6. <u>In cases where Jan didn't pet a cat, Jan didn't sneeze.</u>
7. Therefore, Jan is probably allergic to cats.

This example is slightly trickier. Notice that we need both premises 5 and 6 in order to conclude that petting the cat caused the sneezing. This is because eating hot dogs was also present in both cases of sneezing. So, to conclude the relevant feature is the cat and not the hot dog, we need a premise that eliminates hot dogs. Premise 6 does this because it was also present in premise 4, but did not precede sneezing. Similarly, sitting on shag carpet preceded sneezing in one case, but not in another. The only event that occurred when sneezing was present and did not occur when sneezing was absent was Jan's petting the cat.

The Joint Method of Agreement and Disagreement has the following general form, though the number of cases may vary:

1. Case 1. Features A, B, and C preceded event E.
2. Case 2. Features A, C, and D preceded event E.
3. Case 3. Features A and B did not precede event E.
4. Case 4. Features B and D did not precede event E.
5. All cases of E were preceded by C.
6. <u>In cases where C was not present, E was not present.</u>
7. Therefore, it is likely that C is the cause of E.

4. The Method of Concomitant Variation

In some cases, causes come in greater or lesser frequencies, so it is not easy to identify a specific cause from a set of events. For instance, a drink with a small amount of caffeine may increase alertness only a small degree, while the same drink a large amount of caffeine may increase alertness to the point of jitteriness. In this case, all the same features are present in all cases, only the amount of caffeine varies. In order to overcome this problem and identify the relevant cause of *E*, hold all but one of the conditions or events fixed, vary the frequency of the remaining condition or event, then evaluate the corresponding frequency of *E*.

This is an informal variation on the randomized experimental study. We control for as many features as possible, and treat one of the events as a hypothesis, varying its frequency in order to evaluate its effects on the test implication, *E*.

Imagine that every time Jan visits Brad's house she eats hot dogs, sits on his shag carpet, pets the cat, and sneezes. But sometimes she sneezes much more often than others. What explains the difference in frequency of the sneezes? Brad could set up the following experiment to identify the cause:

1. Brad's house on Monday: Jan eats 1 hot dog, sits on the shag carpet for 15 minutes, pets the cat twice, and sneezes four times.
2. Brad's house on Tuesday: Jan eats 4 hot dogs, sits on the shag carpet for 30 minutes, pets the cat twice, and sneezes four times.
3. Brad's house on Wednesday: Jan eats 1 hot dog, sits on the shag carpet for 20 minutes, pets the cat four times, and sneezes ten times.
4. Brad's house on Thursday: Jan eats 4 hot dogs, sits on the shag carpet for 30 minutes, doesn't pet the cat, and doesn't sneeze.
5. As the frequency of eating hot dogs or sitting on the carpet changes, the frequency of E remains constant.
6. As the frequency of petting the cat increases, the frequency of the sneezes increases.
7. As the frequency of petting the cat decreases, the frequency of the sneezes decreases.
8. Therefore, the frequency changes in sneezing is caused by the frequency changes in petting the cat.

This example is more complicated, but if you read through it closely, you will see that, even though the frequency of eating hot dogs or sitting on the carpet goes down, the sneezing either remains the same or increases. However, the frequency of the sneezing goes up or down as the frequency of petting the cat goes up or down. This allows us to identify the cat as the cause, even though both of the other events were present in all cases.

The Method of Concomitant Variation has the following general form:

1. Features A, B, and C precede event E.
2. As the frequency of B and C are increased or decreased, the frequency of E remains constant.
3. As the frequency of A increases, the frequency of E increases.
4. As the frequency of A decreases, the frequency of E decreases.
5. Therefore, variations in E are probably caused by variations in A.

It is important that both premises 3 and 4 are present. This is because *E* may increase or decrease independently of *A*, *B*, or *C*, in which case, the increase in frequency of both *A* and *E* may be mere coincidence. But if an increase or decrease in the frequency of *E* corresponds to an increase or decrease in the frequency of *A* (they vary "concomitantly"), then it is more likely that *A* causes *E* than that the correspondence is merely coincidental.

Though this is a more complicated argument form to explain, examples of concomitant variation abound. If a funny noise that your car is making gets louder as you press the gas and quieter as you release the gas, it is likely that there is a problem with the engine (or other component of the powertrain system), as opposed to a problem with a wheel or the battery or the fan, all of which operate independently of the gas pedal. Similarly, if an allergic reaction becomes more severe the more shellfish you eat, you are probably allergic to shellfish. And finally, if the academic quality of a school decreases as the population increases, it is likely that overcrowding is affecting the school's educational mission.

5. The Method of Residues

Sometimes an event is complex, and various features of that event have different causes. For example, the words on the page you are reading are a product of at least four groups: the authors, the editors, and the person who types the manuscript for print. Therefore, if there is a mistake in the content, it could be caused by any one of the three (though we poor authors always take the blame). If you discover a mistake and learn that it was not in the original manuscript given to the editor (which it probably would be in our case), and that it was not in the copy given to the person who types the manuscript for print, then the mistake was most likely caused by the last person in that chain. This is an example of the **method of residues**—identify all possible causes, eliminate those that didn't play a role in this case, and conclude that the cause or causes remaining are most likely responsible for the observation.

There is also another way to use the method of residues. Sometimes an event can be explained by multiple causes. If this is the case, it is important to have a test that will help us identify the right cause in a given case. For example, lung cancer can be caused by a number of events, including smoking, being around smokers, breathing coal dust, and genetics. If someone has lung cancer, we can attempt to identify which causes are present and which are absent. If we learn that lung cancer does not run in the family (so it is not likely genetic), the person doesn't smoke, and the person doesn't work in a coal mine, we might conclude that she probably works a job where she is constantly around smokers. In this case, like the one before, we identify all the possible causes, eliminate those that were not involved in this case, and conclude that the remaining cause or causes must be responsible for the observation.

For a more detailed example, consider, again, our allergy-prone friend, Jan. Let's say that her allergy attacks sometimes include more than just sneezing; in some cases, her eyes also water, and her skin itches terribly. Today, at Brad's house, Jan develops itchy skin, but no other allergy symptoms. Brad knows that her sneezing is caused by her petting his cat, and her eyes typically water when it is spring and there is lots of pollen in the air. To explain her itchy skin, Brad could set up the following informal experiment:

1. Jan's bad allergy attacks consist of sneezing, watery eyes, and itchy skin.
2. Itchy skin can be the caused by a pet allergy, a food allergy, or grass pollen allergy.
3. Exposure to cats causes sneezing, but not itching, so a pet allergy is not the cause.
4. Jan just ate hot dogs and has had no reaction to hot dogs in the past, so it is not a food allergy.
5. Jan was sitting in the grass earlier.
6. Therefore, the itching is likely the result of a grass pollen.

The method of residues has the following general form:

1. Event E is known to be caused by feature A, B, or C (or a combination of them).
2. The relevant feature of E (or this instance of E) was not caused by A or B.
3. Therefore, C probably caused the relevant feature of E (or this instance of E).

9.6. Exercises with informal experiments

Exercises 9.d.

For each of the following informal experiments, explain which of Mill's Methods is being used:

1. You get sick after eating lobster for the first time and conclude that it probably was the lobster.
2. "Why in the heck are there dead worms on the front porch for the past three weeks I have taken out the trash for trash collection on Monday mornings," you think to yourself as you step over a dead worm to place the trash in the bin located in your driveway. Then, you remember that it had rained heavily for the past three Sunday nights, which you figure brought out many worms, that subsequently died on the porch because they could not get back to the soil.

3. Susan has to weigh her cat at the vet, but the cat won't sit still on the scale by herself. So, the nurse records Susan's weight first, which is 120 pounds. Then she has Susan and her cat step on the scale, notes that the scale now reads 130 pounds, and records the cat's weight as 10 pounds. Which of Mill's methods did the nurse utilize?

4. Al, Ben, and Courtney go out to eat for dinner and have the following:

   Al: chicken soup, spinach salad, soufflé, ice cream sundae
   Ben: chicken soup, mushroom soup, ice cream sundae, coffee
   Courtney: Soufflé, pie, tea

   Al and Courtney both get sick and vomit all night long. Why do you think so? And which of Mill's methods did you use to arrive at the conclusion?

5. Zoe sneezed every time she went into the basement. Her parents tried to figure out what was causing it by vacuuming, dusting, and scrubbing the floors, in various combinations, and having her go in the basement afterwards. Zoe still sneezed, no matter if the basement was: vacuumed, but not dusted or scrubbed; dusted, but not vacuumed or scrubbed; scrubbed but not vacuumed or dusted; vacuumed and dusted, but not scrubbed; vacuumed and scrubbed, but not dusted; dusted and scrubbed, but not vacuumed; vacuumed, dusted, *and* scrubbed. One thing that stayed the same throughout the vacuuming, dusting, and scrubbing events, however, was that the fabric softener sheets (which gave off a strong lilac smell) were present every time Zoe went into the basement. Zoe's parents then removed the fabric softener sheets and sent Zoe into the basement. Finally, she stopped sneezing! They put the fabric softener sheets back, and guess what happened? She sneezed again. They have since stopped using the fabric softener sheets and Zoe no longer sneezes when she goes into the basement. So, from this whole ordeal, Zoe and her parents reasoned that the fabric softener sheets were what caused the sneezing.

6. You worked on your radio by taking it apart, and now it won't work. You figure it was probably something you did to it.

7. There is a strong correlation between the summer months and the rise in criminal activities in big cities.

8. You wake up in the morning with a headache, which is unusual for you. However, the night before you had worked on several crossword puzzles in bed by the dim light of your nightlight. You infer that the headache has to do with straining your eyes while working on the crossword puzzles.

9. When 10 mice were subjected to heavy metal music for 10 days, they began biting at each other. After 20 days of heavy metal music, they began biting each other to the point of drawing blood. After 30 days, two of the mice had been eaten.

10. There's a strong draft in your room when the door is closed. You put a towel at the base of your door and the draft lessens a little. You then put weather stripping foam around the window and the draft lessens even more, but is still there. You figure that the ceiling vent, which leads directly to the space between your ceiling and the roof, is the cause of the remaining draft.

11. You notice that every time you spin in a circle for more than one minute, you feel nauseated. This has happened at least five times you remember. You figure that the nausea is brought on by your spinning.

12. You have been keeping track of the growth of your plants for six years now. For three of those years, you actually watered your plants weekly, and you noticed that

⇨

they bore fruit. You figure that the water is what assists in helping your plants bear fruit.

13. You have two lawnmowers, and wonder what would happen to the engine of a lawnmower if it is used without oil. So, you mow a half-acre of lawn with lawnmower #1, which contains oil, and you mow another half-acre of lawn with lawnmower #2, which does not contain oil. Then, you open up both engines and discover that lawnmower #2 (the one you used that did not contain oil) has engine parts that are all blackened, dented, and gritty-feeling, while lawnmower #1 (the one you used that did contain oil) has engine parts that are all shiny, smooth, and slick-feeling. You reason that the oil is responsible for the condition of the parts of the engine.

14. Moe, Larry, and Curly have keys to the store, and this morning the store is missing $10,000.00 from the register. The money was there last night, however, when you closed up the store with Moe, Larry, and Curly. Moe and Larry left the store with you last night and spent the night in your guest room, while Curly went his own separate way. You, Moe, and Larry conclude that Curly stole the money.

15. How many more studies do we need to perform in order to show the simple fact that the general increase in smoking leads to a general increase in lung-related and heart-related diseases?

Exercises 9.e.

Set up one of Mill's Methods to identify the cause of each of the following observations:

1. "I suddenly feel sick after eating at that restaurant. How could I tell if it was something I ate?"
2. "I think one of my medications is making me dizzy. How can I tell which one?"
3. "There are at least four reasons for my headaches: stress, allergies, head injury, and brain tumors. How can I tell which one?"
4. "The longer I listen to Dr. Arp, the more tired I become. How can I tell whether it is his lecture-style that's making me sleepy?"
5. "When I visit some people, I get really hungry; when I visit others I don't. What might cause that?"
6. "I think your driving makes me sick. How can we tell?"
7. "I know there are three things that could cause that noise in the attic: gremlins, a wild animal, grandma's ghost. Which do you think it is?"
8. "I think I'm allergic to shellfish. Is there a way to test for that?"

9.7. A problem for causal tests: Underdetermination

A causal claim expressing the results of an experiment (formal or informal) *explains why* we observe what we observe. Why do we observe that group *A* lost more weight than group *B*? Because group *A* was taking Emaci-Great and

Emaci-Great causes weight loss. Sometimes, however, the results of an experiment are ambiguous between two explanations. For instance, we might discover two hypotheses, both of which cannot be true, but which are both sufficient to explain the same test implication:

1. If H_1, then I.	1. If H_2, then I.
2. I._____	2. I._____
3. Therefore, H_1.	3. Therefore, H_2.

A classic case from the history of science illustrates this problem well. In the 1700s, experiments on the nature of heat led to a wide array of explanations. One powerful explanation was the Caloric Theory of Heat, which states that heat is an invisible, liquid-like substance that moves in and out of objects much like water, moving from areas of high density to low density, following a path of least resistance. The Caloric Theory was incredibly useful, allowing scientists to explain why air expands when heated, why warm drinks cool when left on a cool table in cool air, the radiation of heat, and from the theory we can deduce almost all of our contemporary gas laws.

A competing powerful explanation was the Kinetic Theory of Heat (or "Kinetic-Molecular Theory"), according to which solids and gases are comprised of tiny molecules or atoms in motion colliding with one another. The faster the molecules collide with one another, the more energy that is expended. Heat is simply the expended energy of molecular motion. This theory was also incredibly useful in explaining the phenomena the Caloric Theory explains.

So, which is the better explanation? For years, researchers didn't know. Eventually, the debate was settled in the Kinetic Theory's favor, but until then, researchers were stuck evaluating the virtues of the theories themselves.

Many were skeptical of the Kinetic Theory because it involved introducing atoms or molecules as scientific objects. Since we cannot see molecules and they do not intuitively act the way we experience heat acting (flowing from one object into another, radiating from objects, etc.), the Kinetic Theory requires a big change in our previous beliefs about the nature of reality.

On the other side, the material "caloric" was no more directly observable than molecules. And the view must be combined with a few extra physical laws in order to explain the motion of some gases and the speed of sound. Nevertheless, these additions made the theory quite precise and was used to make predictions even after the Kinetic Theory made it obsolete.

Now we find ourselves with an interesting philosophical puzzle. We have two inductive arguments, both apparently strong and both consistent with all available evidence. In cases like this, we say that the theories are *underdetermined* by the data, that is, the data we have is not sufficient for choosing one theory over the other. To resolve this problem, rather than looking for additional evidence, we can turn to some of the features of the explanations themselves.

9.8. A new type of argument: Inference to the best explanation

The features of an explanation that help us determine which is more plausible are called **theoretical virtues**. Theoretical virtues serve as practical reasons for choosing one explanation over another. They serve as *practical*, and not *epistemic*, reasons because there are no arguments to show that they constitute evidence for the *truth* of the explanations under consideration. They have, however, led to important advancements in science and philosophy, and therefore have become important to the process of reasoning about causal explanations. Therefore, an explanation with more theoretical virtues is considered a *better explanation* than an explanation with fewer virtues. An argument that concludes one explanation is better than another by contrasting their theoretical virtues is called an **inference to the best explanation**, or an **abductive** argument.

The American philosopher C. S. Peirce (1839–1914) is thought to be the first to name this method of reasoning, but it was used at least as far back Isaac Newton (1642–1726) and philosopher John Locke (1632–1704).

9.9. Explanatory virtues

The actual number of explanatory virtues is unsettled, but there are six that philosophers widely agree on:

1. Independent Testability
2. Simplicity
3. Conservatism
4. Fecundity
5. Explanatory Scope
6. Explanatory Depth

1. Independent Testability

As we have seen, a hypothesis formulated to explain an observation does not become plausible simply because we were able to think of it. There must be some other implication of that claim that will allow us to confirm or discon-firm that hypothesis. An example would be explaining why coffee in a pot is cool by hypothesizing that "the pot is not plugged in." Noting a second time that "the coffee is cool" does not increase the plausibility that the pot is unplugged. However, noting that "the switch is on but the indicator light is not" *would* increase the plausibility of the hypothesis. This is an *independent* test.

2. Simplicity

Simplicity is a very old theoretical virtue that was expressed famously by William of Ockham (1288–1348) in the phrase, "Do not postulate more gods than you need." Ockham took certain arguments as conclusive that something supernatural was responsible for the creation of the universe. He took this to be the Christian God. He offered this phrase in response to those who asked how he knew there was only one supernatural being and not two or dozens. The idea is that, if one is good enough, it is more likely to be true than two or a dozen; the others are superfluous. The fewer mechanisms or laws a hypothesis needs in order to explain some observation, the *simpler* that hypothesis is. The idea is that, if two hypotheses explain the same observation, but one invokes two laws while the other only invokes one, the hypothesis with fewer laws is more likely to be true. Simplicity motivated much of the Newtonian revolution in physics. Newton's theory could explain most observed motion with only three laws compared to the dozens of laws and conditions required in earlier theories.

3. Conservatism

A theoretical virtue that keeps investigation stable is **conservatism**. An expla-nation is conservative if accepting it requires that we change very little about our previous beliefs. Often, new and exciting theories will challenge some of our previous beliefs. This virtue tells us that the fewer beliefs we have to change the better. In their famous, *The Web of Belief* (1978), philosophers W. V. Quine and J. S. Ullian give an excellent example of how conservatism works:

> There could be . . . a case when our friend the amateur magician tells us what card we have drawn. How did he do it? Perhaps by luck, one chance in fifty-two; but this conflicts with our reasonable belief, if all unstated, that he would not have volunteered a performance that depended on that kind of luck. Perhaps the cards were marked; but this conflicts with our belief that he had no access to them, they being ours. Perhaps he peeked or pushed, with help of a sleight-of-hand; but this conflicts with our belief in our perceptiveness. Perhaps he resorted to telepathy or clairvoyance; but this would wreak havoc with our whole web of belief.[1]

Notice that, in this case, we are forced to change at least one of our previous beliefs. But which one? The least significant is the most plausible weak spot. Quine and Ullian conclude, "The counsel of conservatism is the sleight-of-hand."

4. Fecundity, or Fruitfulness

An explanation is "fecund," or fruitful, if it provides opportunities for new research. Science and philosophy make progress by taking newly successful explanations and testing them against new implications and applying them in new circumstances. If an explanation limits how much we can investigate the hypothesis, it should be preferred less than an explanation that does not limit investigation. A classic example of a hypothesis thought to limit our research capabilities comes from the field of Philosophy of Mind.

"Substance dualism" is the view that mental states (beliefs, desires, reasoning) are products of a non-physical substance called a "mind" or "soul." "Materialism" is the view that mental states are simply products of physical human brains. Many have argued that materialism is much more fecund than substance dualism. Since brains are subject to neurological research and souls, for example, are not subject to any further research, many researchers conclude that dualism's explanation of mental states is "impotent" compared to material-ism's explanation. If this is correct, materialism is a better explanation than dualism because it has the virtue of fecundity, whereas dualism does not.

5. Explanatory Scope

An explanation's **explanatory scope**, also called its "generality," is the number of observations it can explain. The more observations a hypothesis can explain, the broader its explanatory scope. The hypothesis that metal conducts electric-ity to explain our observation that a small bulb lights when connected to a battery by a metal wire, also explains why lightning is attracted to lightning rods, why electricity travels through natural water that is laden with metallic minerals (but not purified water), and why the temperature of wire rises when connected to a power source. The explanatory scope of this hypothesis is limited, however. It cannot explain why smaller wires become warmer than larger wires when attached to the same current. It also cannot explain why some materials do not conduct electricity, like glass and purified water. Nevertheless, if one hypothesis has more explanatory scope than another, the one with the broader scope is a better explanation.

6. Explanatory Depth

An explanation's explanatory depth is the amount of detail it can offer about the observations it explains. The more detailed the explanation, the richer its explanatory depth. For example, pre-Darwinian evolutionary biologist Jean-Baptist Lamarck hypothesized that variation among biological species (a giraffe's long neck, a zebra's stripes) could be explained in terms of two mechanisms operating on organisms through events that happened to a particular generation organisms while they were alive. This generation then passed this new feature on to the next generation. So, a giraffe's long neck can be explained by the fact that each generation of giraffe had to reach higher and higher to eat leaves off certain trees. Each generation stretched its neck slightly and then passed on this stretched feature to the next generation. Unfortunately, except for suggesting some principles of alchemy, Lamarck offered few details of how this could occur. Charles Darwin, on the other hand, argued that each generation passed on some variation to its offspring, but these traits were not a result of any particular events that happened to that generation. Instead, he suggested that the variations were random and offered a single mechanism, natural selection, to explain how these variations were preserved or eliminated from generation to generation. The introduction of a single, detailed explanatory mechanism gave Darwin's theory much more explanatory depth than Lamarck's.

9.10. Applying the virtues

There is no systematic formula for applying the virtues. It could happen that hypothesis 1 has three of the virtues and hypothesis 2 has the other three. In that case it would be difficult to tell which is the better explanation. Which virtues are most important depends on the particular nature and circumstances of the observation in need of explanation. In some cases, we might be willing to sacrifice a great deal of simplicity, if the alternative is a hypothesis with great explanatory scope and depth. Similarly, we might be willing to forego broad explanatory scope, if the alternative is a hypothesis with great explanatory power and fecundity. Therefore, applying the virtues takes a bit of creativity and insight. Here are three examples to help you get the feel for it:

Three Examples

O_1: There is a noise in the attic.

H_1: Gremlins are bowling in the attic.

H_2: A wild animal crawled in.

Which of the hypotheses is a *better* explanation of why we hear a noise in the attic? Most of us would not hesitate in choosing H_2, but why? Surely, a noise in the attic is exactly what we would expect if gremlins were bowling in the attic. And the same goes for the wild animal. But H_2 has several more explanatory virtues than H_1. H_1 is not clearly independently testable, since if we checked the attic, it is unlikely that we would actually see gremlins (they are sneaky devils). H_1 is also more complex than H_2 because it introduces beings that aren't normally found in attics to explain the noise. If there is a more common cause, we should choose that. Similarly, H_1 is less conservative than H_2; it requires that we accept the existence of gremlins—something we may not be prepared to do without a great deal more evidence. And it should be easy to see, now, that we could go on to show that H_2 is more fecund, broader in scope, and richer in depth than H_1.

> **O_2: A rock broke the window on the house.**
> H_3: A piece of gravel from the road was thrown into the window by a passing car's tire.
> H_4: A young boy hit a rock with a stick into the window (accidentally or intentionally).

This is a more commonplace example and slightly more difficult. Both hypotheses seem independently testable, both have sufficient scope and depth for events like O_2, and neither reduce our ability to investigate further. In addition, neither introduces any complex mechanisms or additional laws to explain O_2. Nevertheless, H_3 seems to challenge our belief about the direction car tires typically throw rocks and the force with which they throw them. It seems clear that a tire can throw a rock to the rear of a car with enough force to crack a window. But it is less likely that a tire will throw a rock sideways, and even if it could, it is unlikely that it would have enough force to travel far enough to hit and break a house window. A boy with a bat, on the other hand, is not subject to this concern. Therefore, H_4 is more conservative than H_3, and therefore, probably the better explanation.

> **O_3: My truck has a flat tire.**
> H_5: Someone vandalized my car.
> H_6: I ran over a nail or screw.

In this example, both hypotheses are independently testable, simple, fecund, and have explanatory depth. H_5 has slightly less explanatory scope than H_6, because comparatively few cases of having a flat tire involve vandalism. The key difference in virtue, here, is conservatism. Given only the observation about the tire, it is much more likely to have a flat tire because of a nail or screw than because of vandalism. Similarly, H_5 violates our belief that vandals typically have some purpose to their destruction, either theft or wonton destruction. If only the tire is flat, then there is no sign of theft. And a flat tire is far short of wonton destruction. Therefore, because H_6 has more explanatory scope and is more conservative than H_5, H_6 is probably the better explanation.

9.11. Exercises with inference to the best explanation

Exercises 9.f.

For each of the following, identify *both* the explanation *and* the observation being explained:

1. Flowers are able to reproduce because bees transfer pollen from flower to flower as they gather pollen for honey.
2. Voters turned out in droves for candidate Jones because his television ads were so compelling. (Additional question: is this explanation causal?)
3. Of course your eyes no longer itch. Benadryl stops allergic reactions.
4. Geese fly south every winter. That explains why we've seen so many recently.
5. The car is out of gas. That's why it won't start.

Exercises 9.g.

Construct one plausible and one implausible causal explanation for each of the following observations:

1. I don't have my wallet.
2. That police officer is stopping someone.
3. I feel strange after drinking that glass of milk.
4. That meat looks undercooked.
5. My boyfriend just freaked out when I asked him about his sister.

Exercises 9.h.

In each of the following there is an observation and two possible explanations. Using at least one theoretical virtue, identify the best of the two explanations:

1. Observation: This shrimp tastes funny.
   Explanation A: The shrimp is bad.
   Explanation B: It is not shrimp.

2. Observation: The dryer is making a knocking sound.
   Explanation A: The load is out of balance.
   Explanation B: You trapped the baby inside.

⇨

3. Observation: This guitar string keeps going out of tune.
Explanation A: The string is old.
Explanation B: Someone keeps turning the tuner when I'm not looking.

4. Observation: This shrimp tastes funny.
Explanation A: The shrimp is bad.
Explanation B: I'm getting sick and food tastes differently when I'm sick.

5. Observation: An oil spill in Prince William Sound, Alaska
Explanation A: Members of Green Peace bombed the tanker.
Explanation B: The tanker hit a reef due to the negligence of an over-worked crew.

Exercises 9.i.

In each of the following there is an observation and two more complicated possible explanations. Using at least 2 theoretical virtues, identify the best of the two explanations:

1. Observation: "That landscape is represented perfectly on this photo paper! How is that?"

Explanation A: A small demon lives inside cameras and each has the unique ability to paint pictures very quickly and very accurately.

Explanation B: Thin paper, treated with chemicals to make it sensitive to the light of the three primary colors (yellow, red, blue) are exposed to the light reflected from a scene (such as a landscape). This produces a reverse image of the scene called a "negative." A chemical reaction with silver halide causes the negative to transfer (by a process called "diffusion") into a positive image, or, the image you wanted to capture.

2. Observation: "The sun looks like it moves up into the sky in the morning, then down into the ground in the evening. Why is that?"

Explanation A: The sun is a set of four fiery horses driven by Helios out of his palace by the River Okeanos every morning across the flat disc of planet Earth. It lights the sky for humans and animals and is then driven down into the land of Hesperides, where Helios rests the night in a golden cup that carries him back to his palace in the east.

Explanation B: The earth is spherical in shape and spins on a tilted axis. When the part of the earth you are on turns toward the sun, the sun appears to rise in the east. As your part of the earth turns away, the sun appears to descend in the west.

⇨

3. Observation: "Hey, these two pieces of steel get warm when you rub them together quickly. Why is that?"

   Explanation A: There is a liquid-like substance called "caloric" that is warm. When an object has more caloric it is warmer than when it has less. Caloric flows from warmer objects to cooler just as smoke dissipates into a room. When you rub two pieces of steel together, the caloric from your body flows into the steel.

   Explanation B: Objects are made of molecules. Heat is a function of the speed at which molecules in an object are moving. If the molecules move faster, the object becomes warmer; if the molecules slow down, the object becomes cooler. Rubbing two metal pieces together quickly speeds up the molecules in the metal, thereby making it warmer.

4. Observation: "You say the flagpole is 50 feet high? Why is that?"

   Explanation A: Because the shadow cast by the flagpole is 50 feet long. The shadow's length given the sun's 45° angle to the ground plus the mathematics of an isosceles triangle logically entails that the flagpole is 50 feet tall. Given these conditions, the flagpole couldn't be any other height.

   Explanation B: Because the town decided to make the flag pole one foot tall for each state in the Union.

[This one is tricky. Here's a hint: think about what each explanation is attempting to do. Then think about how well each answers what the question is asking.]

Real-Life Example: A Murder Investigation

In their famous *Web of Belief* (1978: 17), philosophers W.V.O. Quine (1908–2000) and J. S. Ullian (1930–) offer the following example of evidence in need of explanation:

> Let Abbott, Babbitt, and Cabot be suspects in a murder case. Abbott has an alibi, in the register of a respectable hotel in Albany. Babbitt also has an alibi, for his brother-in-law testified that Babbitt was visiting him in Brooklyn at the time. Cabot pleads alibi, too, claiming to have been watching a ski meet in the Catskills, but we only have his word for that. So we believe
>
> (1) that Abbott did not commit the crime,
> (2) that Babbitt did not,
> (3) that Abbott or Babbitt or Cabot did.

⇨

But presently Cabot documents his alibi—he had the good luck to have been caught by television in the sidelines at the ski meet. A new belief is thus thrust upon us:

(4) that Cabot did not.

It seems clear that all four beliefs cannot be true. How should we proceed? Abbott might have had someone forge his name in the hotel register, Cabot might have manipulated the film footage, and Babbitt's brother-in-law might have lied about his being in Brooklyn. Construct two inferences to the best explanation. In the first, identify the two least well-supported claims. In the second, based on your conclusion in the first inference to the best explanation, choose a course of investigation.

Informal Fallacies **10**

We have spent a lot of time looking at how to reason correctly. We have also seen how a few good arguments can go wrong. For example, remember that *modus ponens* becomes **invalid** if we affirm the consequent in the second premise and try to draw a conclusion about the antecedent:

Example 1:

1. If it has rained (antecedent claim), the sidewalk in front of my house is wet (consequent claim).
2. The sidewalk in front of my house is wet (affirming the consequent).
3. Therefore, it has rained (concluding to the antecedent).

WRONG! This conclusion does not follow; it may be that it has snowed, or a water main broke below the sidewalk, or a very, very big dog peed on my sidewalk!

Example 2:

1. You win the lottery (antecedent) only if you play the lottery (consequent).
2. You play the lottery (affirming the consequent).
3. Hence, you win the lottery (concluding to the antecedent).

WRONG! This conclusion does not follow; just try playing the lottery and you'll see how much money you waste *not* winning the damn lottery!

Similarly, we saw that generalizing from a sample that is too small does not support the conclusion strongly enough for a good inductive argument—the generalization is "hasty."

Example 1:

1. I had a lousy meal at Joe's Diner.
2. Therefore, all the meals at Joe's are lousy.

WRONG! This conclusion does not follow; it may be that the meat loaf is terrible, but the chicken salad is amazing, in which case it's not true that *all* the meals at Joe's are lousy. Don't be hasty in your judgment of Joe's Diner food!

Example 2:

1. I had a bad experience with a person A of religion X where that person A was a zealot, and my friend had a similar bad experience with another person B of religion X where that person B was a zealot.
2. Therefore, all the persons C, D, E . . . N of religion X are zealots.

WRONG! This conclusion does not follow. Don't be hasty in your judgment of religion X.

In each of these examples, a fallacy has been committed. Recall that a **fallacy** is *an error in reasoning*. The error is about the relationship between the premise(s) and the conclusion—not the *truth* of the premises. An argument can have false premises and still not commit a fallacy, though a fallacious argument certainly might have false premises.

All of the fallacies in this chapter are called **informal** fallacies. There is a fairly straightforward distinction between **informal** and **formal** fallacies. Formal fallacies are mistakes in the *form* of an argument. Informal fallacies are mistakes in the *content of the claims* of an argument—that is, mistakes in either the *meanings* of the terms involved (e.g., ambiguity, vagueness, presumption) or the *relevance* of the premises to the conclusion. Formal fallacies can be detected regardless of what terms are substituted for the variables. For instance, no matter what terms are substituted for the variables in a case of **affirming the consequent**, the form is fallacious:

Form:	Example:
1. If p, then q.	1. If it's a cat, then it's a mammal.
2. q.	2. It's a mammal.
3. Therefore, p.	3. Therefore, it's a cat.

Informal fallacies, on the other hand, cannot be detected unless you know what terms are involved:

Form:	Example:
1. p.	1. In trial 1 drug y lowered cholesterol.
2. q.	2. In trial 2 drug y lowered cholesterol.
3. r.	3. In trial 3 drug y lowered cholesterol.
4. Therefore, s.	4. Therefore, drug y lowers cholesterol.

Remember from Chapter 8 that the argument above is a generalization because it draws an inference from a sample of a population to the whole population—the sample is a set of specific instances of someone taking the drug; the population is every (past, present, or future) instance of someone taking the drug. In this case the generalization is hasty, because the sample size is too small. (There would need to be hundreds of trials before we could draw a qualified conclusion that drug y lowers cholesterol.) But, we could not have known this from merely looking at the argument's form. In fact, we don't even know whether the form above is a generalization—it could include any number of different kinds of premises. Consider an argument of the form above that is not fallacious:

Form:	Example:
1. p.	1. In game one, Ted beat Jan.
2. q.	2. In game two, Jan beat Ted.
3. r.	3. In game three, Ted beat Jan.
4. Hence, s.	4. Hence, Ted beat Jan two out of three games.

The argument above is perfectly good. If someone doubted whether Ted beat Jan two out of three games, all that is needed is to cite the evidence. If p, q, and r are presented as evidence, the conclusion, s, follows. If someone doubts p, q, or r, more evidence would need to be presented, for instance a score card or an independent witness. But the argument, as it stands, is not fallacious.

Remember, just because an argument has false premises does not mean it is fallacious. Consider the following argument:

Example:

1. Most Republicans are liberal.
2. Sam is a republican.
3. Hence, Sam is probably a liberal.

Since the conclusion receives strong support from the premises, the argument is not fallacious. The premises are relevant to the conclusion and they do not mislead you about what the terms mean. You might not know what a "Republican" or a "liberal" is, but there is nothing misleading about the words themselves—they have clearly definable meanings. However, it is not a good argument, since the first premise is false.

Because informal fallacies have to do with the premises actually given as evidence, they are not as easy to detect as formal fallacies. With formal fallacies, all you need to learn are a set of rules about what makes a form good, then if an argument does not follow those rules, the arguer has committed a formal fallacy. Refer back to Chapter 6 for examples.

However, there are *numerous* ways that arguments can go wrong informally. We can't learn them all, but there are a handful that pop up on a regular basis. If we get a good grasp of these, we will be less likely to commit them and less likely to fall for them, and therefore in a much better position to reason well.

In this chapter, we will spend time looking at twelve fallacies and some of their variations. Before we begin, remember the basic rules of argument evaluation. The most important step is to identify the basic structure of the argument—always ask:

- First: what claim is the arguer asking me to believe? This is the conclusion.
- Second: what evidence is being used to support this claim? These are the premises.

These steps must be completed before an argument can be evaluated. Let's begin.

10.1. *Argumentum ad Hominem,* abusive ("appeal to the man/person")

You've heard it said, "Character counts." And this is right when you are deciding whether to trust someone, for instance, in choosing someone to be responsible with your business's money or your parents' estate. You should be able to trust your accountant or your spouse, and for these decisions, character is paramount. If you find out the guy you're dating cheated on his last girlfriend, warning bells should be ringing in your head. Since character counts so much in so many areas, it is easy to be deceived into thinking it affects whether you should believe about what someone claims—but you must be careful here, for a fallacy lurks.

Imagine you are at a medical conference discussing a new vaccine for the flu virus. A prominent member of the medical community, Dr. *X*, has just given a thirty-minute presentation on the success of this vaccine and its lack of negative side-effects. In response, another prominent member of the medical community, Dr. *Y*, comes to the podium and announces, "I had dinner with Dr. *X* last night and he is obnoxious, selfish, and crude. You should not believe a word he says." Dr. *Y* promptly leaves the podium, having soundly refuted his colleague. Right?

Hardly. In this case, Dr. *Y* has committed what is known as the **ad hominem, abusive** fallacy, or "attack on the person." The conclusion you are asked to draw is, "Dr. *X* is wrong." The evidence is that, "Dr. *X* is obnoxious, selfish, and crude." Dr. *Y* attacked Dr. *X*'s character, not the evidence Dr. *X* presented in favor of his results. The truth of Dr. *X*'s conclusions hangs on whether the experiments produced the results Dr. *X* claims; not whether Dr. *X* is a good person.

But character counts, right? So *why* shouldn't we take Dr. *Y*'s pronouncement as damning evidence against Dr. *X*'s findings? We should ignore Dr. *X*'s character *because it is irrelevant* to the evidence for his findings. Claims stand or fall on the evidence that supports them. A person's character is (most of the time) irrelevant to their claims. Someone can be a good accountant while being a nasty driver. Someone can be a good doctor while being a bad husband and absentee father. Look at these examples:

Example 1:

1. Since, Dr. *X* is obnoxious, selfish, and crude;
2. Therefore, Dr. *X*'s findings should not be trusted.

WRONG! This conclusion does not follow; it may be that Dr. X is the biggest bastard on the planet, but this has nothing to do with his findings.

Example 2:

1. Because he's a bad husband and absentee father . . .
2. Dr. *X*'s claims about medicine should be dismissed as faulty.

WRONG! This conclusion does not follow; his competence with relationships is irrelevant to his competence with medicine.

Consider another example. Imagine your postman leaves you a note telling you there's a package waiting for you at the main branch of the post office. In the mean time you find out that your postman is an adulterer with a gambling problem who was just arrested for drunk driving. Does this in any way affect your judgment about the truth of the note he left? Should you believe that there is a package waiting for you? There seems little doubt: you *should* believe it. In this case, his character is irrelevant to whether the note he left is true or not.

Watch out for this fallacy when politicians and business leaders square off against one another. They will tell horrendous stories of conniving, trickery, and ulterior motives. But when it comes right down to it, this is not your primary concern; you want to know whether what they say is *true,* that is, *whether their platform is worth adopting.*

With that said, we have to be careful not to call an argument fallacious when it is not. There are times when it is appropriate to judge someone's character. For instance, if that lying, son-of-a-so-and-so boyfriend, who (you just found out) cheated on his last girlfriend, says to you, "Honey, I've always been faithful to you," you have no reason to think his claim is true. His testimony is not good evidence because it has been corrupted by his poor character. The same goes for politicians when you have already decided their platform is worth adopting, and want to know *whether they will do what they say they will do* once in office. At this point, you've already accepted the platform, now you want to know whether the politician will keep her promise. And that *is* a character issue.

Now, the previously unfaithful boyfriend *may be completely honest* this time; you *don't* have evidence that he's lying. But his bad character prevents his testimony from functioning as evidence; you just can't judge either way. Similarly, if Dr. Y stood up and recited a list of reprimands given to Dr. X for falsifying test results, you would then have lost any reason believe Dr. X's conclusions based on his testimony. Again, you don't have evidence that his results are false; this may be the one time where Dr. X conducted his research properly and published the actual results—you just can't say either way. Thankfully, these kinds of claims can (sometimes) be evaluated independently of testimony. For instance, if there are doubts about Dr. X's character, other experts can at least check his results.

We often hear appeals to character in crime dramas, where a witness's testimony is undermined because of some inconsistency or because some nefarious character flaw has been exposed: "Didn't you swear in your statement that you were in the ladies room during the murder? Now you're telling us you were in the lounge! Were you lying then or now, Mrs. Henderson? Ladies and gentlemen of the jury, I submit that this witness cannot be trusted to tell the truth!"

> **TIP:** So, here's a way to tell the *ad hominem*, abusive fallacy from an appropriate appeal to character: if the person's character is relevant to whether what they are saying is true, then it is an appropriate appeal to character; if character is irrelevant to whether what they are saying is true, it is an ad hominem fallacy.

Some of you may remember that U.S. President Bill Clinton was accused of having an affair with one of his interns, Monica Lewinski. Clinton said, "I did not have sexual relations with that woman." Let's *suppose*, for the sake of argument, we find out he *was* lying and that he did have an affair with Lewinski. Since Clinton is, and was, a married man, we can safely say this doesn't bode well for his character: he's an adulterer *and* a liar.

Now, let's also suppose that a lawmaker wants to convince his fellow lawmakers that a bill that Clinton has proposed should be rejected. The gist of his argument is that, "I have good evidence that Mr. Clinton is an adulterer and a liar, therefore, this bill should not be passed." In this case, the lawmakers should disregard their colleague's argument—it is irrelevant to whether the bill should be passed; it is an *ad hominem*, abusive fallacy. The bill should be evaluated on its own merits and has nothing to do with Clinton's character even if, as we have supposed, his character is nothing to be proud of.

Now consider an alternative case. Sometime in the future, Clinton is, once again, accused of having a sexual relationship with another woman who is not his wife. Clinton, again, responds, "I did not have sexual relations with *that* woman." In response, a lawmaker says, "I have good evidence that Mr. Clinton is an adulterer and a liar." In *this* case, if the lawmaker can produce substantiate (back up) his evidence, we have reasons to disregard Clinton's testimony. However, we still *do not have reason to think he is lying*, but we also have no reason to think he is telling the truth. His testimony just ceases to count as evidence.

You should also know that the *ad hominem*, abusive fallacy doesn't just apply to appeals to *negative* character traits. Just because someone is a particularly good and honest person doesn't mean that what they have to say is true. It might mean that they will faithfully relay to you what they really believe, but what they believe may be false, or they may be in no position to speak on the matter. I might respect a scientist or philosopher as a moral person, a good friend, and a clear writer, but these have nothing to do with whether what she says is true. Her claims still have to be evaluated on their own merits. On the other hand, her credentials as a particular kind of scholar and the renown of her research do contribute to whether I should believe her testimony. Of course, if she turns out to be a liar, then her testimony without any supporting evidence cannot count as evidence.

The difficulties associated with character and credentials are reasons why expert testimony in legal cases is so controversial. A jury cannot be expected to make these fine distinctions without proper training, and of course the legal system can't afford to train citizens for these types of tasks—they depend on your taking classes that use books like this one.

In court cases, jurors typically *assume* that an expert is of good character ("I swear to tell the truth" and so forth). This presumption simply makes the likelihood of anything she has to say, zero (rather than negative, for instance, if you learned she was a liar). Then, a list of an expert's credentials and accolades serves to make her an *appropriate source* of evidence (you wouldn't want a seven-year-old musing on psychological disorders). Given both of these and your relative ignorance of the subject-matter, you are justified in accepting the expert's testimony.

Let's look at three more examples of the *ad hominem*, abusive fallacy. Be able to explain why each one is an example of this fallacy:

Examples:

a. "Senator Edwards has cheated on his wife. So, I don't believe a word that comes out of his mouth."
b. "That doctor is an arrogant man. There is no way he knows what he is talking about."
c. "Dr. Wilson believes all sorts of crazy things. So, all of his arguments must be taken with a grain of salt."
d. "What an idiot! Mark never reads and he plays video games all day long. He is not qualified to advise the state's finance committee."

10.2. *Argumentum ad Hominem, circumstantial (variation on the ad hominem)*

An arguer does not have to focus only on someone's character to commit an *ad hominem* fallacy. She can also focus on a person's affiliations or circumstances. If you attempt to discredit someone's claim by pointing out that they are affiliated with an unsavory group or that their socio-economic status prohibits them from speaking truly, you have committed an ***ad hominem,* circumstantial** fallacy—*appeal to an arguer's circumstances.*

You've heard political pundits like Keith Olbermann make claims like, "It's just another misleading conservative ploy." It doesn't matter what the policy is for us to evaluate this response. This claim does not give you any reason to believe that the "ploy" is misleading *except* that it was attempted by conservatives. "Ploy" is often used as a derogatory term for a "strategy," for instance, to indicate that it is somehow devious or deceitful or that someone is "trying to get one over on you." But, again, the only reason given for thinking it is devious or deceitful is that it is attempted by "conservatives," so we'll examine this aspect of the argument.

Is a strategy misleading *just because* it is proposed by conservatives? Not obviously. The arguer has committed an *ad hominem,* circumstantial fallacy. "Misleading-ness" is not entailed by conservatism nor is it part of its definition. The arguer might point to a long line of deception from conservatives as support for the claim, but that would not tell you anything about *this* strategy. Maybe this one is *not* deceptive. It must be evaluated on its own merits. Consider this example:

Rachel Carson, *Silent Spring* (1962):

One of the claims Rachel Carson makes in her classic environmentalist text, *Silent Spring* (1962), is that certain pesticides commonly used at the time were harmful to the environment. This text is now recognized as a significant contribution to the environmental movement as well as environmental ethics. At that time, however, the director of New Jersey's Department of Agriculture claimed the book was "typical" of the group of "misinformed . . . organic-gardening, bird-loving, unreasonable citizenry that has not been convinced of the important place of agricultural chemicals in our economy" (see Douglas Walton, *Ad Hominem Arguments*, Tuscaloosa,

⇨

AL: University of Alabama Press, p. xi). In associating Rachel Carson with groups his audience find distasteful or unappealing, the director of New Jersey's Department of Agriculture is attacking the context in which Carson's conclusions are presented. It was meant to get people to draw the fallacious conclusion that what Carson had produced was lousy scholarship and/or that she was some kind of an idiot; hence, don't even listen to what she says. Of course, even if he was completely right to associate Carson with this crowd, it is irrelevant to whether her evidence supports her conclusions.

This fallacy is also common in race and gender debates. Consider the following hypothetical interchange:

Mr. Chauvinist: "The evidence just does not support the claim that women are paid less than men for the same jobs."

Miss Feminist: "As a man, Mr. Chauvinist cannot possibly know what he is talking about."

TIP: If someone responds to a claim by pointing to the arguer's *circumstances*, whether race, gender, political affiliation, religious affiliation, economic status or any other situation, they have committed an *ad hominem*, circumstantial fallacy. This sort of fallacy occurs regularly in many different contexts, so watch out.

Below are three more examples. Make sure you can explain why each one is an *ad hominem*, circumstantial fallacy:

Examples:

a. "It is unlikely that Senator Wilkins can really help the poor because he comes from an Ivy League, oil family."
b. "Dr. Perkins cannot possibly know anything about the origins of the universe since he is a dyed-in-the-wool atheist."
c. "Senator McCain's plan to stimulate the economy cannot possibly benefit the working class because Mr. McCain is a Republican."
d. "Mr. Obama's complaint about the rising price of arugula shows just how disconnected he is from his working-class constituency. His high-brow, idealist, Ivy-League values are so far from blue-collar struggles that it is implausible to think he will do anything to help low-income families."

10.3. *Tu Quoque* ("you, too") (variation on the *ad hominem*)

We predict that you have always thought it was just too easy to win an argument by pointing out that someone is a hypocrite. Out loud you might have exclaimed, "Ha! You're a hypocrite. I win!" But in the back of your mind you were wondering, *Did I really get the best of that interchange? Did I really respond to the worry?* In this case, the little voice in your head was the intuition that claims must be evaluated on the evidence, not on whether someone contradicts himself or does what she says not to do. To be clear, the little voice was right.

Anyone who tries to win an argument against you by pointing out that you are a raging hypocrite commits a variation of the *ad hominem* fallacy known as "*tu quoque*," or "you too" (pronounced: *too-**kwo**-kway*). It is sometimes mistaken for the "I'm rubber and you're glue" fallacy, or the Spanish version, "y tu mama tambien," (and your mother, too!). But really it just means, "You're a hypocrite so I don't have to listen to anything you have to say on the subject."

But, this response is fallacious because it has nothing to do with the *truth* of the claim the arguer is defending. For instance, someone who is currently cheating on his wife might present a convincing argument that adultery is morally wrong. Pointing out the arguer's hypocrisy does not affect the likelihood that the claim is true or undermine the possibility that the argument is a good one. You are simply pointing out an inconsistency between the arguer's actions and beliefs. Big deal! We want to know whether what the arguer is saying is *true*—we need some *reasons* to believe or disbelieve *the claim*. Referring to irrelevant information, such as hypocrisy, just takes the discussion off course.

In fact, the arguer may agree with your assessment and respond, "Yes, that's right, I'm an adulterer. And since I believe that adultery is wrong, I am doing something wrong. But the fact that I'm doing it doesn't change the fact that it's wrong." When someone makes a claim like, "Adultery is wrong," a critical thinker does not evaluate the arguer, the critical thinker evaluates the claim and any evidence offered in favor of it. The proper strategy, whether you already agree with the claim or not, is to demand evidence for thinking the claim is true.

> **TIP:** If someone attempts to reject an argument by pointing out that the arguer believes the opposite or does the opposite (i.e., that the arguer is a hypocrite), that person has committed the *tu quoque* fallacy.

Look at three more examples of the *tu quoque* fallacy. Make sure you can explain why each one is an example of this fallacy:

Examples:

a. *Officer:* "Did you know you were going 20 miles over the speed limit."
   Idiot: "Yes, but officer, you had to go at least that fast to catch me. So, since you would be a hypocrite to give me a ticket, can I assume I'm off the hook?"
b. *Counselor:* "I had an abortion and I have regretted it ever since. I don't think you should do it."
   Pregnant teenager: "Who are you to tell me not to have an abortion? You had one!"
c. "Senator MacMillan can't possibly be serious about his proposal for cutting spending. The senator has more personal debt than any other member of congress."
d. "That doctor smokes and drinks. It is unlikely that he can advise you about a healthy lifestyle."

10.4. *Argumentum ad Populum* ("appeal to the people")

Believe it or not, you are regularly asked to believe something or to do something *just because* everyone else believes it or does it. You might think you are invulnerable to this move since your mother exposed you to this fallacy long ago: "If everyone jumped off a bridge, would you do it?" But since mothers everywhere have done so much to foster awareness of this reasoning pitfall, contemporary versions of it are somewhat disguised.

Perhaps you have been tempted to think that a politician is doing a bad job because everyone else thinks he or she is doing a bad job (the phrase, "job approval rating," should come to mind). Or maybe you have been persuaded to believe there are objective moral facts, like "murder is always wrong," on the grounds that every culture in history has agreed on at least a few basic moral principles. On the behavior side, there is a chance you have considered ingesting certain illegal substances since "*everyone* has tried it" (and, heaven forbid you miss out). And you have probably been tempted to buy something just because it is the "best selling *x* in America," or "Mothers in Europe have been giving it to their children for thirty years."

All of these arguments commit the **ad populum** fallacy, or, appeal to the people. Make sure you recognize that, in each case, the conclusion—"I should believe *x*," or "I should do *x*"—may be true or false. There may really be objective moral facts. Some politicians really do a bad job. But evidence that everyone believes something or that everyone does something cannot help you make an informed decision about whether the claim is true.

What if everyone suddenly came to believe that the world is flat or that God exists? Would everyone's *believing* these things *make* them true? Of course not. They are true or false regardless of what someone believes. Since someone's belief about a claim does not make it true or false, you will need a different sort of evidence to make a good judgment about its truth or falsity.

> **TIP** You can recognize an *ad populum* fallacy if the reasons given for believing a claim (that something is the case) or acting a certain way (for example, buying something) are that everyone else believes it or does it.

WARNING: an *ad populum* fallacy is an appeal to a large number of people, not specific groups. If an argument tries to sway you by pointing out a specific group—for example, "Republicans everywhere believe *x*," or, "The discriminating shopper buys *x*"—the fallacy is a variation on the *ad populum* called an **appeal to snobbery or vanity**. We will look at this fallacy in the next section.

But first, let's look at three more examples of the *ad populum*. Note that many of the conclusions will be left implicit. This means that you will have to figure out what conclusion you are supposed to infer from the claim(s). Be able to explain why each is an example of this fallacy:

Examples:

a. *MonkeyTears Shampoo—used by more salons than any other all-natural shampoo*
b. *Reading—everybody's doing it!* (This is from an actual commercial on PBS during a block of children's programming.)
c. "The majority of congressmen, including members from both parties, believe that Iraq is a threat to the United States. Therefore, we should probably go ahead with the invasion."
d. "Everyone in the PTA believes that the superintendent's policies are biased against male teachers. Therefore, we should not reelect her."

10.5. Appeal to snobbery / vanity (variation on *ad populum*)

Someone who appeals to a group of people to justify a claim need not appeal to *all* people or even a very large group. She may appeal only to a select group. It might be a group you want to be a part of or a group you don't want to be a part of. For instance, if an advertisement appeals to "luxury" or "elegance" or something "fine," it is trying to convince you that you need to be a part of a special group, that your are elite or a VIP. The arguer is appealing to your vanity to get you to do something or believe something. For example, "All university professors believe that progressive policies are better for society." This claim implies that you should believe that progressive policies are better for society, since an envied class (intelligent, informed, dapper university professors) believes they are (well, maybe not because they're "dapper").

Similarly, if an arguer says something like, "Only an *amateur* beer-drinker would drink Pabst Blue Ribbon," or, "No one of any *intelligence* would think that gay marriage is morally permissible," he is appealing to your sense of superiority over amateur beer-drinkers or unintelligent people.

These arguments all commit the fallacy of **appeal to snobbery or vanity**. A good argument does not depend on whether a group is well-regarded or ill-regarded, whether you feel superior to that group, or whether something strokes your ego. None of these are good reasons to accept or reject a belief. Be careful that you are not wooed by these tactics—some people *will* tell you anything you want to hear to get you to join their bandwagon.

> **TIP** If an arguer associates a belief or action with an attractive or unattractive group in order to persuade you to accept or reject the belief or perform or not perform the action, the arguer has committed an appeal to snobbery/vanity.

2 WARNINGS:
(1) This fallacy is easy to mistake for *ad hominem*, circumstantial fallacy. Remember, the *ad hominem*, circumstantial fallacy associates a *person* (the arguer) with an *unsavory* character or set of circumstances or group in order to convince you to reject his or her claims. The appeal to snobbery/vanity associates an idea or action with a *savory or unsavory group* in order to convince you to accept or reject it or its claims.

(2) Some textbooks include "appeals to celebrity" in this category. The idea is that, if a celebrity tries to get you to believe something (e.g., if Edward Norton tries to convince you that Global Warming is true), you are more likely to believe it. We take it that an appeal to celebrity is not an appeal to snobbery or vanity, but an *appeal to inappropriate authority* (see section 10.6). This is because appeals to celebrity are typically about individual celebrities (and not the category of celebrities).This is a minor point, though, and secondary to your recognizing *that* appealing to someone's fame or celebrity as support for a belief is fallacious, regardless of how you categorize that fallacy.

Look at the following three examples of appeal to snobbery/vanity. Make sure you can explain why each argument commits this fallacy. Again, you may have to infer a conclusion if the claim leaves it implicit.

EXAMPLES:

a. "Only a religious fundamentalist would question Darwin's theory of evolution."
b. "You should not adopt that conservative economic policy. Only greedy, blue-bloods adopt such policies."
c. "*Lunar Tan*—used by top supermodels!"
d. "Buy ShamWow! Made in Germany!"

10.6. *Argumentum ad Vericundiam* ("appeal to [inappropriate] authority")

Everyone loves to cite research. Advertisements for cosmetics, weight-loss supplements, car wax, and tooth brushes all cite some form of "research" that supports some claim about their product. One commercial for a diet pill actually had a piece of paper in the background with the words, "Journal of Research," written in bold at the top while the announcer explained the "amazing results!" Just after the terrorist bombings in London in 2005, a CBN (Christian Broadcasting Network) News anchor interviewed a guest, whom they labeled, "Terrorism Expert," to explain just how serious the attacks were. Political pundit Glenn Beck said repeatedly over the span of half an hour that evidence of global warming is "false science."

What do all these sources of evidence have in common? They are not authorities on the claim in question. The "Journal of Research" does not exist, so it can't be an authority, and even if a journal with this name existed, it's not clear why it is relevant to diet pills. It could be dedicated to agriculture or horticulture or veterinary medicine—who knows? Similarly, what is a "terrorism expert" and where does one go for these credentials? Would a radical Islamic suicide bomber count as a "terrorism expert"? Pasting these words under someone's name does not establish his authority to inform a lay audience about terrorism. And finally, Glenn Beck is not a scientist, he did not interview scientists, he did not read scientific research on the air, he cited no independent source whatsoever—he simply authoritatively pronounced a claim (made by scientists) as "false science."

To be clear, the diet pill may work, the terrorism expert may be legitimate, and global warming may, in fact, be a liberal myth. The problem is that you, as a critical thinker, have not been given *appropriate* evidence to think any of these claims are true. All three examples commit the fallacy of **appeal to inappropriate authority**. There are two ways an appeal to authority can be inappropriate:

(1) the authority can be *irrelevant,* or
(2) the authority can be *biased.*

If an authority is irrelevant, he or she is just not in any position to speak on the claim being evaluated. If an authority is biased, he or she pretends (knowingly or unknowingly) to be in a position of authority on the subject.

If your physics teacher drones on and on about the deplorable character development in Jane Austen novels, it might be wise to take her opinions with a grain of salt. On the face of it, she is an *irrelevant* authority. Who cares what a scientist has to say about literature? She might be right, but you should look for independent evidence. On the other hand, if you also learn that one of her long-time hobbies is nineteenth century literature, you can take her claims a little more seriously. In this case, she is a relevant authority.

If a representative from the National Rifle Association (NRA) tells you that it is your Constitutional right to own whatever gun you want, you should look for some independent evidence. Since the NRA is devoted to the promotion of firearm ownership, they are a *biased* authority. This does not mean they are wrong, it just means that they have a *vested interest* in promoting certain claims. This vested interest can bias their testimony, that is, it could lead them to exaggerate the truth or mislead you about a claim. This is tricky because it is not always the case. For example, the Environmental Protection Agency has a vested interest in promoting certain claims. However, it is better for them to be unbiased if they want to keep getting funding.

Consider a more difficult case. What if a publication called *The Journal of New Testament Studies* publishes an article on Jesus of Nazareth? Whether it is an appropriate authority depends on what else you know about the journal. If it is a journal that publishes based on "blind reviews" (the reviewer does not know the author's name) and its editorial board is made up of well-respected scholars who study the New Testament, then it might be a reliable source. On the other hand, if all the editing scholars are known to have a certain take on the New Testament (say, that Jesus didn't exist), or that they only publish scholars who agree with them, then the journal is less reliable—it is not an appropriate authority.

Jamie once saw a billboard with Tiger Woods wearing a Tag Heuer watch. He immediately wondered: *Why should* this *make me want to buy a Tag Heuer watch?* He decided there were two possible reasons, both fallacious. First, the billboard might have been trying to convince Jamie that he "should be like Tiger," join an elite club of celebrities who wear Tag Heuer. This would be the snob appeal twist on the *ad populum* fallacy from 10.4: people of a select group you want to be part of believe *x* or do *x*, therefore you should believe *x* or do *x*—in this case, wear Tag Heuer. But then Jamie thought, *no one in their right minds* [snob appeal?] would really think they should (or could) be like Tiger, so he decided this was not the most likely reason.

Second, the billboard might have been trying to convince Jamie that Tiger Woods, being rich and famous, and having access to the finer things in life, has some *insight* into which things count as "finer." We are supposed to assume, implicitly, that Tiger is a connoisseur of fine watches (or at least fine things) and therefore, *recommends* Tag Heuer. But, Tiger Woods is a golfer. Golf is his realm of authority. If Tiger recommended a brand of golf clubs, fine; he's an authority. But a watch? Hardly. It's like Whoopi Goldberg telling us to vote for Barak Obama, or the Red Hot Chili Peppers telling us to *Rock the Vote!* What authority do these people have to tell us *anything* outside of their realm of expertise? The answer is: none.

TIP If someone makes a claim without providing good reasons to accept it, you should be wary. If the speaker is a relevant authority and asks you to believe on the basis of her authority, you might accept the claim tentatively (a physicist speaking about physics; a mathematician speaking about mathematics; a philosopher speaking about logic). If she is an irrelevant or biased authority and asks you to believe on the basis of her authority, she has committed *an appeal to inappropriate authority*. You have no more reason to accept her claim than if she didn't say anything at all.

Consider the following arguments. Make sure you can explain why each is an example of appeal to inappropriate authority and whether the inappropriate authority is "biased" or "irrelevant":

EXAMPLES:

    a. Actor Edward Norton says: "Save the environment. Buy hybrid cars."
[Though Norton is widely recognized as an "environmentalist," he is not an environmental scientist. So, without offering evidence in support of his testimony, this is an appeal to inappropriate authority.]

    b. "The president of General Motors recently said that American cars are built better than any of their Japanese competitors."

    c. "The *Journal of Paranormal Research* says that 75% of people experience psychic phenomena on a daily basis."

    d. The *National Enquirer* newspaper prints: "Monkey-boy is his own father!"

10.7. *Argumentum ad Baculum* ("appeal to force")

"If you don't make better grades, I'm cancelling your guitar lessons for a month!" This is a pretty compelling argument. Not compelling enough, we're afraid. Jamie never took guitar lessons again. Other arguments like this are much more motivating: "Clean up this mess or you're fired," "Now Timmy, a good little boy wouldn't put all his action figures in the toilet." The argument can also be made without words, for instance, when the bouncer at a bar gives you the angry death stare and points you outside. All of these arguments, compelling as they may be—you don't want to get fired; Timmy wants to be a "good little boy"; and you definitely don't want that bouncer to act on his inclinations—are fallacious. They all commit the *ad baculum* fallacy, or **appeal to threat/force.**

> **TIP** If someone attempts to persuade you to believe a claim or perform an action on the grounds that not doing so will have bad consequences, this is an appeal to force.

Appeals to force have been quite popular throughout history, for instance during the Spanish Inquisition, when Jews, Protestants, and Muslims were "persuaded" to recant their religious beliefs by a machine called "the rack." And, more recently, there have been accusations that suspected terrorists have been waterboarded in attempt to "convince" them to divulge certain information.

However successful these methods may be at eliciting the desired response, it is important to remember that the results are not necessarily related to truth. I might agree that my mother is a butterfly who likes bananas if you burn me with a red-hot iron rod over and over. Timmy might be a good little boy even if he does put his toys in the toilet and despite what his mother thinks. Arguments that appeal to evidence that do not support the truth of a claim, that is, for something you should believe or something you should do, are fallacious.

Consider four more examples of the *ad baculum* fallacy. Make sure you can explain why each one is an example.

EXAMPLES:

a. "You'll support what we're saying here, right? You wouldn't want your windows broken, would you?"

b. "Your answer on the exam was wrong. Why? I'm the professor, you're the student, and I'm the one handing out grades here."

c. "I'd hate to see your career come to an end because you showed the President of sales what the Vice President of sales is up to; so, adjust the numbers."

d. "I will let you go. But first I want you to say, 'I love crepes.'" [In other words: If you don't say, "I love crepes," I will break your arm. From the film, *Talladega Nights*.]

10.8. *Argumentum ad Misericordiam* ("appeal to pity [or other emotions]")

Soft music is playing. A dark screen fades slowly into focus on the frowning face of a young dark-skinned little girl in tattered clothes. A fly crawls across her bottom lip, but the child doesn't respond; she just stares off in the distance. Then, a deep but gentle voice says: "For just twenty-five cents a day, you can save a child like Cassandra from starvation." Of course, you and your (football player) roommates are crying and calling your parents to convince them to send money to Cassandra. "Less than two bucks a week, Mom! We can save lives!"

Well . . . maybe not.

Is it *right* that you help starving kids in Ethiopia? Probably. Should you believe this because you *feel bad*? Absolutely not. Your emotions have nothing to do with the truth of a claim. Just because you feel you deserve a new car for graduating, this does not place any moral obligation on your parents to buy you one. Just because you feel bad for criminals serving life in prison doesn't mean they shouldn't be there. Just because you don't like to go the speed limit doesn't mean you shouldn't. Your *emotions* have nothing to do with whether a claim is *true*. These arguments are fallacious because their premises are irrelevant to the truth of the conclusion. The conclusion might be true or false, but emotions cannot tell you which.

> **TIP** If someone tries to convince you that a claim is true by *appealing to emotions, especially negative emotions like pity*, she commits the fallacy called *ad misericordiam*— **appeal to pity**.

Appeals to pity show up in less conspicuous ways than in the starving kids commercials. Sometimes you can find talk shows where "noted" psychologists try to convince you and the audience that kids who have committed horrible atrocities are not *really* bad at heart, they have just had a difficult childhood and poor role models. They try to convince you to "feel sorry" for them and to not think they should be tried as adults or sent to juvenile detention.

WARNING: These cases are tricky because they can seem like *ad hominem*, circumstantial fallacies. Here's the difference: in the *ad hominem*, circumstantial fallacy, you are directed to a person's circumstances and asked to draw a conclusion about his character, positive or negative, which is then supposed to undermine or support the truth of any claim made *by* him (e.g., my dad might the most honest person I know, but that does not mean he is always right). In the *ad misericordiam* fallacy, you are directed to a person's circumstances and asked to pity him, which is then supposed to support or undermine some claim made *about* him (e.g., "Mr. Smith can't be guilty; just look at that face. Is that the face of a stone-cold killer? I think not.").

> **TIP** If someone attempts to defend a claim about someone by trying to make you feel sorry for them, he has committed the *ad misericordiam* fallacy. This also goes for any other emotions, such as "cuteness," "sexiness," "happiness," or "guilt." Cuteness is often used in advertisements for children's products. Sexiness and happiness are often used in car commercials or beer commercials. Guilt is often used in public service announcements, for instance, about using too much electricity, second-hand smoke, greenhouse gas emissions, voting, etc. Appeals to emotion have nothing to do with whether a claim is true, so be careful not to commit this fallacy or fall for it.

Consider four more examples, and make sure you can explain why they are examples of the *ad misericordiam* fallacy.

Examples:

a. "You'll support what we're saying as being true; you wouldn't want us to lose our land, would you?"
b. *Student*: Please re-think my grade.
   Professor: But your response did not answer the question.
   Student: My mom will kill me if I flunk English.
c. "Don't fire Jim, even if he is incompetent. He has a huge family to provide for."
d. "If I don't get this promotion my wife will leave me!"

10.9. *Argumentum ad Ignorantiam* ("appeal to ignorance")

"There's no evidence against extra-terrestrials. That means they're probably out there, somewhere!" Right? Who knows? The lack of evidence against something does not entail anything about its truth. Similarly, the lack of evidence for something does not entail anything about its falsity. An atheist may argue, "There is no evidence for God's existence, therefore, it's likely he doesn't exist." But even if he is right that there is no evidence, this tells you nothing about whether God exists. Maybe God really does require us to have faith without evidence. Lack of evidence alone is not compelling. What's more, the theist could offer a counterargument along the same lines, "There's no evidence that God *doesn't* exist, therefore, it's likely that he does." But both of these arguments are fallacious. Though they may sound interesting, the evidence appealed to (in this case, the lack of any evidence) does not support the truth of either conclusion.

> **TIP** Any time someone tries to convince you that a claim is true or false by *appealing to a lack of evidence against or for a claim*, they have committed an *ad ignorantiam* fallacy—an **appeal to ignorance**.

This fallacy can be expressed in one of two **argument forms**:

1. There is no evidence for x.
2. Therefore, x is false.

1. There is no evidence against x.
2. Therefore, x is true.

Consider the following example:

1. There is no evidence that there is pot in the brownies.
2. Therefore, these aren't pot brownies.

1. There is no evidence that there isn't pot in these brownies.
2. Therefore, I bet these are loaded, dude.

This fallacy is popular with conspiracy theorists. There are many people who believe that the terrorist attacks on the United States on 09/11/01 were part of a government plan to embroil the United States in a Middle-Eastern military conflict. The reasons for wanting such a conflict are various: to increase military payroll, to boost political relations with large corporations that produce military equipment, to secure more oil reserves, and so on. You might attempt to engage someone who holds beliefs likes, and attempt to explain that the terrorists who took responsibility for the attack express severe hatred for the United States and that the consequences of anyone finding out would be more than devastating to the acting administration. If your conspiracy-fan responds by pointing to pictures that apparently show bombs attached to the bottom of planes and documents apparently condoning insurrectionary activity, then you at least have some evidence to discuss. However paltry the argument, it is not fallacious. On the other hand, if your conspiracy-fan responds by saying, "There's no evidence the government wasn't involved," he has committed a fallacy.

WARNING: Good scientific research can sometimes sound like an argument from ignorance. If a scientist says, "We found no evidence linking *x* and *y*" or "We found no evidence of cancer," she is not appealing to ignorance. She has conducted experiments in attempt to prove a hypothesis. If the experiments do not produce the hypothesized result, she has some reason to believe the hypothesis is not true. In this case, there *is* evidence; it just came up negative. An argument from ignorance would be to argue that there is no evidence of cancer *before* conducting the experiment.

Malaria is a disease that can be carried for a long time without producing any symptoms. Imagine that I have spent a period of time in an area known for malaria. Just because I haven't been tested for malaria, I cannot conclude that I don't have malaria. But similarly just because I don't have any evidence that I don't have malaria, does not mean that I do have it. Both of these are arguments from ignorance. However, if I take a blood test and it comes back negative, then I have reason to think I do not have the disease. This is a non-fallacious argument.

Consider four more examples. Make sure you can explain why each is an example of an argument from ignorance.

EXAMPLES:

a. God must exist, because no one has been able to prove decisively that God does not exist.
b. *Student*: Ronald Reagan was a socialist.
   Professor: How did you arrive at *that* conclusion?
   Student: Show me the evidence that he wasn't one.
c. During the Cold War in the United States, Senator Joe McCarthy is noted for having said: "I do not have much information on this except the general statement of the agency that there is nothing in the files to disprove his Communist connections" (see *Senator Joe McCarthy*, by Richard Halworth Rovere, Berkeley: University of California Press, 1996, p. 132).
d. "There is no evidence that this pesticide doesn't kill small animals. Therefore, it should be illegal."

10.10. *Circular argument* ("begging the question")

You will often hear the phrase, "that begs the question," but few people use it the way philosophers and logicians do. This is because the phrase has come to have two uses in the English language. One is rhetorical, and means "raises the question, . . ." or "demands an answer to the question, . . .," and is typically followed by an actual question. This is the meaning you're probably familiar with. The other use is logical, and it means to assume a claim you are attempting to prove, that is, to present a circular argument. The latter is the phrase's original meaning, but clever journalists co-opted it for rhetorical purposes, and now both meanings are accepted. We, however, will only use the logical meaning—a circular argument.

The fallacy of **circular argument**, or **begging the question**, is an argument that includes or implies the conclusion in the premises. For example:

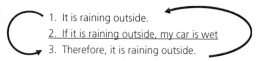

1. It is raining outside.
2. If it is raining outside, my car is wet.
3. Therefore, it is raining outside.

In this argument, the conclusion is already assumed in the premises. The arguer assumes that it is raining outside in order to support the claim that it is raining outside. This is called a "circular" argument because, though the premises are intended to support the conclusion, we need to know the conclusion is true in order to believe the premises. So, support seems to be running in two directions, forming (metaphorically) a circle:

1. It is raining outside.
2. If it is raining outside, my car is wet.
3. Therefore, it is raining outside.

Now, you might wonder: why in the world would anyone construct such a foolish argument? It's actually much easier to commit this fallacy than you might think. Consider a subtler version of this fallacy. Imagine someone attempts to convince you that God exists by giving you the following argument:

1. The Bible says God exists.
2. The Bible is true because God wrote it.
3. Therefore, God exists.

The arguer is attempting to prove that God exists. But if God wrote the Bible, then God exists. So, God's existence is implied in premise 2, the very claim the arguer is trying to support in the conclusion.

The next example is even subtler:

1. Murder is morally wrong.
2. Abortion is murder.
3. Therefore, abortion is morally wrong.

In this argument, someone is attempting to convince us that abortion is morally wrong because abortion is murder. But most of us already believe that murder is, by definition, morally wrong. "Murder" is defined as an *immoral killing*. So, this conclusion follows only if we already believe that abortion is murder; but this is the claim the arguer needs to prove.

The tricky aspect of this fallacy is that all question-begging arguments are *valid* arguments. The conclusion is, either implicitly or explicitly, a premise of the argument, so, if the premises are true, the conclusion is also. Consider the first example, again. If premise 1 is true (it is raining outside), then the conclusion must be true (it is raining outside). Consider also the last example. If premises 1 and 2 are true and an action's being murder entails that it is morally wrong, then premise 3 follows with certainty. So, we would be quite content with this argument if we accepted the premises. However, it is premise 2 that needs support; and that requires a different argument. So, while valid, it is unclear that this argument is sound without an additional, independent argument for the premise in question. And, if such an argument is available, this one is unnecessary.

TIP Any time someone assumes in the premises, implicitly or explicitly, a claim being supported in the conclusion, he or she has committed the fallacy of **begging the question.**

In addition to question-begging arguments, there are question-begging *sentences*. These sentences assume a claim that has yet to be supported. For instance, the question: "Have you stopped beating your wife yet?" presupposes that you have, at some point in the past, beaten your wife. Answering either yes or no commits you to this claim even if it is not true. Unless there is already evidence that you beat your wife, this question begs the question. Another example is: "Will you continue to support unnecessary spending?" This question presupposes that you have been supporting unnecessary spending. Again, answering either yes or no commits you to this claim even if it is not true. Unless there is evidence that you supported unnecessary spending, this question begs the question.

To sum up: if an argument presupposes, or assumes, in the premises the claim being supported as the conclusion, the argument begs the question. Similarly, if a sentence presupposes a claim that has not yet been established, that claim begs the question. Here are four additional examples. Identify whether each is an instance of a question-begging *argument* or *sentence*. And be sure you can explain why each begs the question.

Examples:

a. "I believe Professor Williams that X. Look; it's even in his textbook on page 322!"
b. "Of course the government should provide health care for all citizens. Health care is a basic human right."
c. "Cheating violates academic integrity. Therefore, it is wrong to cheat."
d. An illegal abortion is the termination of a pregnancy during the last trimester which does not meet the requirements of a legal abortion. (Florida abortion statute.)

10.11. Straw man

Imagine two boxers enter a ring to fight. Imagine also that just before the fight begins, one of the boxers pulls out a dummy stuffed with straw and dressed like his opponent. The boxer pummels the dummy to pieces, then struts around as if he were victorious and leaves. Clearly no one would accept this is as a legitimate victory. Now imagine that two politicians are debating. One politician argues that some claim, X, is the case. The other politician proceeds to offer a compelling argument against X*, a slight variation on X. Has the second given good reasons to doubt X? Surely not. He has simply committed a fallacy known as "straw man."

A **straw man** fallacy is an argument in which an arguer responds to a different argument than the one presented, though he treats it as the one presented. If the alternate argument is subtle enough, it is easy to be deceived by a straw man. Politicians often use straw man arguments to rally voters against their opponents. For instance, during the American invasion of Iraq, members of the Republican party disagreed with members of the Democratic party about the duration of the American occupation. Democrats accused Republicans of supporting an unqualified "stay-the-course" campaign, which would lead to great financial and political losses. Republicans accused Democrats of supporting a "cut-and-run" campaign, which would leave Iraq in political, social, and religious chaos. Interestingly, neither side advocated either of these extreme positions. Each committed the straw man fallacy against the other.

Consider another example from political pundit Rush Limbaugh:

> Joe Biden also said that if you don't pay your taxes you're unpatriotic. You're paying taxes, you're patriotic. It's a patriotic thing to do. Paying increased taxes is a patriotic thing to do, so I guess we're to assume under Biden's terminology that Tim Geithner was unpatriotic (Jan. 15, 2009).[1]

To be sure, Tim Geithner *might* have been unpatriotic to ignore several thousand dollars of tax debt, but this is not what Biden said. Biden was referring to the higher taxes for wealthy citizens proposed by, then presidential hopeful, Barack Obama. The online news site MSNBC reports Biden's actual words: "Noting that wealthier Americans would indeed pay more, Biden said: 'It's time to be patriotic . . . time to jump in, time to be part of the deal, time to help get America out of the rut.'"[2] This is quite different from, "If you don't pay your taxes you're unpatriotic." Limbaugh gets it right the second time: "Paying increased taxes is a patriotic thing to do." But then he conflates *paying taxes* with *paying increased taxes*: "I guess we're to assume under Biden's terminology that Tim Geithner was unpatriotic." Geithner didn't pay at all, and Biden didn't comment on whether this was unpatriotic (though Biden supported Geithner's appointment as US Secretary of the Treasury). Therefore, Limbaugh has set up a straw man against Biden.

TIP Any time someone changes her opponent's conclusion, even the slightest bit, and attempts to show that the changed conclusion should not be believed, she has committed the **straw man fallacy**—often called "setting up a straw man."

Here are four more examples of the straw man fallacy. Be sure you can explain why each is an example of this fallacy.

Examples:

a. "Mrs. Crowder has argued that birth control should be available to every student. But folks, if every student is using birth control, then every student is engaged in sexual activity. Thus, Mrs. Crowder says she promotes sexual activity among students. Are you comfortable knowing that your child is sexually active? If not, you should reject her proposal."

b. "Governor Thomas objected to the board's proposed increase of the school janitorial budget. In doing so, he denied a clear promise he made during his campaign to increase the quality of education in this state. Governor Thomas cares very little about education; you should not re-elect him."

c. "Mr. Turner argues that the potholes in the roads can wait until next season because the crack in the dam is a financial liability to the community. Mr. Turner is saying that the welfare of this community's drivers is less important than its financial stability. You cannot vote for this man."

d. "I talked to Jane this morning, and she said that the economic crisis was caused by people agreeing to loans they could not afford. But surely people know whether they can afford a home or not. She can't seriously think those people didn't know they might foreclose. I don't believe her."

10.12. Exercises

The informal fallacies explained in this chapter:

Argumentum ad Hominem, Abusive
Argumentum ad Hominem, Circumstantial
Tu Quoque
Argumentum ad Populum (appeal to the people)
Appeal to Snobbery/Vanity
Argumentum ad Verecundiam (appeal to [inappropriate] authority)
Argumentum ad Baculum (appeal to force)
Argumentum ad Misericordiam (appeal to pity)
Argumentum ad Ignorantiam (appeal to ignorance)
Petitio Principii (begging the question)
Straw Man

Exercises 10.a.

In each of the following exercises:

a. identify the informal fallacy that is committed, and
b. explain why each is an example of that fallacy.

1. "Mr. Bush regularly works on his ranch and goes hunting. He is a down-to-earth, regular guy, just like you. You should vote for Bush for President."
2. "How could a blue-collar, state-college graduate responsibly protect the company's investments?"
3. Your math professor says: "You should be buying government bonds. They're really a good investment right now."
4. *Jury Foreperson*: "Listen people, we've been here for a month. Do you want to spend another month here? Let's find him guilty of the crime already!"
5. *Lawyer*: "My client is the victim of incest himself. How can you convict him of this crime of incest?"
6. *Lawyer*: "In my country, someone is guilty until proven innocent."
7. "My doctor says the tests showed no cancer. So, I'm cancer-free!"
8. Your parents say: "Einstein's theory of special relativity is a load of bunk."
9. "I've known Mr. Smith for twenty years. He is a good, hard-working person. He is a deacon in his church and a good husband. There is no way he could have murdered Congressman Dooley."
10. "You support universal health care? That idea has been supported by God-hating liberals for the last fifty years."
11. Dale Earnhardt, Jr. says: "I only drink Budweiser." [Of course, this is before he dropped their endorsement.]
12. "Jones is a left-wing, fascist pig. Falsehoods drip from his mouth like honey from a comb."
13. "Introducing the Lexus HS 250h: The World's Only Dedicated Luxury Hybrid." (Found on the Lexus website.)
14. *Child*: "Why do I have to do it?"
    Mother: "You will not be happy if you don't!"
15. "It is immoral to assign grades according to relative student performance. Grading on a curve does just that! Therefore, grading on a curve is immoral."
16. "The doctor in this town warns us not to smoke, yet she smokes. What the F?"
17. Teenage son to father: "You can't tell me not to do drugs! You did it!"
18. "Jenny, you can't possibly believe that premarital sex is wrong. You've done it, like, a hundred times!"
19. "Everyone else is having sex. Therefore, I should be having sex, too."
20. "*GatorAde—is it in you?*"
21. "You believe in God? Well, beliefs like that are common among the uneducated working class."
22. "It's not like you to keep this office so sloppy. You know, your job is on the line here. You'd better clean up this mess."
23. "Are you still cheating on your exams?"
24. "Muslims are a bunch of hypocrites and bigots. Anything they say must be false."
25. "Almost every culture holds that it is morally wrong to kill for no reason, rape, and lie. Therefore, it is morally wrong to kill for no reason, rape, or lie."

26. *Cop to suspect*: "Tell the truth now and it'll be easier on you later. Keep on lyin' and I'll make it even harder on you."

27. "No one has ever shown me any convincing evidence for evolution. Therefore, it must be false."

28. "Look at little Jenny. She is malnourished, weak, anemic, plagued with rats on a nightly basis. But there is still a light in her eyes, hope for tomorrow. For just pennies a day, you could sponsor a child like Jenny, and give her the hope she so desperately needs. Give to the Christian Children's Fund."

29. "It is not morally wrong for me to have premarital sex because everyone does it."

30. "My opponent in this campaign has failed to reveal to you his background. He comes from a poor family, his father was a liar, and his mother was a drunk. Therefore, you definitely should not vote for him."

31. "The surgeon general says that smoking is linked to cancer. But I know lots of people who smoke and don't have cancer. So, it easy to see that it is false that *everyone* who smokes will get cancer. Thus, the surgeon general is just wrong."

32. "My opponent in this campaign has been two-faced with you. He was a horrible man to have dinner with this afternoon. Therefore, you definitely should not vote for him."

33. "The *Journal of Psychic Research* showed that remote viewing was used successfully in military operations during the Cold War."

34. "Biologists argue that humans and chimpanzees share a common ancestor. But it is foolish to think that humans evolved from chimps. The theory of evolution says that new species are selected because they are better suited to their environments than their predecessors. So if humans evolved from chimps, the chimps would have gone extinct. Since there are still chimps, it is absurd to think we evolved from them."

35. "All the reports of alien abductions come from people of exceptionally low intelligence. This is further supported by the fact that they make claims about alien abductions."

Real-Life Example 1: Rush Limbaugh

Identify and explain at least three fallacies in the following excerpt from an article by political pundit Rush Limbaugh:

"What can make the recession worse is the wrong kind of government intervention. I believe the wrong kind is precisely what President Barack Obama has proposed. I don't believe his is a 'stimulus plan' at all. I don't think it stimulates anything but the Democratic Party. This 'porkulus' bill is designed to repair the Democratic Party's power losses from the 1990s forward, and to cement the party's majority power for decades. Keynesian economists believe government spending on 'shovel-ready' infrastructure projects—schools, roads, bridges—is the best way to stimulate our staggering economy. Supply-side economists make an equally persuasive case that tax cuts are the surest and quickest way to create permanent jobs and cause an economy to rebound. That happened under JFK, Ronald Reagan and George W. Bush. We know that when tax rates are cut in a recession, it brings an economy back." (From Rush Limbaugh, "My Bipartisan Stimulus," *Wall Street Journal*, Jan. 29, 2009, http://online.wsj.com/article/SB123318906638926749.html)

Real-Life Example 2: National Center for Science Education

Find and explain at least three fallacies in the following article from the website of the National Center for Science Education (NCSE). This article is part of a larger discussion about the state of Texas's right to dictate the information about evolution in their biology textbooks. There are fallacies made by the author as well as those quoted, so be careful to note who is committing the fallacy.

"Consequences of the flawed standards in Texas?"

April 17th, 2009

Since the March 2009 decision of the Texas state board of education to adopt a set of flawed state science standards, media coverage has increasingly emphasized the possible consequences. As NCSE previously reported, although creationists on the board were unsuccessful in inserting the controversial "strengths and weaknesses" language from the old set of standards, they proposed a flurry of synonyms—such as "sufficiency or insufficiency" and "supportive and not supportive"—and eventually prevailed with a requirement that students examine "all sides of scientific evidence." Additionally, the board voted to add or amend various standards in a way that encourages the presentation of creationist claims about the complexity of the cell, the completeness of the fossil record, and the age of the universe. The result, NCSE's executive director Eugenie C. Scott commented, was "a triumph of ideology and politics over science."

The board's antics seem to have caught the attention of legislators in Texas. There are now no fewer than six bills in the Texas legislature—HB 710, HB 2261, HB 3382, SB 440, SB 513, and SB 2275—that would reduce the state board of education's power. As the Wall Street Journal (April 13, 2009) reported, "The most far-reaching proposals would strip the Texas board of its authority to set curricula and approve textbooks. Depending on the bill, that power would be transferred to the state education agency, a legislative board or the commissioner of education. Other bills would transform the board to an appointed rather than elected body, require Webcasting of meetings, and take away the board's control of a vast pot of school funding." To be sure, it is not only with respect to evolution that the board's actions have been controversial, but the recent decision about the state science standards seems to have been the last straw.

Gaining the most attention recently is SB 2275, which would transfer authority for curriculum standards and textbook adoption from the board to the Texas Commissioner of Education; the bill received a hearing in the Senate Education Committee on April 14, 2009. The Dallas Morning News (April 15, 2009) reported that one of its sponsors, Senator Kel Seliger (R-District 31), told the committee, "The debate [over the science standards] went on with almost no discussion of children," adding, "The fact is there is nothing that makes the board particularly qualified to choose curriculum materials and textbooks." The Texas Freedom Network's Kathy Miller was among the witnesses at the hearing testifying to "the state board's unfair processes, divisive ideological history and outright ineptitude."

⇨

Texas Citizens for Science's president Steven Schafersman (<u>writing</u> on the *Houston Chronicle*'s Evo.Sphere blog on April 14, 2009) and the *Waco Tribune* (<u>writing</u> in its April 17, 2009, editorial) have both expressed their support for the bill.

Unless such a bill is enacted, it seems likely that the board will pressure textbook publishers to dilute the treatment of evolution in the biology textbooks submitted for adoption, probably in 2011. As Lauri Lebo <u>explained</u> in a story on Religion Dispatches (April 14, 2009), "With almost $30 million set aside in the budget, Texas is second only to California in the bulk purchase of textbooks. But Texas, unlike California, approves and purchases books for all the state's school districts. Publishers often edit and revise textbooks in order meet the specific demands of the Texas board members." NCSE Supporter Kenneth R. Miller, coauthor (with Joe Levine) of several widely used textbooks published by Prentice-Hall, told the *Wall Street Journal* that "We will do whatever we think is appropriate to meet the spirit and the letter of Texas standards," but firmly added, "We will never put anything in our books that will compromise our scientific values."

Lebo discussed the possibility of litigation over the board's decision: "Now the issue is whether there is enough prima facie evidence to challenge the Constitutionality of the wording now, or wait for the textbook review process in two years." It is not surprising that she thought of the possibility, since she wrote a book, *The Devil in Dover* (The New Press, 2008), about the *Kitzmiller* case, which she covered for a local newspaper, the *York Daily Record*. That newspaper's report (April 6, 2009) on the situation in Texas <u>opened</u> with a noteworthy quotation from one of the eleven plaintiffs in the *Kitzmiller* case, which established the unconstitutionality of teaching "intelligent design" creationism in the public schools: "Steve Stough was silent. He had just heard a passage from Texas' new public school science standards, and was processing. Then: 'Oh ----,' he said. 'That's intelligent design without using the nomenclature. It really, truly is.'"

Part Four
GRADUATE SCHOOL ENTRANCE EXAMS

Reasoning on the GRE, LSAT, GMAT, and MCAT

11

11.1. Introduction to graduate school entrance exams

We hear it over and over. Students who have taken a graduate school entrance exam such as the GRE or the LSAT tell us they wish they had taken a logic course or more philosophy courses. For this reason, many professors are including a section on these exams in their critical thinking and introductory logic courses. One of the main purposes of this textbook is to help students and to help instructors help students who plan to take one of these exams.

This section of the book is not a substitute for a more comprehensive test preparation guide or course. Those materials are designed to teach you how the test designers construct questions and to provide strategies for answering questions based on those assumptions. You'll still want that information since they'll decrease the amount of time you spend on each question. But this section of the book is designed to help you develop such an in-depth grasp of reasoning that you would do well even without those strategies. It will also help you see why those strategies work. In addition, this book only covers the reasoning portions of those tests, whereas you'll still need a guide for the verbal, quantitative, and other non-reasoning sections. But reasoning questions make up at least half of the LSAT and a third of the GRE and GMAT, so you can never go wrong with more training in logic.

There are several kinds of reasoning questions asked on each of the Big Four entrance exams. The kinds of reasoning questions that are regularly asked on these exams can be grouped into two general categories: (1) analytical reasoning and (2) inductive reasoning. For the analytical reasoning questions, you'll need a solid grasp of the concepts presented in the first three chapters of this book and many of the skills covered in the chapters on deductive reasoning, Chapters 3–6. For the inductive reasoning questions, you'll need many of the skills covered (surprise, surprise) in the chapters on inductive reasoning, Chapters 7–11 of this book. Don't forget to refer back to these chapters if you have difficulty with any of the concepts in this chapter.

The kinds of questions asked on graduate school entrance exams can be grouped as follows:

Analytical Reasoning

- What is the main point of the argument?
- What are the author's reasons?
- What assumption supports the claim that ____?
- What's missing?
- Compare the following arguments
- Logic puzzles, or "games"

Inductive Reasoning

- Which premise strengthens the argument/weakens the argument?
- Inference questions (identify a conclusion, though not necessarily *the* conclusion)
- Flaw questions / Fallacies (identify a mistake in reasoning, a counterexample, or an unwarranted assumption)

- Parallel-the reasoning / classification / "reasoning" questions (is the argument an "analogy," "generalization," or "causal argument"? or Choose the argument with the pattern of reasoning that best follows the pattern of reasoning of the argument given.)

We have listed the kinds of reasoning questions regularly asked on each of the Big Four in the chart below:

LSAT
Analytical reasoning:
  All of the above

Inductive reasoning:
  All of the above

GRE
Analytical reasoning:
  None[1]

Inductive reasoning:
  All of the above

GMAT
Analytical reasoning:
  All of the above

Inductive reasoning:
  Classification
  Fallacies

MCAT
Analytical reasoning:
  What is the main point of the argument?
  What are the author's reasons?

  Inference questions
  What assumption supports the claim that ___?

Inductive reasoning:
  None

Having a good grasp of arguments and how they work from the previous sections of this text will help with the majority of reasoning questions. Always feel free to go back to the basics. Knowing and recognizing the components of an argument (Chapters 1 and 2) underwrites every reasoning question. Make sure you can: identify the main point (typically the conclusion of the argument), identify the assumption (typically a central premise of the argument), answer "why" questions (also typically a premise).

Since we've covered so much of this material in earlier chapters, here we'll focus on applying and reinforcing those skills as they will be used on grad school entrance exams. We'll also cover the questions unique to those exams: **11.4: "strengthen/weaken" questions; 11.5: inference questions; 11.6: logic puzzles/ games; 11.7: flaw questions; 11.8: and parallel-the-reasoning questions**.

Before we discuss the more specific kinds of questions, let's take a look at how information from the previous chapters can be used to solve the basic analytical reasoning questions. Afterward, in section 11.3, we'll offer some tips for interpreting some of the more complicated instructions you'll find on your exam.

11.2. Basic analytic reasoning questions

Consider the following argument you might find on any of the Big Four:

> ## Example 1:
>
> The mayor of the village of Bree sent a letter to the townspeople instructing them to stop watering their lawns in the middle of the day to conserve the reservoir during the summer. A few weeks after the letter was delivered, there was a noticeable decrease in the amount of water the townspeople of Bree was using on a daily basis. Therefore, it is obvious that the letter was successful in conserving the reservoir during the summer.

If you were asked to identify the author's ma in point, you would simply point to the conclusion of the argument. You would locate the conclusion by looking for a conclusion- indicating word. In this case, we find "therefore" and no others, and can, therefore, assume with some safety that we have identified the main point:

> **(C)** Therefore, it is obvious that the letter was successful in conserving the reservoir during the summer.

If you were asked the author's reasons for drawing the conclusion she does, the "why" question, you would simply identify the premise or premises of the argument. Since you've already identified the conclusion, you can assume that the rest of the paragraph contains the premises. But watch out for extraneous material. In this case, there doesn't seem to be any extraneous material, so we pick out the premises by picking out the claims:

> **P1)** The mayor of Bree sent a letter telling people to use less water.
> **P2)** People started using less water.

Notice that both premises are required to answer the why question. You can see this if you **diagram** the argument as follows:

We can see that (P1) cannot support (C) without (P2) and vice versa. Therefore, the premises work jointly to support (C).

If you were asked a "what's missing" question, you would consider whether (P1) and (P2) are sufficient to guarantee (C), that is, whether (C) follows necessarily from (P1) and (P2). If so, the argument is deductive and nothing is missing. Though we might question the truth of the premises, the premises, *if true*, guarantee the conclusion. On grad school entrance exams, however, *few arguments will be deductive*. The exceptions are logic puzzle, or "game," sections, which we will discuss later in this chapter.

If (P1) and (P2) only grant (C) a degree of probability, then the argument is inductive, and (C) might not be true even if (P1) and (P2) are true. The quickest test to determine whether an argument is deductive is the counterexample. Could anything make the conclusion false and keep the premises true? In this case, we want to know whether we can conceive of *anything* other than the letter causing the lower water usage. And the answer is, of course. Here is a short list:

- It rained profusely in the days after the letter was sent.
- Many people from the village left to visit friends in nearby towns for the holidays.
- A dam broke and flooded the village.
- The price of water rose sharply in the days following the letter being sent.

Though a counterexample is often the fastest way to see how something might be wrong with the argument, it is not always the best option. For example, even though it is *possible* that many villagers left for holiday just after the letter was sent, it is not a *plausible*, or likely, alternative explanation for what caused the drop in water usage. If you can't think of a plausible counterexample, the next step is to *look for a fallacy*.

If the conclusion generalizes from a survey or poll, challenge the strength of the generalization: Is it random? Is the sample large enough? Were the questions organized to avoid framing or ordering biases? If the conclusion draws an analogy between two sets of properties, challenge the closeness of the analogy: Are there many disanalogies? Are the compared properties relevant? If the conclusion is a causal argument, challenge the relationship between the correlation and causation: Might both have a common cause? Might the event being explained have actually been the cause?

Having a good grasp of inductive arguments and their limitations will greatly increase your ability to accurately analyze arguments on your exam. Here's another example. This one might be found on the GRE or GMAT.

Example 2:

A recent study shows that people living in the United States suffer 8 times more from arthritis and 30 times more from headaches than do people living in India. Interestingly, Indians, on average, drink two cups of green tea per day, whereas Americans drink virtually none. It turns out that green tea contains antioxidants, which have been found to possess disease-preventing properties. Thus, Americans should consider drinking green tea on a regular basis as a way of preventing fatigue and depression.

If you are asked to find the author's main point, look for the conclusion. We find the conclusion indicating word "thus" just before, "Americans should consider drinking green tea on a regular basis as a way of preventing arthritis and headaches," so this might be our conclusion. The phrase, "it turns out that," can sometimes indicate a conclusion so read the claim following it carefully. It says: "Green tea contains antioxidants, which have been found to posses disease-preventing properties." If this claim is the conclusion, there should be premises supporting. Since no other claims mention the relationship between green tea, disease-prevention, and antioxidants, we should assume it is another premise. So, with this option eliminated we have identified the author's main point:

(C) Americans should consider drinking green tea on a regular basis as a way of preventing arthritis and headaches.

If you are asked the author's reasons for drawing the conclusion, identify the premises. Since there is only one conclusion, the remaining claims comprise the author's reasons:

P1) A recent study shows that people living in the United States suffer 8 times more from arthritis and 30 times more from headaches than do people living in India.
P2) Interestingly, Indians, on average, drink 2 cups of green tea per day, whereas Americans drink virtually none.
P3) It turns out that green tea contains antioxidants, which have been found to possess disease-preventing properties.

Notice that the phrases "interestingly" and "it turns out that" aren't doing any work in supporting the conclusion. They are merely stylistic additions to make the paragraph flow smoothly. These are extraneous to the argument and should be eliminated. So our argument now looks like this:

P1) A recent study shows that people living in the United States suffer 8 times more from arthritis and 30 times more from headaches than do people living in India.

P2) Indians, on average, drink two cups of green tea per day, whereas Americans drink virtually none.

P3) Green tea contains antioxidants, which have been found to possess disease-preventing properties.

C) Americans should consider drinking green tea on a regular basis as a way of preventing arthritis and headaches.

Notice that (C) requires all three premises to support it. (P1) alone doesn't mention soy or disease-preventing. (P2) doesn't mention disease-preventing properties. (P3) doesn't mention North Americans or Asians. Since the conclusion includes all these elements, all three premises are required to support it. This means the premises jointly support the conclusion and we could diagram it thus:

If you were asked a "What's missing?" question, you would consider whether (P1)-(P3) adequately support (C). You might question (P1) by asking whether the sample is representative. Is it random? Are the sample sizes large enough? Also, who conducted the survey? Do they have a vested interest in the outcome? Are they a reputable organization such as the UCLA or Johns Hopkins medical schools?

You might question (P2) on the grounds that, while Americans may eat virtually no soy on average, there are plenty of Americans who eat soy on a regular basis. Are these Americans subject to the same frequency of arthritis and headaches? The argument doesn't tell us, but if so, then green tea is a very unlikely solution. Without this information the argument is very weak.

You might question (P3) on the grounds that the argument doesn't indicate which diseases antioxidants have been found to prevent. It is one thing for them to ward off the flu or a pollen allergies, but quite another for them to ward off heart disease. We need to know whether antioxidants have a causal effect on arthritis and headaches. Without this information the argument is very weak.

11.3. Interpreting complicated instructions

Being able to decipher complicated instructions will significantly increase the speed and accuracy with which you answer questions. Always read a set of instructions twice, once before you read the argument, and once after. When you get to the exercises of this chapter, take a minute to write out an interpretation of the questions before you try to answer them. After you've completed your answers to a couple, check the answers provided to see how well you understood the question. You won't have time to sketch your interpretation on the test, but practicing now saves time later.

Consider the following set of instructions that may precede a series of arguments on the GRE, LSAT, or GMAT.

Example 3:

Discuss how well reasoned you find the following arguments. In your discussion be sure to analyze the line of reasoning and the use of evidence in the argument. For example, you may need to consider what questionable assumptions underlie the thinking and what alternative explanations or counter examples might weaken the conclusion. You can also discuss what sort of evidence would strengthen or refute the argument, what changes in the argument would make it more logically sound, and what, if anything, would help you better evaluate its conclusion.

The instruction to "discuss how well reasoned" you find an argument, without any qualification is vague. Do they want you to reconstruct the argument? Criticize it? If no further information is given, evaluate it very systematically like we just did with the two arguments above. Here, however, this instruction is followed by a series of qualifiers that narrows the information the testers are looking for.

"Analyze the line of reasoning." This is a request for the basic form of the argument. They are looking for the specific conclusion and the premises from which the conclusion is inferred.

"Analyze the use of evidence." This is a request for the kind of evidence being used and what claims it is being used to support: Is the evidence scientific (empirical)? Is it testimony from an expert? Is it a poll or a survey? Is the evidence being used to support a premise (sub-conclusion)? Is it being used to support the ultimate conclusion?

"For example, you may need to consider what questionable assumptions underlie the thinking and what alternative explanations or counterexamples might weaken the conclusion." This instruction *qualifies* your answer to the evidence question. Not only are they asking what the evidence is and what it's supporting, they want to know what information might undermine this evidence: Is the scientific evidence current? Is that testimony reliable? Is the survey random and representative? Is there evidence that supersedes the evidence cited? In addition, this qualification asks you whether you can think of any alternative explanation for this conclusion than the evidence cited or whether you can think of a counterexample. For a refresher on evidence and counterexamples, refer back to Chapter 2.

"You can also discuss what sort of evidence would strengthen or refute the argument." This request is similar to the "strengthen" and "weaken" questions we will evaluate in the next section, except here you are not given any options. You must think quickly and come up with some evidence that either increases the likelihood that the conclusion is true, decreases the likelihood that the conclusion is true, or makes the conclusion impossible (a counterexample). This will get easier with practice.

"You can also discuss . . . what changes in the argument would make it more logically sound." This is clearly a bad request, but it is certainly one you may encounter. Recall from Chapter 2 that an argument cannot be more or less sound. Soundness applies only to deductive arguments and a deductive argument is sound if it is valid and its premises are true. Since an argument is either valid or invalid and premises are either true or false, soundness does not come in degrees. This request, then, must be interpreted in one of two ways.

Remember that we always assume the premises of an argument on these exams are true, so the request will either be about validity or strength. If the argument under consideration is deductive (which is unlikely on graduate entrance exams), it can be interpreted as asking what would make the argument valid, as opposed to invalid. If the argument is inductive (very likely), it can be interpreted as asking what would make the argument stronger.

Always assume the argument is inductive unless you have some very specific reason for thinking otherwise. Information that would make an inductive argument stronger is information that increases the likelihood that the conclusion is true given the premises. So to answer this question you should either: *provide more evidence for the conclusion,* or *strengthen the evidence already presented.* For instance, consider an argument with the premises: 35% of males over 40 admit to cheating on their spouses and 15% of males under 40 admit to cheating on their spouses, and the conclusion is: a large percentage of marriages are adulterated. You could increase the strength of this argument by providing more evidence for the conclusion: for example, studies might also find that 20% of females over 40 admit to cheating on their spouses and 10% under 40. You could also increase the strength of this argument by strengthening the evidence already given: for instance, new studies might find that the number of males over 40 who cheat has increased 3 percent since the earlier findings.

And finally, "You can discuss . . . what, if anything, would help you better evaluate its conclusion." This is an open-ended opportunity to list any additional information that would be relevant to assessing the argument. For instance, in the adultery argument just mentioned, we would like to know at least the following: how recently were these surveys conducted? How many subjects were surveyed? Was the survey random? Were the subjects previously married? How many of the subjects were in "common-law" versus legal marriages? Etc. Refer back to your answer about what evidence might "strengthen or refute" the argument for help.

Here's another example of a set of instructions you may encounter:

Example 4:

Discuss the extent to which you agree or disagree with the opinion stated below. Support your position with reasons and/or examples from your experience, observations, or reading.

Don't get thrown the term "opinion." Recall from the very first chapter of this book than an opinion is just a claim that is either true or false. Whether you agree with this claim will depend on how much evidence supports it. Begin answering this question by clearly stating your conclusion: "I agree that . . . ." Be sure to include the claim with which you agree. It will not be sufficient to say: "I agree with the author." The testers want to know what about the author's argument you agree with. State it clearly.

"Support your position with reasons and/or examples." This is a request for premises. What evidence supports your conclusion? Try not to use phrases such as "in my opinion," or "it seems to me." These phrases express hesitation. It is your essay, so of course it is your view; no one needs to be reminded. State your view clearly and forcefully. Don't, however, use rhetorical phrases such as, "it is obvious that," or "no one can deny," unless it really is obvious or unless no one really can deny it. These phrases express carelessness or overconfidence. Let your evidence do all the work.

". . . from your experience, observations, or reading." Technically speaking, there is no big difference between your experience and your observations. Observations are a subset of your experiences, so don't get too hung up here trying to distinguish them. If you can cite sources, do so as completely as possible, giving author, title, and page number. But if you only remember the title, put the title.

These are just a few of the kinds of argument evaluation questions that earlier chapters of this book will help you answer. See the Exercises section of this chapter for lots of practice problems. Let's turn now to one kind of inductive reasoning question you will encounter: strengthen/weaken questions.

11.4. "Strengthen/weaken" questions

"Strengthen/weaken" questions ask you to either construct a premise that would make the argument stronger or weaker, or choose from a set of premises which would make the argument stronger or weaker. "Strengthen/weaken" questions apply only to inductive arguments. Recall that deductive arguments can be evaluated in terms of validity and soundness, neither of which admits of degrees. Therefore, no new premise can make a deductive argument stronger or weaker. New evidence may leave a deductive argument as it is, or render it unsound. Remember also that, in inductive arguments the conclusions do not follow necessarily from their premise or premises; the conclusion follows only with some degree of probability.

For these questions on graduate school entrance exams, you will be asked to assess whether the probability of a conclusion given a set of premises is changed by the addition of a new premise. The new premise might increase the likelihood of the conclusion given the premises (it might "strengthen" it), it might decrease it (or "weaken" it), or it might be irrelevant to the conclusion, in which case the likelihood of the conclusion given the premises remains the same. In some cases you will be asked which of a set of premises would strengthen or weaken an argument, in others you'll be asked to come up with a premise that either strengthens or weakens an argument.

Here's an example of an inductive reasoning question you might find on the LSAT:

Example 5:

Most major home improvement chains experienced a significant increase in the amount of merchandise lost to shoplifting during the late 1990s. By 2000, however, all chains had instituted theft prevention strategies, including electronic anti-theft devices, in their stores. Since then, the number of shoplifting incidents in those stores has declined.

Which of the following, if true, would most strengthen the claim that theft prevention strategies were responsible for the decrease in shoplifting?

    (A) The average size of the merchandise stolen from home improvement stores is now small enough to fit into a person's pocket.
    (B) The average cost of home improvement merchandise has declined since 2000.
    (C) Each item in the store was clearly marked with a permanently attached security number.
    (D) Shoplifting has increased at independently owned home improvement stores since 2000.
    (E) Shoplifting has increased in the retail industry overall since 2000.

Notice that our conclusion has been clearly identified for us in the question: "... the claim that *theft prevention strategies were responsible for the decrease in shoplifting.*" The premises for this argument can easily be identified in the paragraph above the question:

    P1) There was an increase in shoplifting at home improvement chain stores in the later 1990s.
    P2) By 2000, home improvement chain stores implemented theft prevention strategies, including electronic anti-theft devices.
    P3) Since 2000, shoplifting has decreased at home improvement chain stores.
    C) Theft prevention strategies were responsible for the decrease in shoplifting.

We must be careful how strongly we couch this inference. Remember from Chapter 8 that just because two events are correlated does not mean that one causes the other. The premises clearly indicate a correlation between the implementation of theft prevention strategies and a decrease in shoplifting. The question is whether we can legitimately infer (C) from the premises. Correlations do increase the likelihood that one event causes the other, so there seems to be some degree of support for the conclusion. The question asks us to choose a premise from the list to add to the argument to make the inference stronger.

There are two ways to make an analogical argument stronger: (1) increase the similarities between the things compared, and (2) increase the dissimilarities of alternative options. Look at each possible premise, then determine whether it does (1) or (2) or neither.

(A) The average size of the merchandise typically stolen from home improvement stores is now small enough to fit into a person's pocket.

This premise does (2). The alternative is that something else is causing the decrease in shoplifting. If items are easier to shoplift, we might expect that the number of shopliftings would not go down or that there was something in the store keeping them from being taken. Since we know they've gone down, perhaps the theft prevention strategies are doing their job. This premise plausibly strengthens the argument. But the question asks us to identify the premise that most strengthens it, so we'll have to come back to this one after all the evidence is in.

(B) The average cost of home improvement merchandise has declined since 2000.

The premise does the opposite of (2). It increases the plausibility of an alternative cause. If the average cost of merchandise has decreased, then this might better account for a decrease in shoplifting than theft prevention strategies. This premise does not strengthen the case.

(C) Each item in the store was clearly marked with a permanently attached security number.

This premise seems to fulfill (1). If items are clearly marked with theft prevention information, this increases the likelihood that potential shoplifters would know about the theft prevention strategies and might shy away from stealing. This definitely strengthens the argument. Let's come back to it after all the evidence is in.

(D) Shoplifting has increased at independently owned home improvement stores since 2000.

This premise certainly makes it seem like something has made shoplifters shift from chain home improvement stores to locally owned stores. This premise would certainly strengthen the argument if we had more information, such as, that the locally owned stores do not have theft prevention strategies. Since we don't have any information correlating independently owned stores to chain stores, this premise is neutral.

(E) Shoplifting has increased in the retail industry overall since 2000.

This premise is promising. If shoplifting is going up everywhere except in the home improvement chain stores and since shoplifting stopped increasing in 2000 when they implemented the theft prevention devices, this premise definitely strengthens the argument.

So we're left with three plausible choices (A), (C), and (E). Let's look first at (A). To infer from the premises that items are easier to shoplift yet they're being shoplifted less, to the conclusion that the theft prevention strategies are working, we need some big assumptions. We need to assume that people typically steal what they can hide and that the theft prevention strategies involve enough technology to detect even items carried in pockets. This is too much of a jump for this to be the premise that most strengthens the argument.

Let's look at (C) again. The items are now marked with security information which, if potential shoplifters recognize these and think they would increase their chances of being caught, they might not shoplift those items. But these are big IFs.

Looking again at (E), we know that since 2000 shoplifting is going up everywhere except at home improvement chain stores. The only relevant difference we know of starting at 2000 is the implementation of theft prevention strategies by home improvement chain stores. This means that the introduction of (E) into the argument would strengthen the argument more than any of the others.

You'll need to process all this information fairly quickly on the exam and getting the hang of this kind of reasoning will take some time and patience. Having a clear grasp of the rules of inductive and deductive inference will speed up this process.

Example 6:

A recent study has shown that, for our vitamin needs, seaweed has none of the drawbacks of beef. Seaweed contains neither the high levels of saturated fat nor the chemical hormones that commercially grown beef does, and its harvest doesn't require the vast amount of energy and resources that beef production does. In light of this evidence, it is clear that people must change their diet from one consisting mainly of beef to one consisting mainly of seaweed.

Which one of the following statements, if true, most seriously weakens the argument above?

(A) Relatively few scientific studies have been done on people's willingness to radically change their diets.

(B) The only reports containing information on the drawbacks of seaweed as a vitamin substitute have been funded by the United States Department of Agriculture.

(C) Greater federal regulation of the beef industry could reduce the amount of chemical hormones used in beef production.

⇨

(D) The costs incurred in harvesting enough seaweed to substitute beef as a vitamin source greatly exceeds the cost of beef production.

(E) To date, there are no practical methods in place to make seaweed commercially available to consumers.

We are looking to weaken the above argument, so it is important to know what premises are doing the work. The case for substituting seaweed for beef is based on beef's drawbacks, which seaweed apparently doesn't have. What are these drawbacks? Hormones and production costs. If seaweed doesn't have these, then perhaps we should consider changing our diet. Therefore, if new evidence undermines one or both of seaweed's advantages, the argument is weakened. Keep in mind, we are also looking for the evidence that most weakens it, so just finding evidence against one of these premises might not be good enough.

(A) Relatively few scientific studies have been done on people's willingness to radically change their diets.

This information is irrelevant to the argument, which says people should change their diet. It has nothing to do with their willingness. In addition, the merit of an argument does not depend on whether people actually change because of it. Maybe they don't understand it, maybe they've never heard it, or maybe they just don't care about evidence and reasons. Regardless an argument may be a good argument.

(B) The only reports containing information on the drawbacks of seaweed as a vitamin substitute have been funded by the United States Department of Agriculture.

This claim might weaken the argument if we had some additional reason to think the Department of Agriculture has a vested interest in beef production and against seaweed harvesting. However, we don't have that information, and it would be quite a leap of reason to assume that, because they fund these projects, they must be influencing the results.

(C) Greater federal regulation of the beef industry could reduce the amount of chemical hormones used in beef production.

This evidence could undermine one of the premises if and when it is carried out. But the mere possibility that such legislation could be put into action doesn't weaken the original argument.

(D) The costs incurred in harvesting enough seaweed to substitute beef as a vitamin source greatly exceeds the cost of beef production.

If this evidence came out, the seaweed supporter should be seriously worried. One of their premises is that it would require fewer resources and less expense to harvest seaweed. If this turns out to be false, as (D) suggests, half of the case is undermined. Let's keep (D) in mind.

(E) To date, there are no practical methods in place to make seaweed commercially available to consumers.

This weakens the argument, as well, because one claim is that seaweed harvesting is less expensive and uses fewer resources than beef production. If, however, the scale at which this harvesting is currently operating isn't comparable to beef production, then the author doesn't really know it is less expensive and uses fewer resources. This definitely weakens the argument. Does it weaken it as much as (D)? (E) only claims that we don't know how much it will cost, which means the arguer could still turn out to be right. (D), on the other hand, is evidence that it definitely costs more, and therefore knocks out one of the premises. (D) is the correct answer.

Example 7:

In the wake of large numbers of violent crimes using assault rifles, many people have argued for a federal law making it illegal for civilians to own assault rifles anywhere in the United States. It is clear, however, that any such proposal would have the opposite of the desired effect. When assault rifles were banned in Atlanta in 1980, the number of violent crimes committed with assault rifles increased by 9% by 1982. Further, such a proposal violates the Second Amendment, which gives civilians the right to bear arms.

Which of the following, if true, would most strongly support the conclusion above?

(A) The number of assault rifle crimes in Atlanta increased 15% from 1979 to 1980.
(B) The number of assault rifle crimes in the United States increased by 1% from 1980 to 1982.
(C) The number of assault rifle crimes in Atlanta in 1982 was not as great as the number of assault rifle crimes in the entire country.
(D) The attempt to ban assault rifles in Argentina in 1975 also led to an increased number of assault rifle crimes.
(E) Canada, which has an assault rifle ban, has a faster growing rate of crimes from firearms than does the United States.

Let's start at the beginning:

(A) The number of assault rifle crimes in Atlanta increased 15% from 1979 to 1980.

This evidence would weaken the conclusion, rather than strengthening it. Since we know that the number of assault rifle crimes increased 9% from 1980 to '82, (A) is evidence that the ban worked to reduce the number of violent crimes committed with assault rifles, the opposite of the author's intent. (A) is out.

(B) The number of assault rifle crimes in the United States increased by 1% from 1980 to 1982.

Since the rest of the nation had no ban and assault rifle crimes increased only 1% and Atlanta had a ban and assault rifle crimes increased 9%, this would indicate the ban had the opposite of the intended effect. This strengthens the argument, let's keep it in mind.

(C) The number of assault rifle crimes in Atlanta in 1982 was not as great as the number of assault rifle crimes in the entire country.

The actual number of crimes is not the point. We need to know something about deviations from the norm over time. Comparing the actual numbers from one year won't affect the argument either way. (C) is out.

(D) The attempt to ban assault rifles in Argentina in 1975 also led to an increased number of assault rifle crimes.

This is interesting evidence, and potentially telling, but the circumstances (political and social) in Argentina could be much different from ours, making this evidence irrelevant to the case at hand. Without more information, (D) is out.

(E) Canada, which has an assault rifle ban, has a faster growing rate of crimes from firearms than does the United States.

Notice that this evidence is about "firearms" generally, and doesn't refer to assault rifles. This cannot be used in the present argument. If the evidence was about assault rifles, it would be useful to the author, since the political and social climate of Canada is much closer to the United States than, for instance, Argentina. Therefore, we have eliminated all choices except (B), which is the correct answer.

11.5. Inference questions

Inference questions ask you about the relationship between the premises and the conclusion. Some questions indicate that some piece of information is missing and ask you to choose the claim that would make the argument work, as in Example 8 below. In other questions, the argument may be missing a conclusion, and you have to choose which claim follows from the premises. In still other questions, there may already be an ultimate conclusion and the question may ask you what other claim follows or doesn't follow from the premises.

Here's an example of an inference reasoning question you might find on the GMAT. Try this one on your own, first, then read the solution.

Example 8:

British soldiers in the southern Sahara in the early 1700s observed the natives using rifles to hunt with. The rifles had flint-lock firing mechanisms, which involve a locking hammer on top of the rifle's stock that, when the trigger is pulled, releases the lock, allowing the hammer to strike a flint stone, igniting the gun powder. Flint was not introduced into North Africa until the 1500s. Thus, we can conclude that natives developed the rifle sometime between the introduction of flint to the North Africa and the time of the British soldiers in the early 1700s.

Which one of the following assumptions is critical to the passage's conclusion?

(A) Natives used flint-lock rifles in ceremonial as well as military exercises.
(B) Using flint as a firing mechanism was one of the natives' earliest use of flint stone.
(C) This kind of firing mechanism was used by natives throughout North Africa.
(D) Since the rifle was first developed in Africa, it had a flint-lock firing mechanism.
(E) British soldiers in the 1700s were the first to document the natives' use of flint-lock rifles.

Narrow your choices as quickly as possible. Notice the word "critical." This is an indication that you're looking for an important connection between the premises and conclusion. Make sure you can pick out the conclusion. In this case, "Thus, we can conclude that," tips us off:

(C) Natives developed the (flint-lock) mechanism sometime between the introduction of flint to the North Africa and the time of the British soldiers in the early 1700s.

(A) is irrelevant to the inference, so it's out. (E) might be relevant, but we would need to know much more about the natives' documented history. If there is none, (E) is irrelevant, since it wouldn't help us narrow the gap between 1500 and 1700. If there is a lot right up to the 1700s, (E) would strengthen our inference. Either way, (E) is not *critical* to the conclusion, so it's out. (C) would depend on a lot of information about the timeline of other native groups and it is not clear it is critical to an inference about *South Saharan* natives. (C) is out.

This leaves us with (B) and (D). Is (B) critical to the conclusion? The passage tells us of only one kind of rifle. There may be many other types of rifle, and so perhaps the natives didn't need flint for rifles prior to 1500. If it is possible the natives had non-flint-lock rifles prior to 1500, (B) is out. This clearly seems possible, leaving us with (D). (D) tells us that, if the North Africans had rifles, they were flint-lock. This entails that the rifles were developed between 1500, when flint was introduced, and 1700, when they were observed using them. (D) is the correct answer.

If you're not getting the right answer on your first read through, don't get discouraged. Go back through both examples. Make sure you clearly understand each solution before moving on to the exercises. Prep guides will give you a set of strategies to use to get you through the exam. But strategies often require more time and memorization than just understanding the concepts to begin with. In addition, if you clearly understand how an argument works, you won't get frazzled when you run into a question that your strategy won't work on. Getting the concepts right takes a lot of practice, but it will pay off in more ways than just getting you through the entrance exam. Let's look at another:

Example 9:

Some of the people on Mars are Martians; others are aliens. No Martians can swim. All aliens can swim. Therefore, Martians are not aliens. Everyone who is not an alien is a cave dweller.

Assume that each of the above statements is true. Which of the following must be true if it is also true that no aliens are cave dwellers?

(A) The only people who can swim are cave-dwelling Martians.
(B) Anyone who is not a Martian is an alien.
(C) All who can swim are cave dwellers.
(D) All cave dwellers must be Martians.
(E) All Martians are cave dwellers.

Notice all the quantifiers: some, no, all. This means that a quick Venn diagram might be the key to answering this question quickly. The problem is that there are five categories: people who live on Mars, Martians, aliens, swimmers, and cave dwellers. Recall that categorical logic can't handle more than three categories. So you'll have to reason through the answers.

Since we know no Martians can swim, (A) is out. We also know that no Martians are aliens, but we can't conclude that Martians and aliens aren't the only kinds of people, so (B) is out. By saying anyone who is not a Martian is an alien, it implies that there are only two kinds of people, which we don't know. (C) is tricky, let's save it.

(D) tells us all cave-dwellers are Martians, presumably because everyone who is not an alien is a cave-dweller. But, again, this assumes that there are only two kinds of people. Since we don't know this, (D) is out. (E) looks like just a restatement of (D), but be careful. (D) says cave-dwellers *must* be Martians, (E) says only that all Martian are cave-dwellers. Since we know that no Martians are aliens, (E) follows directly from the claim that everyone who is not an alien is a cave-dweller. This looks promising, but we still need to rule out (C).

(C) tells us something about all people who can swim: they are cave-dwellers. We know that Martians can't swim. Does this mean they don't live in caves if (C) is true? No, (C) only tells us that people who can swim also live in caves. We know that everyone who is not an alien is a cave-dweller, does this mean that aliens can't live in caves? No, everyone who is not an alien lives in caves, but aliens might also. But the instruction tells us that no aliens live in caves. Since (C) says all who swim live in caves and since aliens swim but don't live in caves, (C) can't be true. Therefore, (E) is the correct answer.

Before leaving this section, let's look at an example that really is discouraging, but which you might run into on your exam.

Example 10:

Geordi can get a promotion unless he doesn't close the Morgan deal or he gets fired.

Which one of the following statements cannot be validly drawn from the above statement?

(A) Geordi got a promotion. Therefore, he closed the Morgan deal and didn't get fired.

(B) Geordi got a promotion and closed the Morgan deal. So he must not have been fired.

(C) Geordi did not close the Morgan deal. So he will not get a promotion.

(D) If Geordi does not get a promotion, then he did not close the Morgan deal or he got fired.

(E) If Geordi does not close the Morgan deal and he gets fired, then he will not get a promotion.

TAKE NOTE! This question appears to be *deductive*. The instructions ask you to find the statement (claim) that "cannot be validly drawn." Since in a valid argument the conclusion follows necessarily from the premises, the letter you are seemingly asked to fill should be the only claim that doesn't follow necessarily from the premise. But the qualifier "can" severely weakens the claim, making it difficult to see what follows necessarily from it.

Unfortunately, the instructions do a very poor job of instructing. They imply that there is only one statement, or claim, in each answer. This is clearly not true. There is an additional premise in some of the answers ((A), (B), and (C)) and an inference drawn from the set of premises. This is distracting and disheartening. Unfortunately, that is the goal of these tests. You must muster the will to overcome shoddy questions and choose the most rational answer.

The "can" plays tricks on you if you try to symbolize it. So just keep in mind that "unless" can be translated "if not." If it is not the case that Geordi doesn't close the Morgan deal or get fired, then he **can** get a promotion. It doesn't entail that he **will** get a promotion. On the other hand, in order for him to be able to get the promotion, he must have closed the Morgan deal and he must not have gotten fired. Therefore, since (A) says he got the promotion, he must have met both criteria. So the conclusion in (A) follows from the premises.

(B) says that Geordi got the promotion and he closed the Morgan deal, but the info that he closed the Morgan deal is irrelevant. If he got the promotion, he met the criteria. So the conclusion in (B) follows from the premises. (C) says Geordi didn't meet one of the criteria. If he didn't meet one, then he can't get the promotion, so the conclusion in (C) follows from the premises. (D) says that if Geordi meets the criteria, he **will** get the promotion. But does this follow? No, we only know that he **can** get the promotion; the criteria must be met to allow him to get the promotion, they don't guarantee the promotion. (D), therefore, is promising. Let's look at (E) just to be sure.

(E) says that, if Geordi doesn't meet both criteria, he won't get the promotion. This is right, so the conclusion in (E) follows from the premises. Therefore, (D) is our answer.

11.6. Logic puzzles, or games

Graduate school entrance exams such as the GRE, the LSAT, and the GMAT pose problems similar to those found in logic puzzle books, which you can find in almost any grocery store. Working logic puzzles will help increase your score on grad school entrance exams and keep your mind sharp for real life decision problems, plus they're a lot of fun once you get the hang of them.

To solve logic puzzles you must draw a series of conclusions from a list of clues (a list that often seems a little too short). The reasoning used in logic puzzles is deductive, that is, your conclusions will follow necessarily from the premises. This means there's usually only one right answer. Every now and then you'll get a puzzle where a couple of variables could be switched without your answers being inconsistent with the clues. This is very rare; your clues will almost always prevent multiple right answers, and they will never allow you to make only one mistake. If you're wrong about one answer in the puzzle, you'll be wrong about at least one other. You'll probably want to read this section over after working a few puzzles to be reminded of things to look out for.

A logic puzzle will always begin with a little background story. This story will orient you to the elements of the puzzle, which can be almost anything (e.g., people's names, places, events, times, days, animals, countries, foods, planets, etc.). This story won't have any of the clues in it so you won't have to refer back to it while trying to solve the puzzle. Here's an example of a typical background story:

Example 11:

Five animals were adopted from the shelter last week, each on a different weekday. From the information provided, determine which owner (one is Cathy) adopted which animal (one is Drake), as well as the day on which each animal was adopted.

Notice that two names are mentioned in the story. If names are mentioned in the background story, it means you'll be using them in the puzzle though your clues probably won't mention them. This does not mean there's a clue to the puzzle in the story; they merely complete your list of puzzle **elements**, in this case, the name of an owner and an animal.

Here's an example of a set of clues:

1. Anne adopted an animal on Monday, but she did not adopt Wally.
2. Star was adopted on Wednesday. Rolph was adopted on Friday, but not by Ida.
3. Vic (who was adopted by Fran) was adopted the day after Eve adopted an animal.

From the clues you have a complete list of the puzzle elements. You have a list of people who adopted animals:

Cathy
Anne
Ida
Fran
Eve

A list of animals adopted:

Drake
Wally
Star
Rolph
Vic

And a list of days on which they were adopted (the puzzle says "each on a different weekday"):

Monday
Tuesday
Wednesday
Thursday
Friday

The challenge is to link all the pet owners with their pets and the day on which each adoption took place. Logic puzzle books start you off with a grid so you can chart your conclusions as you reason through the clues. The grid for our puzzle would look like this:

	Drake	Wally	Star	Rolph	Vic	Monday	Tuesday	Wednesday	Thursday	Friday
Cathy										
Anne										
Eve										
Fran										
Ida										
Monday										
Tuesday										
Wednesday										
Thursday										
Friday										

To begin working this puzzle, look at clue #1. It gives us two pieces of information: that Anne adopted her animal on Monday, and that Anne did not adopt Wally. Choose a symbol you will use to match one element of the puzzle with another, and choose a different symbol to show that two elements do not match. We'll choose "•" to match one element with another and "X" to show a mismatch. Marking our chart according to clue #1 looks like this:

	Drake	Wally	Star	Rolph	Vic	Monday	Tuesday	Wednesday	Thursday	Friday
Cathy										
Anne		X				•				
Eve										
Fran										
Ida										
Monday										
Tuesday										
Wednesday										
Thursday										
Friday										

But we actually know quite a bit more than this from clue #1. We know that, if Anne adopted her animal on Monday and each of our five people adopts an animal on *only one day* of the week, she did not adopt it on Tuesday, Wednesday, Thursday, or Friday, which we can represent on our chart as follows:

	Drake	Wally	Star	Rolph	Vic	Monday	Tuesday	Wednesday	Thursday	Friday
Cathy										
Anne		X				•	X	X	X	X
Eve										
Fran										
Ida										

(Continued)

	Drake	Wally	Star	Rolph	Vic	Monday	Tuesday	Wednesday	Thursday	Friday
Monday										
Tuesday										
Wednesday										
Thursday										
Friday										

And we also know that, if each of our five people adopted an animal on a *different* day of the week, and Anne adopted on Monday, then neither Cathy, Eve, Fran, nor Ida adopted their animals on Monday. This leaves our chart looking like this:

	Drake	Wally	Star	Rolph	Vic	Monday	Tuesday	Wednesday	Thursday	Friday
Cathy						X				
Anne		X				•	X	X	X	X
Eve						X				
Fran						X				
Ida						X				
Monday										
Tuesday										
Wednesday										
Thursday										
Friday										

So, for every match between two elements of the puzzle, you can X-out all the other options horizontally and vertically FOR THAT ELEMENT.

Notice that we can't deduce any more information about which animal she adopted from learning the name of one she didn't adopt. We can't match her to any one of the other animals yet, and we can't eliminate her from any of the others. All we know is that she didn't adopt Wally.

Now let's look at clue #2. We now know that Star was adopted on Wednesday, which means she wasn't adopted any other day of the week, and no other animals were adopted on Wednesday:

	Drake	Wally	Star	Rolph	Vic	Monday	Tuesday	Wednesday	Thursday	Friday
Cathy						X				
Anne	X					●	X	X	X	X
Eve						X				
Fran						X				
Ida						X				
Monday			X							
Tuesday			X							
Wednesday	X	X	●	X	X					
Thursday			X							
Friday			X							

We know that Rolph was adopted on Friday, which means that he wasn't adopted on any other day of the week, and no other animal was adopted on Friday:

	Drake	Wally	Star	Rolph	Vic	Monday	Tuesday	Wednesday	Thursday	Friday
Cathy						X				
Anne		X				●	X	X	X	X
Eve						X				
Fran						X				
Ida						X				
Monday			X	X						
Tuesday			X	X						
Wednesday	X	X	●	X	X					
Thursday			X	X						
Friday	X	X	X	●	X					

We know that Rolph wasn't adopted by Ida:

	Drake	Wally	Star	Rolph	Vic	Monday	Tuesday	Wednesday	Thursday	Friday
Cathy						X				
Anne		X				●	X	X	X	X
Eve						X				
Fran						X				
Ida				X		X				
Monday			X	X						
Tuesday			X	X						
Wednesday	X	X	●	X	X					
Thursday			X	X						
Friday	X	X	X	●	X					

Now we're ready for clue #3. Vic was adopted by Fran.

	Drake	Wally	Star	Rolph	Vic	Monday	Tuesday	Wednesday	Thursday	Friday
Cathy					X	X				
Anne		X			X	●	X	X	X	X
Eve					X	X				
Fran	X	X	X	X	●	X				
Ida					X	X	X			
Monday			X	X						
Tuesday			X	X						
Wednesday	X	X	●	X	X					
Thursday			X	X						
Friday	X	X	X	●	X					

We are also told that Vic was adopted the day after Eve adopted an animal. This is where we have to begin reasoning. We don't know when Fran or Eve adopted their animals, but we do know that it wasn't on Monday, since Anne adopted her animal on Monday. This means the earliest Eve could have adopted is Tuesday and the latest is Thursday, since Fran adopts Vic the day *after* Eve adopts. So now we know two additional pieces of information: we know that Fran did not adopt Vic on Tuesday and that Eve didn't adopt on Friday:

	Drake	Wally	Star	Rolph	Vic	Monday	Tuesday	Wednesday	Thursday	Friday
Cathy					X	X				
Anne		X			X	●	X	X	X	X
Eve					X	X				X
Fran	X	X	X	X	●	X	X			
Ida					X	X	X			
Monday			X	X						
Tuesday			X	X						
Wednesday	X	X	●	X	X					
Thursday			X	X						
Friday	X	X	X	●	X					

We've now done all we can do working straight from our clues. Here's where we really have to dig in and reason about our puzzle.

If we look at our column for Vic, we'll see that he couldn't have been adopted on Tuesday. And if we compare our row for Fran to our column for Vic we'll see that Fran couldn't have adopted Vic on WEDNESDAY or FRIDAY:

	Drake	Wally	Star	Rolph	Vic	Monday	Tuesday	Wednesday	Thursday	Friday
Cathy					X	X				
Anne		X			X	●	X	X	X	X

(Continued)

	Drake	Wally	Star	Rolph	Vic	Monday	Tuesday	Wednesday	Thursday	Friday
Eve					X	X				X
Fran	X	X	X	X	•	X	X	X		X
Ida				X	X	X				
Monday			X	X						
Tuesday			X	X	X					
Wednesday	X	X	•	X	X					
Thursday			X	X						
Friday	X	X	X	•	X					

This leaves only one day that Vic could have been adopted: Thursday. And since we have just learned that Vic was adopted the day after Eve adopted her animal, we can infer that Eve adopted on Wednesday:

	Drake	Wally	Star	Rolph	Vic	Monday	Tuesday	Wednesday	Thursday	Friday
Cathy					X	X		X	X	
Anne		X			X	•	X	X	X	X
Eve					X	X	X	•	X	X
Fran	X	X	X	X	•	X	X	X	•	X
Ida				X	X	X		X	X	
Monday			X	X						
Tuesday			X	X	X					
Wednesday	X	X	•	X	X					
Thursday			X	X	•					
Friday	X	X	X	•	X					

We can also see that, since Star was adopted on Wednesday, and Eve adopted her animal on Wednesday, we can match Eve to Star:

	Drake	Wally	Star	Rolph	Vic	Monday	Tuesday	Wednesday	Thursday	Friday
Cathy			X		X	X		X	X	
Anne		X	X		X	●	X	X	X	X
Eve	X	X	●	X	X	X	X	●	X	X
Fran	X	X	X	X	●	X	X	X	●	X
Ida			X	X	X	X		X	X	
Monday			X	X						
Tuesday			X	X	X					
Wednesday	X	X	●	X	X					
Thursday			X	X	●					
Friday	X	X	X	●	X					

Now that we're out of clues, what do we do? When you get the hang of logic puzzles, you'll develop a set of strategies for determining your next move. One general strategy is to start looking around for logical connections. For instance, notice that Anne adopted on Monday and she could only have adopted Drake or Rolph. But, looking down the columns for Drake and Rolph, we see that Rolph couldn't have been adopted on Monday because he was adopted on Friday. Therefore, Anne must have adopted Drake on Monday:

	Drake	Wally	Star	Rolph	Vic	Monday	Tuesday	Wednesday	Thursday	Friday
Cathy	X		X		X	X		X	X	
Anne	●	X	X	X	X	●	X	X	X	X
Eve	X	X	●	X	X	X	X	●	X	X
Fran	X	X	X	X	●	X	X	X	●	X
Ida	X		X	X	X	X		X	X	
Monday	●	X	X	X	X					

(Continued)

	Drake	Wally	Star	Rolph	Vic	Monday	Tuesday	Wednesday	Thursday	Friday
Tuesday	X		X	X	X					
Wednesday	X	X	•	X	X					
Thursday	X		X	X	•					
Friday	X	X	X	•	X					

With what's left we can see that Ida must have adopted Wally and Cathy must have adopted Rolph. Since Ida either adopted Wally on Tuesday or Friday and she didn't adopt him on Friday (since Rolph was), Ida adopted Wally on Tuesday and Cathy adopted Rolph on Friday:

	Drake	Wally	Star	Rolph	Vic	Monday	Tuesday	Wednesday	Thursday	Friday
Cathy	X	X	X	•	X	X	X	X	X	•
Anne	•	X	X	X	X	•	X	X	X	X
Eve	X	X	•	X	X	X	X	•	X	X
Fran	X	X	X	X	•	X	X	X	•	X
Ida	X	•	X	X	X	X	•	X	X	X
Monday	•	X	X	X	X					
Tuesday	X	•	X	X	X					
Wednesday	X	X	•	X	X					
Thursday	X	X	X	X	•					
Friday	X	X	X	•	X					

Therefore, we have our solution:

Cathy / Rolph / Friday
Anne / Drake / Monday
Eve / Star / Wednesday
Fran / Vic / Thursday
Ida / Wally / Tuesday

Each person has a unique animal and day, so our answer is internally consistent. As long as it doesn't conflict with any of our clues, then it is correct. Logic puzzle books provide the answers and explanations to each puzzle in the back so you can check your work.

You probably won't have time to draw a grid for each logic problem on your exam—remember the tests are timed. You'll want to develop a handful of very simple charts that are quick to draw and that will help you keep the elements of the puzzle and their relationships sorted clearly. Try the next two logic puzzles using one or each of these simple chart examples. The solutions are at the end of the chapter.

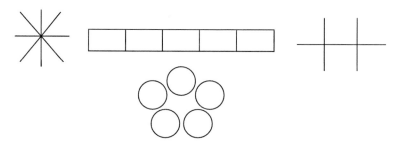

Example 12:

For her daughter's birthday, Alice went to Toy City to purchase a very special gift— one of the new Betty dolls. She went directly to the doll section, where she found five different Betty dolls (A through E) comfortably on a shelf. Alice noticed that each doll (including Office Betty) wore a different color outfit and was holding a small bag with a different pattern (one was stars). After examining each doll, Alice made her selection and tucked the doll under her arm. From the information provided, can you determine the color of the outfit of each doll and the pattern on her bag, as well as which doll Alice ultimately purchased?

1. The five dolls are Simply Betty, the one with the white outfit, the doll in position B, the one with the flowered bag, and the doll Alice purchased.
2. Prissy Betty (who isn't the one with the grey outfit) is to the immediate left of the doll with beige outfit (who isn't carrying a flowered bag) but somewhere to the right of the doll with the polka-dot bag.
3. Alice didn't buy the doll with the dark-brown outfit and the striped bag. Always Betty (the millennium edition, who isn't carrying the bag with hearts on it) has a white outfit.
4. Thrifty Betty (the most controversial release) is either exactly three places to the right or exactly three places to the left of the doll with the black outfit (who isn't in either position A or E). Simply Betty is not wearing the Beige outfit.

Example 13:

Actress Orta Bloom is on tour with the off-Broadway production of Quick Ari Brown, and last week performed in five different venues in the mid-west. From the clues below, can you work out which theatre she performed at on each night, which town it's in, and how many people came to see the show?

1. Orta performed in Franklin on Saturday; the theatre there is not the Arch, where she had a smaller audience than she did in Garrison.
2. Orta performed in Garrison the night after she was at the Prime Theatre, which is a converted barn.
3. 65 people came to see the show in Oldham, which wasn't where the Tuesday show was played.
4. At the Drover Theatre, Illingham, Orta performed to an audience of fewer than 75 persons.
5. On Wednesday, 45 people came to see Quick Ari Brown.
6. There were 75 people in the audience at the Median Theatre; Orta did her Thursday show at the Finders Theatre, a former pub.

Let's now look at a few examples of logic, or "game," puzzles you are likely to see on your exam:

Example 14:

A designer is building a booth for a design show and wants to display four dresses and three pairs of pants. The only dresses being considered are A, B, C, D, E, and F. The only pants being considered are J, K, L, M, and N.

If A is displayed, then neither B nor L can be displayed.
B is displayed only if D is displayed.
C cannot be displayed unless J is displayed.
D can only be displayed if K is displayed.
If L is displayed, then M must be displayed.
F cannot be displayed unless D is not displayed.

You may then be asked a set of questions like the following. We'll start with two, but there will probably be four or five on your exam:

1. Which one of the following is a possible display of dresses in the window?

(A) A, B, C, F
(B) A, C, D, E

(C) A, D, E, F

(D) B, C, D, F

(E) B, C, E, F

2. If F is displayed, which one of the following must be true?

(A) A is not displayed.

(B) B is not displayed.

(C) K is not displayed.

(D) L is displayed.

(E) M is displayed.

This is a really complicated puzzle with a lot of operations, "If, then," "Only if," "unless," etc. One simple strategy for a puzzle like this (if you can spare the time) is to symbolize the clues:

If A is displayed, then neither B nor L can be displayed. =	A ⊃ (~B & ~L)
B is displayed only if D is displayed. =	B ⊃ D
C cannot be displayed unless J is displayed. =	~C v J
D can only be displayed if K is displayed. =	D ⊃ K
If L is displayed, then M must be displayed. =	L ⊃ M
F cannot be displayed unless D is not displayed. =	~F v ~D

Let's look at question 1. You'll need to consider each possibility in turn:

(A) **A, B, C, F** This won't work because if A is in, B is out (by modus ponens).

(B) **A, C, D, E** There is nothing obviously inconsistent about this, so let's keep it in mind.

(C) **A, D, E, F** This won't work because if D (~~D), then ~F (by disjunctive syllogism).

(D) **B, C, D, F** Again, D and F are inconsistent (by disjunctive syllogism), so this option is out.

(E) **B, C, E, F** This won't work, but it's hard to see. If F is in (~~F), then ~D is true (by Disjunctive Syllogism). But if ~D is in, then ~B is true (by modus tollens).

This leaves us with (B) as the correct answer. This example shows that understanding deductive logic is incredibly helpful in solving these kinds of problems. The more you practice, the easier this will get. On to question 2.

Using our derivation rules, we can see quickly that, if F is in, then ~D is in by disjunctive syllogism (because F is equivalent to ~~F). In addition, if ~D is in, then B is out by modus tollens (so ~B is true). Therefore, (B) must be true.

Example 15:

Eight managers—A, B, C, D, E, F, G, and H—work in a five-story office building. On each floor, there is a corner office and a double-sized office. From the ground floor up, the floors are numbered one through five. The following is known about the managers' office arrangements:

> No manager shares an office with any other manager.
> No one works in the fifth-floor corner office.
> No one works in the third-floor double-sized office.
> D works in the second-floor corner office.
> G words in the fourth-floor corner office.
> D and F both work on a higher floor than H.
> B, E, and H work in double-sized offices.

1. If B works on a lower floor than G, then who must work in the second-floor double-sized office?

   (A) A
   (B) B
   (C) C
   (D) E
   (E) H

2. What is the maximum number of managers any one of whom could be the one who works in the fifth-floor double-sized office?

   (A) 1
   (B) 2
   (C) 3
   (D) 4
   (E) 5

To solve a puzzle like this, look for an element that can be used to sort the others. In this case, they're all on one of five floors. Draw a quick diagram with five categories. Perhaps something like this:

Don't try to solve the puzzle outright, as you would with normal logic puzzles. There isn't enough information for that. Just take the questions one by one. Since there are two elements for each floor (corner, double-sized), you might divide your chart and enter the clues like this:

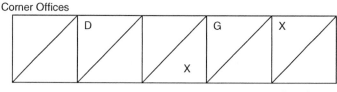

Corner Offices

B, E, and H = double-sized   D and F = higher floor than H

Double-sized Offices

Now let's start with question 1. If B works in a lower floor than G, then B either works on the first or second in one of the double-sized offices. In addition, if D works on a higher floor than H, there is only place for H to be-first floor. This puts H in the double-sized office on the first floor and B in the double-sized office on the second floor:

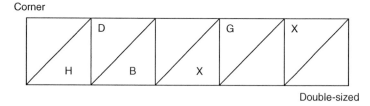

Corner

Double-sized

This means (B) is the answer. On to the next question.

Question 2 is tricky. It is asking how many possible people are eligible to work in the fifth-floor double-sized office. Try to keep in mind: the information introduced in question 1 DOES NOT transfer to this question. So forget anything about B working on a lower floor than G. B, E, and H are all in double-sized offices, so they're all candidates. We're up to three. D and F must be higher than H, but we already have a place for D, so F is available, that's four. What about A? There don't seem to be any restrictions on A, so that's five. (E) is the correct answer.

Example 16:

Five women—Frances, Gloria, Heather, Jackie, and Kit—and four men—Al, Bishop, Cliff, and Dan—carpool to work in three different cars.

Al and Frances always ride together.
Gloria and Heather always ride together.
Jackie and Kit never ride together.
Dan always rides in the car with the fewest people.

Men cannot outnumber women in any car.
The maximum number of people in any car is four.

1. The car in which Dan rides can hold how many people?

   (A) 1
   (B) 2
   (C) 3
   (D) 4
   (E) 5

2. If Bishop rides with Frances, Gloria must ride with which one of the following?

   (A) Cliff
   (B) Dan
   (C) Frances
   (D) Jackie
   (E) Kit

To solve a puzzle like this, look for an element that can be used to sort the others. In this case, all persons are distributed among three cars. So quickly draw a diagram with three sections to represent the cars:

Let's take question 1. Since Al and Frances always ride together, put them in one of the cars:

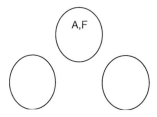

Gloria and Heather always ride together, but you don't know whether they ride with Al and Frances, so put them together but off to the side. Jackie and Kit never ride together, so make sure you don't put them together. Put the others off to the side also, so you can keep up with them.

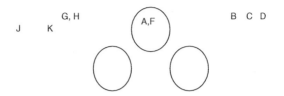

Since the largest number in any car is four, your distribution will be one of the following:

> 4, 4, 1; 3, 3, 3; or 4, 3, 2. Since we know that Dan is in the car with the least number of people, the distribution 3, 3, 3 is out.

Don't try to assign all the names out, as you would in a regular logic puzzle. You don't have enough information for that. Take them on a question-by-question basis. The first question asks how many people can fit in the car with Dan. Since he is in the car with the fewest people, the answer is either 1 or 2. Since Dan would make 3 in the car with Al and Frances or Gloria and Heather, Dan is in a different car from both pairs. This leaves us with two possible scenarios:

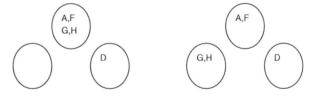

Our only other constraints are that Jackie and Kit can't be in the same car and men can't outnumber women in any car. If Dan is in a car alone, he will be the only man, and therefore, outnumber the women in the car. This means the 4, 4, 1 distribution won't work. Therefore, Dan will always be in the car with one other person who is a woman. 2 is our answer.

Now, for question 2. If Bishop rides with Frances, he also rides with Al. Since Gloria must be with Heather and there can't be more than four people in a car, then Gloria and Heather are in one of the other cars. Since we know Dan rides with only one other person (we know this from the last question), then Gloria and Heather are in the third car.

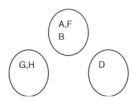

Who else is in the car with them? It can't be either Jackie or Kim, since they can't be together, one has to be with Dan (since there are no other women left) and the other has to be with Bishop, Al, and Frances (in order to keep the men and women even).

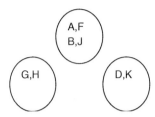

This leaves only Cliff. (A) is the correct answer.

11.7. Flaw questions

Flaw questions simply ask you to identify a fallacy in the argument. The difficult thing about these questions is that there are so many fallacies that can be made. You'll need a good grasp of every fallacy in this book, plus whatever fallacies are covered in the most recent editions of your Exam Prep book. Since the tests change year to year, Exam Prep books are your best guide for which fallacies are most likely to be used in the questions. This section will give you an idea of the kinds of flaw questions you will encounter and tips on how to answer them.

Example 17:

We are faced with a choice between freedom of speech and a book-burning kind of censorship. Since the latter is immoral and undemocratic, we must preserve free speech.
   The conclusion above is unsound because:

   (A) censorship doesn't involve book burning.
   (B) the author places too much emphasis on free speech.
   (C) the author fails to consider an accommodation between the two positions.
   (D) the phrase "freedom of speech" has not yet been defined.
   (E) censorship is a threat to our way of life.

This fallacy might be a **false cause** fallacy if presented a little differently; for example, if the author had said, "Rejecting freedom of speech leads to censorship and censorship to book burning and government surveillance." In this case we are merely presented with two extreme choices. A choice between two extreme positions is rarely a legitimate choice. If there might be more than two options, but only two are presented, this is a fallacy called false dilemma, or bifurcation. A person who commits a false dilemma fails to consider another option. Do any of our answers reflect this criticism? (C) does, and it is the correct answer.

Example 18:

At a recent press conference, the Governor announced an increase of 25 cents on all the state's toll roads, arguing that it would raise almost a quarter of a million dollars a year at the current traffic levels. She continued to argue, a toll increase of 2 dollars would raise more than a million dollars per year, and would completely solve our state's budget shortfalls. The toll increase would also likely lower the volume of traffic on our toll roads, resulting in fewer maintenance costs, accruing even more savings.

Which of the following identifies most accurately the governor's fallacious reasoning?

(A) She mistakes correlation for causation.
(B) Her figures are inaccurate.
(C) She makes inconsistent assumptions.
(D) She assumes what she is trying to prove.
(E) Her argument depends on political factors and not sound reasoning.

Look carefully at the argument again before re-reading the answers. It is reasonable to assume that increasing tolls will raise money, so there is no problem with causation. We know nothing about her figures, so we can't assume their wrong. She does, however, seem to assume something strange near the end. Though her first argument is based on keeping current traffic levels fixed, her second argument assumes the increase this would bring, then tries to add more increase by arguing that traffic levels would be decreased. This is clearly inconsistent, so (C) is the correct answer.

Just to be sure, look at (D) and (E). She doesn't assume anything that requires proving, though she may have to provide the sources for her numbers. And we're given no political information, so (E) is out of the question. We were correct with (C).

Example 19:

Since no one has been able to prove the existence of God, there must not be a God.

Which of the following best exposes the fallacy in the above argument?

    (A) The author is personally attacking those who believe in God.
    (B) The author is assuming what he needs to prove.
    (C) The author is appealing to an inappropriate authority.
    (D) The author is presenting a false dichotomy.
    (E) The author is arguing that something is true because there is no evidence to the contrary.

Consider (A). The author doesn't mention any specific person or group and doesn't say anything particularly disparaging, so he is not committing an *ad hominem*. And he is assuming that someone has tried to prove the existence of God, but this is not question-begging since this assumption does not appear in his conclusion, so (B) is out. The author doesn't appeal to any authority, so (C) is out. (D) is tempting, since one might assume that there may be some middle ground available. But remember that mutually exclusive claims cannot both be true. The claims, "God exists," and "God does not exist," can't both be true, therefore, the author isn't presenting a false dichotomy. The author does, however, seem to argue that God doesn't exist merely from the evidence that no proof has been given. This is an **argument from ignorance** and (E) is the correct answer.

11.8. Parallel-the-reason / classification / "reasoning" questions

Parallel the reasoning questions are simple once you realize that they are asking for you to classify the argument structure. If you have a clear grasp of the various types of inductive arguments, these questions can be fairly straightforward. A difficulty you may find is when a question asks you to choose from a set of arguments that have the same structure as the original. We'll look at three of these.

Example 20:

Just as a bow can be strung too tightly, so too the life of a king can become so stressful that one's body can give out.

Which of the following most closely parallels the reasoning used in the argument above?

(A) Just as the fishing line becomes too taut, so too may one's life be wasted in pursuit of pleasure.

(B) Just as an athlete's prospects change unexpectedly, so are life's pleasures unexpected.

(C) Just as grass can be killed by overwatering, so too can drinking too much lead to laziness.

(D) Just as the pistons may pump too quickly, so too may hard living lead to early demise.

(E) Just as a singer may become anxious before a performance, so too may brooding cause mental illness.

The original claim is an analogy, a comparison of two things, events, or concepts. This is slightly different from our arguments from analogy in Chapter 8, but the idea is similar. The biggest difference for this problem is that we don't have a list of similarities to evaluate. It is simply a claim that two events are alike without any specification of how. This makes answering the question difficult, but not impossible.

In the claim, tautness is compared to stress, and the body giving out is compared, implicitly, to a bow line breaking. Let's see which options match up.

(A) Just as the fishing line becomes too taut, so too may one's life be wasted in pursuit of pleasure.

Here we have tautness, but a wasted life is hardly comparable to a body giving out or a bow line snapping. (A) is out.

(B) Just as an athlete's prospects change unexpectedly, so are life's pleasures unexpected.

Here we have similar events being compared, unexpected prospects and pleasures. The results however are incongruous. The athlete's prospects may be good or bad, and a good athlete can be injured easily. Pleasures, however, are always good. (B) is out.

(C) Just as grass can be killed by overwatering, so too can drinking too much lead to laziness.

Here we have excesses similar to tautness, and grass being killed is similar to the breaking of a bow line. But the laziness caused by drinking is hardly comparable to either. (C) is out.

(D) Just as the pistons may pump too quickly, so too may hard living lead to early demise.

Here we have the stress of pistons pumping and hard living, both of which can reasonably compare with excess tautness and stress. The implication is that pistons pumping too quickly can cause the engine to break down and an early demise is comparable to this and the breaking of a bow line and bodily break down. (D) is promising. Let's keep it.

(E) Just as a singer may become anxious before a performance, so too may brooding cause mental illness.

It is not clear that anxiety and its consequences are comparable to either excess tautness or excess stress. The same goes for a breaking line and mental illness. (E) is out. Our only clear answer is (D).

Example 21:

A black cat is known to cause bad luck when it crosses your path. You're having a string of bad luck, so a cat probably crossed your path.

Which of the following most closely parallels the flawed pattern of reasoning used in the argument above?

(A) A full moon is known to cause strange behavior in people. People are behaving strangely, so there is probably a full moon.
(B) A recent study has shown that seatbelt usage reduces the likelihood of automobile accidents. There has been a steady decrease of automobile accidents over the past few months, so people are probably wearing their seatbelts.
(C) Gas has expanded when heated for as long as gas has been observed. Therefore, it will probably always expand when heated.
(D) Low levels of activity have been linked to increased illness. Therefore, if you're relatively healthy, you're probably active.
(E) People who are good at math are often good at logic. Joe isn't good at math, so he probably won't be good at logic.

Notice that the question is about a *flawed* pattern of reasoning. You'll find this often on your exam, but remember to focus on the pattern of reasoning. You're not looking to name a fallacy here. However, being able to identify a fallacy can be quite helpful. For instance, in this problem, there is a faulty claim about black cats and bad luck. This can be formulated as a conditional: if a black cat crosses your path, then you'll have bad luck. Notice the author concludes someone's path was crossed by a cat (the antecedent) from the premise that he has bad luck (the consequent). This fallacy is affirming the consequent, and it may help you parallel the reasoning. Let's see.

> **(A) A full moon is known to cause strange behavior in people. People are behaving strangely, so there is probably a full moon.**

This is very similar: If there is a full moon, then people behave strangely; you're behaving strangely, therefore, there's a full moon. This also affirms the consequent. Let's keep it in mind.

> **(B) A recent study has shown that seatbelt usage reduces the likelihood of automobile accidents. There has been a steady increase of people wearing seatbelts, so there will probably be fewer automobile accidents.**

This reasoning, while flawed (mistaking correlation for causation), doesn't match the original pattern. It is a valid modus ponens argument. (B) is out.

> **(C) Gas has expanded when heated for as long as gas has been observed. Therefore, it will probably always expand when heated.**

This is an inductive generalization. It infers from past experience something about the future. It does not reflect our original pattern, so it is out.

> **(D) Low levels of activity have been linked to increased illness. Therefore, if you're relatively healthy, you're probably active.**

As flawed as this is argument is (mistaking correlation for causation), it is of the valid form, modus tollens: If you're inactive, you'll get sick more often. You don't get sick often. Therefore, you're not inactive. (D) is out.

> **(E) People who are good at math are often good at logic. Joe isn't good at math, so he probably won't be good at logic.**

This argument is fallacious, but not in the same way as our original. This argument could be formulated: If you are good at math, then you'll be good at logic. You are not good at math. Therefore, you won't be good at logic. This commits the fallacy of denying the antecedent. Since our original argument affirmed the consequent, (E) is out and we're left with (A) as the correct answer.

Example 22:

During the early eighties when German auto makers were making their way into the American automobile marker, Ford surveyed owners of Ford vehicles and asked whether they would be more willing to purchase an American-made or Foreign-made vehicle. Seventy-five percent of those who responded said they prefer American-made vehicles. On this basis, Ford decided to continue at their current production rate. Yet, throughout the eighties, Ford lost more and more of the market to foreign-made vehicles.

Which one of the following, if true, would best explain this discrepancy?

(A) Only 8% of those who were polled replied.
(B) GM conducted a similar survey with similar results and also lost business to foreign automakers.
(C) Those who preferred American-made cars also preferred American-made clothes.
(D) Ford decided it would be more profitable to continue at its current production rate.
(E) 80% of the owners who prefer American-made cars replied but only 40% of owners who preferred foreign-made cars replied.

This question is somewhat different than other parallel-the-reasoning questions. In order to answer it, you'll need to clearly identify the argument structure, then infer the best explanation for why Ford's inference turned out to be a poor one.

You'll notice that this is an **inductive generalization** if you see that Ford inferred from a sample of its current customers a claim about their future purchasing preferences. To accurately answer this question, remember all the things that can go wrong with a generalization from Chapter 8: too small of a sample, nonrandom selection, biased questions, etc.

(A) Only 8% of those who were polled replied.

This is a good possibility. If only 8% responded, then the sample was not large enough and therefore not representative. If this were true, Ford should have caught it before basing a production decision on it.

(B) GM conducted a similar survey with similar results and also lost business to foreign automakers.

Far from explaining the discrepancy, this is merely another instance of it. It might suggest that the numbers were good (i.e., the sample was representative), but that something else is happening that we just don't know about.

(C) Those who preferred American-made cars also preferred American-made clothes.

This seems irrelevant. What do the participants' other preferences have to do with their car preferences. If this pattern holds true, then Ford should not have lost out to foreign automakers. (C) does not explain the discrepancy.

(D) Ford decided it would be more profitable to continue at its current production rate.

This is merely a restatement of their behavior based on their conclusion. It won't explain what went wrong.

(E) 80% of the owners who prefer American-made cars replied but only 40% of owners who preferred foreign-made cars replied.

This is more promising. It suggests that the sample was nonrandom in some way. Rather than gathering data on their entire constituency, those with a vested interest in American-made vehicles responded, biasing the results. This problem would be much harder to detect, unlike (A), and could indeed explain why the markets shifted away from American-made cars despite the survey results. So, for the record, (A) would have explained it, but that should have been obvious to anyone conducting surveys and making decisions about billions of dollars in production. (E) would easily fly under the radar and still explain what went wrong.

Preparing for grad school entrance exams is largely a matter of **practice, practice, practice.** But a solid grasp of good reasoning skills goes a long way toward increasing your speed and accuracy. Don't forget to review material from earlier chapters as you work the exercises that follow in this chapter and the exercises in your Exam Prep guides.

11.9. Exercises

Exercises 11.a.

Analytical Reasoning

1. According to evolutionary theory, humans and monkeys evolved from a common ancestor. People should stop believing that humans evolved from monkeys. Most people believe that humans evolved from monkeys, which is incorrect. Anything that is incorrect should not be believed, in my opinion.

   a. What is the main point of the argument?

      (A) Most people believe that humans evolved from monkeys, which is incorrect.
      (B) Anything that is incorrect should not be believed, in my opinion.
      (C) People should stop believing that humans evolved from monkeys.
      (D) According to evolutionary theory, humans and monkeys evolved from a common ancestor.

   b. Which of the following would be the best completion of this passage?

      (A) Congress should enact legislation enforcing the teaching of evolutionary theory in public schools.
      (B) I am going to stop thinking that humans evolved from monkeys.
      (C) The theory of evolution has been shown to be true by science.
      (D) DNA studies have shown that humans and monkeys have evolved from a common ancestor.

   c. Which of the following would the author utilize in direct support of the argument?

      (A) The theory of evolution has been shown to be true by science.
      (B) DNA studies have shown that humans and monkeys have evolved from a common ancestor.
      (C) Congress should enact legislation enforcing the teaching of evolutionary theory in public schools.
      (D) A person's beliefs should be guided solely by science.

2. Rhinos in India are threatened with extinction because poachers are killing them for their horn. Rhinos have no natural predators and, hence, don't need their horns to survive. There should be an organized program to capture rhinos in the wild and remove their horn. Such a program would eliminate the incentive of the poachers.

   a. What is the main point of the argument?

      (A) Rhinos in India are threatened with extinction because poachers are killing them for their horn.
      (B) Since rhinos have no natural predators, it does not need its horn to survive.
      (C) There should be an organized program to capture rhinos in the wild and remove their horn.
      (D) Such a program would eliminate the incentive of the poachers.

 b. Which of the following supports the claim that rhinos don't need a horn to survive?

  (A) Poachers kill rhinos.
  (B) A program can be organized to remove the rhino's horn.
  (C) Rhinos don't have natural predators.
  (D) It's not the case that rhinos don't have natural predators.

 c. Which of the following is inconsistent with what is communicated above?

  (A) The horn of the rhino is worth a lot of money within the context of illegal markets
  (B) An organized program to remove the horn of the rhino would be expensive to fund.
  (C) Even if the rhino's horn were removed, poachers would still want to kill the rhino.
  (D) Rhinos in other parts of the world might need their horns.

3. Fred lives in Billings, Montana, and I know he has a mountain lion that he keeps as a pet. Any kind of cat normally found in the wild is classified as a non-domesticated animal, and mountain lions are normally found in the wild. Fred is on the cops' radar, for sure. You need a permit to keep a mountain lion as a pet in Billings, and I know Fred does not have one.

 a. What is the ultimate conclusion of the argument?

  (A) Mountain lions are classified as non-domesticated animals.
  (B) Fred will be arrested for sure.
  (C) Fred is on the cops' radar.
  (D) Anyone who does not have a permit in Billings is on the cops' radar.

 b. Which of the following can be directly deduced from what is claimed above?

  (A) Fred won't be arrested if he hides his mountain lion.
  (B) People who live in Billings, Montana with non-domesticated cats all have permits.
  (C) Mountain lions are classified as non-domesticated animals.
  (D) Mountain lions might not be classified as domestic animals.

4. Five people ran a race, Amy, Beth, Cory, Don, and Ed. From the information below, figure out who finished in 1st, 2nd, 3rd, 4th, and 5th place.

– Ed was neither 1st nor last.
– Don was neither 1st nor last, but finished immediately after Ed.
– Amy finished immediately before Cory, who was either in 2nd or 5th place.
– There were two people, and only two people, who finished after Ed.

 a. Who came in 1st ?

  (A) Amy
  (B) Beth
  (C) Cory
  (D) Don
  (E) Ed

 b. Who came in 2nd ?

  (A) Amy
  (B) Beth
  (C) Cory
  (D) Don
  (E) Ed

c. Who came in 3rd ?

(A) Amy
(B) Beth
(C) Cory
(D) Don
(E) Ed

d. Who came in 4th ?

(A) Amy
(B) Beth
(C) Cory
(D) Don
(E) Ed

e. Who came in 5th ?

(A) Amy
(B) Beth
(C) Cory
(D) Don
(E) Ed

5. The Johnson family is getting ready to have a baby. The Johnson's are made up of a mom, a dad, a daughter, an older son, and a younger son. From the information below, determine the girl's name and the boy's name suggested by each family member.

  – Neither of the women in the family suggested a girl's name beginning with the letter "D"; however, the woman who doesn't think that a girl should be named Laura thinks that a boy should be named Dan, and the girl's name should start with the letter "M."
  – The person who suggested Will as a boy's name also suggested Daphne as a girl's name; however, this was neither of the two sons.
  – The person who suggested Rich as a boy's name did not suggest Donna as a girl's name.
  – The three children are: the younger son (who suggested Mike as a boy's name), the one who suggested Dianne as a girl's name, and the one who suggested Seth as a boy's name.
  – Marie is one of the girl's names chosen by one of the women.

  a. Mom suggested Dan as a boy's name.

  (A) True
  (B) False

  b. Dad suggested Daphne as a girl's name.

  (A) True
  (B) False

  c. Mom suggested Laura as a girl's name.

  (A) True
  (B) False

⇨

d. Donna was not suggested by the younger son as a girl's name.

(A) True

(B) False

6. Five people were in line at the grocery store getting ready to pay for steak, pudding, pie, bread, and ham. They all bought something different. Their first names were: John, Martin, Amy, Ned, and Leroy. Their last names were: Suiter, Trent, Breed, Hazelton, and Page.

– Trent had the steak.

– The fourth customer bought the pudding.

– Leroy Page was served later than the person who had ham, but before Suiter.

– The second customer was Martin.

– The pie was purchased by the customer directly after John.

– Ned was the person who bought the bread, and he was served after Amy.

a. What was the last name of the person who purchased the pie?

(A) Page

(B) Hazelton

(C) Breed

(D) Trent

(E) Suiter

b. Ned was which place in line?

(A) First

(B) Second

(C) Third

(D) Fourth

(E) Fifth

c. What was purchased by the third person in line?

(A) Pie

(B) Steak

(C) Pudding

(D) Bread

(E) Ham

7. The White Killer Sharks soccer team has a starting lineup that is selected from two groups of kids: Group #1: Jim, Dan, Ben, and Ed; Group #2: Lee, Ron, Gus, Zoe, and Pete. Coach Roy has the following requirements for the starting lineup:

– Two players are always chosen from Group #1

– Three players are always chosen from Group #2

– The 4 slowest players are: Jim, Ben, Gus, and Pete

– 3 of the 4 slowest players will always be chosen

– If Gus starts, Zoe can't start

– Gus will only start if Ben also starts

– Dan and Ben can't start together

    a. Which of the following can't start together?

       (A) Pete and Zoe

       (B) Ron and Jim

       (C) Jim and Ben

       (D) Ed and Dan

    b. If Gus starts, who must also start?

       (A) Zoe or Ron

       (B) Jim or Pete

       (C) Dan or Jim

       (D) Dan or Lee

       (E) Zoe or Jim

    c. If Zoe starts, who will also be starting?

       (A) Jim, Ed, and Ben

       (B) Jim

       (C) Jim and Dan

       (D) Jim, Dan, and Ben

    d. Of the following players, who must start?

       (A) Ben

       (B) Jim

       (C) Pete

       (D) Zoe

       (E) Gus

Exercises 11.b.

Inductive Reasoning

1. Smith winds up dead, and it looks like murder.

    a. The female district attorney (DA) handling Smith's case finds out that Smith and Brown hated each other, and she concludes that Brown is likely responsible. Is her conclusion justified in any way?

       (A) Yes

       (B) No

    b. Along with the fact that Smith and Brown hated each other, the DA finds out also that Brown and Smith were seen arguing with one another on the day of Smith's death, and she concludes that Brown is likely responsible. Does her conclusion now follow with less likelihood or more likelihood?

       (A) Less likelihood

       (B) More likelihood

⇨

c. The DA finds out further that Anderson and Brown hate each other, too, since Brown has been having an affair with Anderson's wife. And, it is learned that Anderson witnessed Brown and Smith arguing with one another on the day of Smith's death. Yet, the DA still concludes that Brown is likely responsible. Does her conclusion now follow with less likelihood or more likelihood?

(A) Less likelihood
(B) More likelihood

2. If you want to see the best version of that movie, rent the 1948 version. Rent it. It's a must. The acting in the 1948 version is way better than the acting in the 1978 one. What a great movie! Which of the following is the ultimate conclusion of the above argument?

(A) What a great movie!
(B) Rent it.
(C) It's a must.
(D) If you want to see the best version of that movie, rent the 1948 version.

3. Just before a major quake near Beijing, China, hundreds of snakes suddenly appeared from hibernation and froze to death in the snow, fish were seen leaping from the half-frozen rivers and lakes, and many horses and cows refused to enter barns. Prior to a quake in Los Angeles, California, many people reported strange behavior from their pets and domestic animals.

Which of the following is the conclusion that most likely follows from the above claims?

(A) Earthquakes occur in China only when animals are acting strangely.
(B) All animals may be able to predict earthquakes.
(C) Some animals may be able to predict earthquakes.
(D) There is an obvious correlation between earthquakes and animals acting strangely.

4. She can't do the things she used to do. She probably should be allowed to commit suicide if she wants to. I say 'probably' because I'm not 100 percent sure, but darn near close! Her quality of life is horrible since she is confined to a wheelchair. Eating has become a several-hour ordeal. In fact, anyone in her condition should not be denied the second most foundational right next to the right to life, namely, the right to do with one's body what one sees fit.

a. Which of the following is a conclusion supported by reasons in the above argument?

(A) She probably should be allowed to commit suicide if she wants to.
(B) Doing what one wants to with one's body should be a right.
(C) Her quality of life is horrible.
(D) She can't do the things she used to.

b. Which of the following would count against the argument above?

(A) Women view quality of life different from men.
(B) The speaker above is not 100 percent sure of a claim that is significant to the argument.
(C) Eating for this woman has become more than a several-hour ordeal.
(D) The woman above is suffering from dementia.

5. Logic is beneficial in that it gives you the skills needed to construct good arguments. It instills a sensitivity to language, a command of which is essential to clear, effective, and meaningful communication. Also, logic offers a common, leveled playing field, so to speak, where anyone can play on the field, provided they abide by the rules—such rules include, for example, "make sure your premises support your conclusion" and "do not *ad hominem* your opponent."

a. Which of the following is the conclusion of the argument above?

    (A) Logic allows you to construct good arguments.
    (B) Logic offers a common, leveled playing field, so to speak, where anyone can play on the field.
    (C) Logic is beneficial.
    (D) One should not *ad hominem* one's opponent.

b. Which of the following statements most clearly strengthens the argument above?

    (A) Logic is like a sport in that, just as one gets better at a sport with practice, one also gets better at logic with practice.
    (B) Logic is beneficial to any society.
    (C) Another rule of logic is "provide evidence for your claims."
    (D) Using logic will enable you to evaluate the arguments of others, which is a helpful skill to have.

c. Which of the following statements might follow from what has been communicated above?

    (A) You can't communicate anything without logic.
    (B) There are bad arguments that appear as good ones.
    (C) You should study logic.
    (D) Logic can be learned at a very early age.

6. A trip to Mars is a good idea since it gives us a good opportunity to explore the emergence of life. Yet, landing on the tiny Martian moons, Phobos and Deimos, might be more practical. Given that the Martian terrain is rugged, humans would not be able to venture far, and robotic vehicles would have a hard time navigating its myriad hills and valleys. On Phobos and Deimos, robots could easily navigate on the surface. Plus, Phobos and Deimos could be used as base stations from which we would be able to study Mars.

a. Which of the following would further justify a trip to Mars?

    (A) Exploring Mars would give us an opportunity to explore the origins of the universe.
    (B) Mars has a sufficiently rugged terrain.
    (C) We could use Mars' moons as base stations.
    (D) Mars is the fourth planet from the sun.

b. Which of the following can be inferred from the information above?

    (A) Exploring Mars gives us an opportunity to explore the origins of the universe.
    (B) Mars has a sufficiently rugged terrain.
    (C) The terrain on Phobos and Deimos is not rugged.
    (D) Humans would definitely learn more about the emergence of life as a result of a trip to Mars. ⇨

7. Animal cells use energy, and one of the primary functions of the mitochondrion of an animal cell is to produce energy for the cell by converting sugars into a nucleic acid called adenosine triphosphate (ATP). However, this can happen only if there is a line of communication between other organelles of the cell and the mitochondria themselves. ATP acts as the material catalyst of information communicated between mitochondria and other organelles. When sugars are converted, the other organelles receive this information and cellular homeostasis can be maintained.

a. Given the information above, when there are low levels of ATP, what is most likely to occur?

   (A) Mitochondria receive the information about low levels of ATP and convert more sugars.
   (B) Other organelles immediately die.
   (C) ATP itself converts into a nucleic acid.
   (D) The animal cell immediately dies.

b. Which of the following can be inferred from the information above?

   (A) Animal cells use more energy than plant cells.
   (B) ATP is essential to animal homeostasis.
   (C) There are many different types of nucleic acids at work in an animal cell.
   (D) Different organelles perform different functions in the typical animal cell.

8. Research has been conducted on animals to determine how the external environment affects the functioning of various systems of the body. One experiment has to do with occluding or removing the eyes of cats, rats, and birds at various stages of development to see if the neural connections of the brain necessary to the visual system either would develop abnormally or would cease to function altogether. These studies indicated that when occluding or removing the eyes, certain neural connections in the brains of these animals would not be made. This resulted in the cessation of certain visual processes, causing the overall subsystem to be underdeveloped in relation to other animals (cats, rats, and birds) that had not had their eyes occluded or removed.

a. Given what is communicated above, which of the following statements is accurate?

   (A) The visual system is wholly dependent upon the environment for its functioning.
   (B) Animals with normal functioning sight have an overdeveloped visual system.
   (C) This research illustrates what could happen when information is not exchanged between the external environment and organism.
   (D) A visually-stimulating environment is absolutely essential to the normal functioning of the visual system of animals.

b. True or false: given what is communicated above, by analogy it's likely that a human's visual system would be underdeveloped if the eyes are occluded or removed.

   (A) True
   (B) False

c. True or false: given what is communicated above, a visually-stimulating environment is absolutely essential to the normal functioning of the visual system of animals.

   (A) True
   (B) False

Notes

Chapter 1

1. We are taking for granted that claims are the sorts of things that describe states of affairs, and that the relevant states of affairs are most often those that are or are not facts about our world. Some philosophers might object to defining claims as having unqualified values such as "true" and "false." For instance, it might seem strange to say that it is "true" that "Abel Magwitch is Pip's benefactor," since neither Magwitch or Pip exist in our world. But it does make sense to say that, "In the book, *Great Expectations*, it is true that Magwitch is Pip's benefactor." Therefore, it might be more convenient to say that a claim is either "satisfied" or "unsatisfied" with respect to some set of states of affairs (our world, the world of *Great Expectations*, etc.).

Chapter 2

1. *On Writing Well*. (New York: HarperCollins, 2001), p. 8.

Chapter 3

1. This is the classic Venn diagram method. Twentieth century logicians and mathematicians developed Venn diagrams for non-syllogistic arguments and for arguments with more than three categories, but these revisions typically involve trigonometry or calculus. The interest in these more complicated methods diminished with the advent of propositional logic (see Chapters 4, 5, and 6).

Chapter 5

1. From Rush Limbaugh, *Wall Street Journal*: http://online.wsj.com/article/SB123318906638926749.html.

Chapter 7

1. *Foundations of Scientific Inference* (1967), Pittsburgh: University of Pittsburgh Press, pp. 12–13.
2. Ibid., p. 14.
3. John Hospers, *An Introduction to Philosophical Analysis* (1996), Upper Saddle River, NJ: Prentice-Hall, p. 102.

Chapter 9

1. *The Web of Belief* (1978), New York: McGraw-Hill, p. 67.

Chapter 10

1. http://www.rushlimbaugh.com/home/daily/site_011509/content/01125108.guest.html.
2. http://www.msnbc.msn.com/id/26771716/.

Chapter 11

1. The GRE tests analytical reasoning through a writing assignment. It does not include the analytical reasoning questions that we have categorized above.

Index